PRAISE FOR
DANCING IN THE FACE OF DEATH

"Dr. Koen's memoir paints a poignant and realistic portrayal of the devastation of FTD; the resilience of love in the face of a progressive, terminal diagnosis; and the optimism that participating in research brings. Everyone touched by a life-altering diagnosis will benefit from reading this book."

—SHANA DODGE, PhD, Director of Research Engagement, The Association for Frontotemporal Degeneration (AFTD)

"In *Dancing in the Face of Death*, Susan Koen has written a brave, luminous memoir about love in the midst of unimaginable loss. With tenderness, honesty, and extraordinary clarity, she chronicles her partner's dementia and battle with FTD without ever turning away from the hardest truths. Yet what makes this book so powerful is the humanity at its core and Koen's insight into the complexity of caring for a beloved spouse through illness. Beautifully written and deeply moving, this is an essential book for anyone who has experienced deep love and loss."

—DANIELLE TRUSSONI, *New York Times* best-selling author of *Falling Through the Earth* and *The Fortress*

"As someone who has loved, cared for, and lost someone to FTD, I am deeply moved by Dr. Koen's ability to articulate the arc of this disease. She captures how it progresses through the initial development of hallmark symptoms, the daily struggle of managing new ones, the impossible conversations about end-of-life, and ultimately the loss and grief that eventually transform into immense gratitude for the opportunity to have loved and cared for someone so special. My hope is that anyone who has struggled to make sense of loss from FTD or other dementias will find that this book lends words to the ineffable, and in doing so, inspires them to become engaged in the ongoing research to cure these difficult diseases."

—JOSEPH MARQUEZ, MD, Board of Directors,
The Association for Frontotemporal Degeneration (AFTD)

"Susan writes with grace, courage, and an unflinchingly honest voice as she chronicles the transformation of her forty-year marriage when a degenerative brain condition slowly takes hold of her beloved. In this deeply moving memoir, she shows how love endures, evolves, and even expands in the face of profound loss. Everyone will benefit from reading this powerful, compelling book."

—CHRISTA HILLHOUSE, Founding Member, 4 Non Blondes

"This memoir is an insightful read for anyone who is losing someone to dementia but also for anyone experiencing the anticipatory grief that comes when your loved ones are diagnosed with a fatal illness or condition of any kind. Give yourself the gift of being guided and supported on your journey by this author."

—BOARD MEMBER, CureGRN; AFTD Ambassador

DANCING
IN THE FACE OF
DEATH

A Journey of Love, Caregiving, and
Courage amid a Dementia Diagnosis

SUSAN L. KOEN, PhD

RIVER GROVE
BOOKS

Published by River Grove Books
Austin, TX
www.rivergrovebooks.com

Distributed by River Grove Books

Design and composition by Greenleaf Book Group
Cover design by Greenleaf Book Group

Publisher's Cataloging-in-Publication data is available.

Print ISBN: 979-8-90052-029-2

eBook ISBN: 979-8-90052-030-8

First Edition

To my precious BiBi, the love of my life in this world and the next. You blessed my life and enriched me with our shared adventures. Your bravery and desire to help others birthed this book.

CONTENTS

AUTHOR'S NOTE

The author will donate all profits from this book to The University of Pennsylvania's FTD Center to advance knowledge and improve health for individuals and families affected by frontotemporal degeneration (FTD) and related dementias through comprehensive, specialized clinical care, innovative research, and education.

PROLOGUE

The morning was ablaze with fall colors; I walked the Eastern Promenade overlooking Casco Bay. The cool breeze sweeping Portland, Maine, this early September day enlivened me. The crashing waves added a distinct rhythm to my walk while swooping gulls captured my gaze. I savored the varied hues of blue from the sky, to the bay, to the distant ocean.

A water baby through and through, water always stirred me. I was a double Pisces after all—both my sun and rising sign—and a Scorpio moon. My mind floated out to sea, envisioning the myriad adventures Barbara and I would be undertaking soon. She had been my life partner for the past thirty-seven years, and we had an upcoming retirement trip planned to Sicily and Puglia. We also had an extended trip to our beloved Paris booked for the spring. A spontaneous smile spread across my face. We were finally embarking on the carefree traveling phase of our lives we had worked so hard to achieve. While we had seen much of the world together, including two trips to China and one to Africa, we planned to expand our cultural experiences by visiting Japan, Norway, New Zealand, Morocco, and Vietnam over the next five years. There were so many countries, cuisines, and bodies of water to explore.

Giddy at the prospect of upcoming adventures, I strolled into the living room of our condo in search of Barbara. The sunlight streaming in from the sliding doors added to my buoyant mood. I wanted to sweep Barbara into my arms for a spontaneous dance, to celebrate our new era of freedom and connection. I wanted to dance with her and hold her close, thankful we had weathered the periodic strains over three decades of owning and running a business together. We would be together in the same place every day instead of navigating continuous separations due to my work travel.

Barbara's name was on my lips when I rounded the corner of the kitchen island and saw her napping on the couch. She had always loved to nap on the weekends, but in the last month she had drifted off nearly every day. I attributed this new midday sleep practice to her recent release from the presidency of our condo association, making up for the exhaustion the role had caused her. I approached on tiptoes, eager to kiss her awake. Instead, the sight of Barbara's face stopped me cold.

A stranger might have seen Barbara and thought she was simply a slack-jawed woman, peacefully napping. But I could see subtle differences beyond a typical resting face. Barbara's cheeks collapsed inward and her eyes sagged at the edges. Her mouth turned down in a pained frown so uncharacteristic of Barbara's normally sparkling face I could scarcely find her in this face at all. And worst of all, I had seen this exact face before when Barbara's mother, Peggy, started declining from the genetic brain disorder known as frontotemporal degeneration (FTD).

The memory of her mother's drooping face and shriveled frame curled up in a fetal position filled my brain. Silently, I screamed. *NO! This can't be happening!* I closed my eyes tightly, willing the dreadful family disease to disappear from Barbara's beautiful face. I begged the universe to replace the face in front of me with My Barbara. But deep down I knew no amount of pleading would change the harsh truth staring back at me.

I didn't run from the room or try to rationalize what I couldn't escape. I just stood and stared without a word, examining every inch of the face in front of me, desperate to find the energetic, cheerful woman Barbara always had been. Just three years prior, when Barbara turned sixty-five, she had announced she'd won the 50/50 genetic coin toss hanging over her head our whole relationship. She was nearly ten years beyond the age her mother was at the onset of her FTD journey, so Barbara declared herself beyond the point of fear. I desperately wanted her declaration to be true, but my intuition, which always served me well, kept me wary. The age of onset for this little-known brain disorder could range from mid-thirties to early eighties, although it typically manifested between mid-forties to mid-sixties. Barbara was six- ty-eight now, and I couldn't ignore the truth of her face.

As I stared at my beloved, a number of recent mysteries solved themselves. Several months before, Barbara had lost interest in cooking elaborate meals, a prior passion of hers. She was an amateur chef, and I missed her cioppino, moussaka, and her Sunday morning popovers. Barbara had also suddenly stopped reaching out to friends, as well as many family members, which was a significant departure from the norm. She was a caring woman who had remained connected to her friends from elementary and high school. On top of these, she had stopped initiating outings of any kind, which was unlike her.

Now it all made sense. I'd incorrectly attributed these changes to her preoccupation with the many problems going on in our brand-new condo building. But no. Her slack, sleeping face told me her apathy derived from the early stages of the same behavioral variant of FTD (bvFTD) that had taken her mother and other precious family members.

The behavioral variant, also known as *GRN*-FTD, results from a defunct or mutated progranulin gene in one of a person's biological parents. Insufficient progranulin, the protein responsible for cell survival, leads to the eventual loss of brain cells in the frontal and/or temporal lobes, the centers of thought, personality, decision-making, language, and memory formation. This family curse had begun to overtake Barbara in such subtle and minute ways that the real cause of her changed attitude and behavior had escaped even my watchful eyes.

As the reality began to sink in, the room started to spin around me. *I should have known* ricocheted inside my head. *I should have known tragedy wasn't through with me.* I collapsed into the chair across from the sofa, grabbing my head and rocking. I pled silently with the spirits who'd looked after me my whole life and helped me weather one family health crisis and death after another. I didn't want another deep loss in my life. *Not now, and please not Barbara.* Despair enveloped me as I silently begged, *Don't let this happen. Don't let me be right.*

SHIFTING GROUND

September 2019
–
Early December 2020

The longer I live, the more deeply I learn
that love—whether we call it friendship or family
or romance—is the work of mirroring and
magnifying each other's light.

—Maria Popova

FINDINGS AND FEARS

In the spring of 1981, Barbara and I met in the most serendipitous way. I was conducting research on self-defined feminist businesses for my PhD in organizational psychology and women's studies, and one group I selected for my heuristic study was a four-woman restaurant/bookstore collective in Bridgeport, Connecticut. During the one-on-one interviews with each collective member, they told me I had to talk with Barbara, their unofficial fifth member, who had helped them start their business. While Barbara had a full-time job as an agent for illustrators, she still worked at the restaurant every Sunday to support the owners and their purpose, which was to provide a safe space for women to gather, learn, and connect. I scheduled an interview with Barbara during my next visit to Bridgeport.

I can recall our first meeting like it happened yesterday. When Barbara walked into the room, the energy shifted. She flashed me a broad, genuine smile, reached out her hand, and said, "Hi!

I'm Barbara." Her kinetic force was like a strong yet gentle spring breeze—simultaneously enlivening and comforting. Her groundedness, confidence, and pragmatism were immediately evident, and I was struck by how different she was from the other collective members. While all five women were attractive, the first four presented plainly and often expressed reticence, anger, and negativity. Barbara, by contrast, was colorful, sophisticated, relaxed, and vibrant. She exuded positivity.

Although I was the designated interviewer, Barbara's natural curiosity led her to ask me more questions than I asked her.

"How did you select your doctoral thesis? What made you think you could develop a feminist theory of business organizations?" she asked.

She wasn't doubting my capability; she just wanted to know more about my history, thoughts, and ideas. I'd interviewed hundreds of women across nine different feminist businesses by then, and no one else had shown the insight and interest in my studies that Barbara did. Her genuine engagement was intoxicating, sparking an instant attraction. The more we talked, the clearer her depth of insight and emotional maturity became. By the end of the interview, I was entranced by her energy and spirit, and I wanted to be the main recipient of her light-up-the-room smile.

Five months later, I moved into the same neighborhood as this collective. Six months later, Barbara and I declared ourselves a couple. By simply listening and talking about our beliefs, interests, ideas, and vulnerabilities, we had reached deeply into the other's heart. We spent hours discussing politics, books, feminism, family dynamics, travel, and home renovations. We could talk about anything except fashion (I could never hold up my end of that conversation).

I distinctly remember one exchange we had on a lazy Saturday afternoon in early summer 1982, three months into our romantic relationship. Barbara paused in her explanation of the writings of a prominent French feminist, and I interjected.

"Is there anything you don't know about?"

She laughed her rich belly laugh.

"Lots," she replied.

"I'm just amazed at what you know about art, literature, food, music . . . everything that makes up culture."

"But you know about things I don't . . . like how the American government works . . . and science, even neuroscience."

"Yeah. I guess we complement each other," I said contentedly.

And we did, throughout our decades together. Barbara's grounded personality calmed my fiery one, and my expressive enthusiasm inspired her to shine more brightly.

Barbara always said I was easy to talk to, and I listened well. But the truth is, I never listened to anyone as much or as patiently as I did Barbara. It wasn't just because I was intrigued by her thoughts and emotions, which I was. I also loved her melodious and strong voice. The first time I heard Barbara sing, she blew me away. She'd just moved into my house in Bridgeport and was taking a shower before we went out to dinner. I was in the adjoining bedroom when the jazzy lyrics of Billie Holiday's "Blue Moon" came belting out of the bathroom, followed by a cool scat. Happiness permeated my body when I heard her rich alto voice. Barbara and I shared a love of traditional jazz, which our respective fathers introduced us to as children. Barbara's singing stirred deep feelings in me, and I relished them. She brought out a fierce protectiveness in me with her bright, resonant energy.

My love for Barbara soared the most when we danced. Moving our bodies in harmony with one another was simultaneously sexual and spiritual for me. I'd never seen another white woman who could move her hips like Barbara. I'd acquired my own hip-gyrating skills as a teenager with the persistent help (and accompanying laughter) of my fellow officers in the New Orleans Y-Teens Association, which was the only racially integrated youth organization in that city in the mid-1960s. When my friends finally told me, "Girl, you've got it! You've unlocked those rigid white hips of yours," I felt like I'd earned a degree in dance.

I lived mostly in my head, except when I danced. Barbara's moves, on the other hand, were the result of a deep connection with her physical body I found both fascinating and foreign. Barbara and I danced together in so many places over the years— gay bars on both coasts, outdoor women's music festivals, and friends' weddings in the fields of New England. Dancing was our shared language; we naturally took turns leading without having to exchange a word.

||||||||||||||||||||

I don't know why I thought hiring Barbara into my start-up business was a terrific idea, but I did. Three years into our life partnership, I began begging her to join my company as director of sales and client services. Having finished my PhD program the year before, I had launched a training and consulting business focused on optimizing workforce safety and error-free performance within twenty-four-hour industrial operations, including mines, manufacturing sites, and electric generating stations.

I was the subject matter expert, while Barbara had finely honed relationship sales skills from her role as an artist agent. This skill set came with the gift of making easy, authentic, personal connections, and I needed her abilities to build my business into what I envisioned it could be. I wanted to grow an organization from a foundation of trusting relationships with the world's major companies and unions, along with quality services and proven outcomes. I finally convinced Barbara our synergy would work in business too, and she joined my company in 1986. We worked together for thirty years improving safety, reliability, and quality of life for shift workers across the globe, and eventually sold our company to a larger international consultancy.

As anyone who has owned a business with their life partner knows, working together isn't always easy. Barbara and I had different work styles, expertise, and levels of reputational risk involved. We could have been torn apart by the stresses these differences created. Instead, we committed to building and sustaining an effective work relationship based on respect, understanding, and utilization of our differences to the company's advantage. Perhaps most critically, we focused on eliminating power differences at work that could have strained our relationship at home.

Even as we lived and worked together, Barbara and I maintained a great deal of independence. I traveled continuously in the early years of the business, flying around the United States and Canada on a weekly basis. Barbara was content to stay home and run the business while pursuing her many interests like singing, knitting, cooking, and gardening.

In 1990, we moved our home and business from the greater New York City area to Portland, Maine, in favor of a less stressful place to live and work. Within four years of our move, we purchased a seasonal cottage on Great Pond in the Belgrade Lakes region of central Maine. This weekend retreat became a haven where our relationship thrived as we made time in our busy lives for relaxation together.

One day, soon after buying our cottage (or "camp," as Mainers say), Barbara presented me with the challenge of swimming the one and a half miles across the cove and back. She was an accomplished swimmer, and even though I was not, I was never one to turn down a dare. Barbara volunteered to go first, but I didn't want to compare myself to her, so I insisted on starting the challenge. In my mid-forties, I was still athletic and began with a strong crawl stroke I maintained the whole way across.

The return was a different story. As I became tired and shifted to a sidestroke, Barbara shouted encouragement to me from her accompanying kayak.

"You're doing great. Just take your time!" she shouted.

I broke into a smile, inhaling water unexpectedly and almost sabotaging my chances of meeting her challenge. However, after a few coughs and deep breaths, I recovered and completed the return swim back to shore. Following a short rest, we switched roles. As I accompanied Barbara in the kayak and watched her glide across the water with her champion's backstroke, I was struck by the deeper symbolism of this challenge. In our relationship, we were each strong in different ways, and we both flourished with one another's encouragement.

From the mid-1990s onward, Barbara and I poured most of our time and energy into building our business, expanding our consulting work into Europe, South America, and Asia. While preferring to stay home when I traveled domestically, Barbara willingly joined me internationally. Our favorite business and pleasure combination trip was to France in 1991. A true Francophile, Barbara had been to France many times, even living abroad in Paris her junior year of college. This was my first time here, and she couldn't wait to show me why she loved this country so much.

We spent two weeks driving through the Bordeaux, Dordogne, and western Occitanie regions, exploring the ancient cave art, vineyards, châteaus, and towns before spending a week in Paris. Once there, we stayed in Saint-Germain-des-Prés on the Left Bank. We explored the entire city, revisiting Barbara's favorite college haunts. I'm a Monet lover, so viewing the *Water Lilies* series in the Musée de l'Orangerie and taking the train to Giverny made an indelible impression on my soul. For years, I chuckled every time I remembered Barbara's frustration as we viewed the *Mona Lisa* over the heads of a large group of Japanese tourists. I could see it perfectly, while her short stature made it impossible.

And the food. Every food experience we had on this first trip was especially memorable. One meal stands out as pure joy. Barbara introduced me to the Belgian specialty of *moules-frites*, steamed mussels and crispy fries. The garlicky, slightly sweet and briny flavor of the mussels contrasted perfectly with the savory crunch of the fries. I was delighted, and again, a deeper meaning jumped out at me from this experience. We continuously introduced each other to the richness of life because when we were together, we were willing to get outside our comfort zones and take risks.

Almost thirty years later, in the fall of 2019, we were finally free of the pressures of entrepreneurship. Barbara retired in early 2016 when we sold our business, after which I worked with the buyers for a three-year transition period. When the transition period was finally over, I began to relish the freedom and potential of my newly won retirement. No more stress or financial worries burdened me; I had become my most open, relaxed self. We stood at the beginning of a third chapter together filled with great love and adventure—or so we thought.

For weeks after the shock of seeing Barbara's haunting, tell-tale face on the couch, I wanted to pretend I hadn't seen it, but I couldn't. The signs of her likely brain disorder kept forcing themselves on me. I'd been researching <u>f</u>ronto<u>t</u>emporal <u>d</u>egeneration (FTD) since the early months of our relationship when Barbara's mother had been diagnosed with "dementia of unknown histology."* Because of my own family's complicated medical history,

---

* Histology is the study of the microscopic structure of tissues; in this case, brain tissues.

medical science was one of my passions—I had even started college planning to become a physician. I was still as curious as a premed student, especially about the human brain. With my ongoing FTD research, and after watching the slow, devastating demise of both Barbara's mother, Peggy, and her maternal aunt, I recognized every FTD symptom Barbara was exhibiting. Their brain degeneration journeys were unforgettable, having been the centerpiece of the first two decades of our relationship.

It bothered me from the start that Peggy's diagnosis was so difficult. She had been accused of alcoholism before anyone determined the real cause of her erratic behavior. After she died in the early 1990s and her brain autopsy was completed, the best science could do was give Peggy a vague dementia diagnosis; no genetic testing was available at the time.

But I wasn't satisfied with such a vague disease description. I needed to understand more, even if Barbara never wanted to dig deeper into her family's disease. I needed to know everything I could about her family's brain disorder in case Barbara manifested this condition someday. I even got her uncle to tell me stories about Barbara's grandmother, whose behavior led to her placement in a private home for "the afflicted." (Translation: the insane.)

In retrospect, Barbara's grandmother clearly had been the first one in the current family lineage with inexplicable personality and behavior changes. I didn't want any cruel misdiagnosis to happen to Barbara if she started acting strangely. So, over the years, I explored every source I could find on this vague dementia disorder, which was later identified as FTD.

Now that I suspected this dreaded disorder had a hold on Barbara's brain, I documented every physical and behavioral change I observed. In the early months, I was trapped in a state of isolation from my beloved. We had always talked about everything, including her genetic risk for FTD when her aunt first contracted the disease in the early 1990s. Yet, with the reality manifesting before my eyes, I couldn't bring myself to talk to Barbara about my increasingly strong suspicions she had bvFTD.

One day she ate sweets incessantly, which was highly uncharacteristic. A week later she lost interest in knitting, which was a longtime passion of hers. Within two months, she no longer sang in southern Maine's Oratorio Chorale or even graced me with her resonant alto voice around our house. My concerns heightened when Barbara, a highly coordinated and athletic person, lost her balance and fell off her bicycle.

Barbara seemed disconnected from these changes, neither noting nor questioning them. That is, until she had an overdraft in her bank account. I had noticed the increase in her online shopping, but it was her money to spend; we had never joined our money. When the bank called to let Barbara know she'd bounced a check, she seemed bewildered. This had never happened before. And, perhaps more concerningly, she didn't make the connection between her increased spending and the overdraft. Yet even that episode didn't sound the same alarm bells for her as it did me. Instead, she just asked me to take over balancing her checkbook.

"I never liked doing this anyway," she stated flatly.

The overdraft episode was not the first time Barbara had ignored the risk of FTD in our lives. When her oldest cousin started acting strangely and eventually was diagnosed with FTD, upsetting the whole family, Barbara refused to accept the intrusion of this brain disorder into her generation held any meaning for her personally. When the first genetic test for FTD was announced in medical journals, she said it didn't concern her.

"I'm not taking that test," she declared. "I'm going to continue doing my *New York Times* Sunday crossword puzzle and living my life. Why would I want to know if I have the gene that causes that horrible disease?"

I couldn't argue with her at the time. No treatments or even clinical trials were available, so what good would it do for her to know she carried a genetic defect? Regardless, I kept up my research. I needed to know everything I could—every new finding about the causes, types, and potential treatments for this family curse—in case we had to deal with it sometime in the future. I was raised by my scientist parents to face illnesses head-on and be as knowledgeable and proactive as possible. I tracked everything, yet I couldn't find the words or the will to tell her or anyone else about the obvious signs she displayed that indicated her brain wasn't working the same anymore. Naming Barbara's changed behaviors out loud made them too real for me, and I wasn't ready to face the whole truth of what they meant for her or, frankly, for me.

Instead, I kept my growing list of FTD symptoms hidden in my study, tucked in a drawer I knew Barbara would never open. I applied my research skills to each symptom, scouring medical articles for alternative explanations. The evidence of Barbara's brain degeneration kept mounting. Her increasing apathy toward our closest friends and family finally tipped the scale, coming to a head when I came home from shopping one afternoon in early December to find Barbara reading.

"Did you call Cheryl and Norine about coming for dinner tonight?" I asked.

"No," she stated, not taking her eyes from the page.

"But I bought food for all of us. Remember, you were supposed to call them, then call me if they weren't available," I continued, irritation creeping into my voice. "I wouldn't have bought so much food if they weren't coming for dinner."

"Oh," she responded, not even looking at me.

I dropped into a nearby chair as my agitation mounted and my future shattered to the floor. Barbara's indifference was so out of character, it was painful to experience. I couldn't deny any longer the shifting ground in my long, wonderful life with her. I had to tell Barbara what I saw. But how? When? There simply isn't a good time or a good way to tell your beloved they have the fatal genetic brain disorder they intentionally avoided thinking about for decades.

While I pondered how to tell Barbara my suspicions, my mind kept reliving the nine years of pain and, at times, horror caused by her mother's slow brain degeneration. At first Peggy's brain issues caused lots of napping, reduced talking, and lack of motivation. Then, the semipro tennis player stopped caring about the game at all, even stopped watching her beloved tennis stars on TV. She stopped talking altogether a year after her diagnosis of early-onset dementia. No one ever knew whether she had full-blown aphasia, or if she just stopped talking because she often slurred and forgot words. She was a proud, determined woman, just like her daughter.

When Barbara's father took away her mother's car for fear of an accident, Peggy defiantly traversed a busy road with no sidewalks from her house to her favorite local diner to get lunch. Impulsivity kicked in with endless shopping for unneeded items. This advanced to ravenous overeating, consuming food at a speed previously reserved for her powerful tennis backhand. Tension reigned as Barbara's father simply couldn't handle this change in his previously slim, beautifully coiffed, and fashionably dressed spouse.

As I processed what was happening with Barbara, I kept revisiting one interaction I'd had with Peggy thirty-four years before. We were in the den of Barbara's family home in Yardley, Pennsylvania. Barbara and her father had gone out to dinner to discuss some difficult matters, and I had stayed home to be with her mother. We were watching a movie, although it may have been just me doing the watching. Peggy started rocking back and forth in her chair. She was agitated, but I wasn't sure why and she couldn't (or wouldn't) tell me.

I took a guess.

"Do you need to use the bathroom, Peggy?" I asked.

She nodded, so I leapt up off the couch and gave Peggy my hands, helping pull her out of the chair she now was incapable of exiting herself. I knew Peggy wore diapers by that time, but I didn't want her to suffer any unnecessary indignities. I held her elbow and guided her to the powder room. When I positioned her with her back to the toilet, she just stood there. I wasn't sure what to do next, realizing I hadn't gotten sufficient instructions on how to care for her in her husband's absence.

"Do you need me to help you pull down your pants?" I asked.

I didn't want to be intrusive, but my instincts told me she needed help. Again, she signaled yes with her head. Wanting to make light of an awkward situation, I smiled at her.

"Well, no worries. It's just us girls here," I said.

Peggy's mouth turned up slightly, and a twinkle sparked to life in her bright blue eyes. I had the go-ahead. After situating Peggy on the toilet seat, I walked out and closed the door to give her as much privacy as I could. Five minutes later, hearing no stirring inside, I opened the door a crack.

"Do you need me to help you again?" I asked.

From her position on the toilet, she smiled and answered my question with the up-and-down motion of her head. I was not a nurse or caregiver of any kind, and I certainly had never wiped the butt of any adult in my life. Yet I did that night, as graciously and calmly as I could while my stomach churned.

Each time this memory of Peggy surfaced, it stirred up so many questions for me. *Is this what I have to look forward to with Barbara? Are our lives really heading toward another decade of FTD care with the angst and pain it caused?*

CHAPTER TWO

HONESTY AND HOME

By early December, I still hadn't told Barbara my observations. Also, we had gotten the disappointing news that the Smithsonian canceled our two-week spring trip to Paris. This major letdown hit hard, as I desperately needed an escape from my rising fears about Barbara's brain. So, we made a spontaneous decision to go for a two-week Christmas holiday to San Miguel de Allende, a beautiful town in the Colonial Highlands of Mexico known as the *Corazón de México*—its heart.

On the third day of our holiday, we were having lunch on the covered patio of a restaurant facing El Jardín, the central square of the town. Sounds of balloon peddlers and a small mariachi band filled the air. The pink hues of La Parroquia, the parish church that towers over the neatly trimmed laurel trees in the square, had become heightened by the midday sun. We already had fallen in love with this *pueblo mágico*, or magic town.

However, I wasn't as relaxed as I typically would be on vacation. The secret I held weighed on me. I bounced my right leg nervously while I tried to focus on my *chilaquiles verdes con pollo*. Barbara noticed my agitation, a rare event these days. She had been so perceptive before, but I still didn't expect it based on all my recent data gathering on her condition. She paused her focused eating, taco in midair, and looked me in the eye.

"What's going on?" she asked.

Although I was surprised she asked, I felt the warm heat of relief flow through my body. I already had decided that morning I would talk to her before the day's end about what I'd been seeing. Barbara and I had always been intentional and forthright with each other, no matter how difficult the topic, trusting our love to carry us through any challenge. I needed to stay true to the foundation of our relationship and what connected us so deeply. I also knew this would be the most difficult conversation we would ever have. I had needed the last few months to garner the strength for this discussion, but I couldn't put off the dreaded exchange any longer.

I drew in a breath to steady my nerves. Every sight and sound around me disappeared—only we mattered in this moment. Locking eyes and trusting, I rushed right into the abyss.

"I need to have a difficult conversation with you, one I hoped never to have."

Barbara cocked her head. She said nothing but gave me the signal to proceed. I decided to rip the Band-Aid off.

"I've been seeing changes in you," I began in a rush. "Cognitive and behavioral changes. I believe these are signs you have your family's brain disorder, a situation we hoped would never happen."

We had had so many what-if discussions on the topic of FTD during the early years of our lives together that I didn't need to spell my concern out in any greater detail. Barbara's first instinct was to look away and focus on the sounds of the nearby mariachis and the colorful buildings surrounding us. When she turned back, she held my gaze and scoffed at me.

"I'm fine. You worry too much," she said firmly.

I gulped, not sure what to do next.

For Barbara, the conversation was over. She turned her focus back to keeping her taco from falling apart, which wasn't a symptom of any disease. Barbara always had difficulty with sandwiches. It didn't matter if she was eating po'boys, tacos, banh mi, or bao buns, the contents always spilled out as she tried to eat them. I wanted to laugh at her taco troubles like I usually did and continue with my own lunch in pretend ignorance. But having started this dreaded conversation, I couldn't drop it. I plowed ahead and shared my fears.

"No, honey, this is not needless worry on my part. We have to talk about this."

When she turned back toward me, I continued.

"We agreed I wouldn't bring this topic up again unless I saw unmistakable signs. I've seen those signs over the last several months."

I didn't tell her I had a list of eight changes I'd painstakingly compiled across the ten weeks since I was first alerted by her distorted napping face. I needed to share these changes judiciously so I didn't overwhelm and depress her. Without responding, Barbara finished her last bite of taco and wiped her hands on her napkin. Then, she looked directly into my eyes. Her face held no signal of her feelings—no signs of irritation, fear, anger, or any emotion really. The flat facial expression staring back at me had been the most recent and agonizing sign I added to my list of her bvFTD symptoms. After this silent pause, Barbara thrust her pointed chin up in the air and gave me a sideways glare.

"Like what?" she finally asked with an edge of defensiveness.

Declining self-awareness and irritation were common among people in the early stages of bvFTD, so I didn't let Barbara's attitude stop me.

"Well, you don't smile much anymore, for one."

My voice caught as I conjured her radiant smile in my mind. A smile that brought me instant delight for decades. I quickly continued.

"And you don't seem to care about seeing our friends or talking to your family . . . even the ones I know you love dearly."

Barbara kept her eyes on mine, but I still couldn't read her face. I called up all the love I could muster into my eyes, while struggling to hold back my tears. I held her gaze while considering whether my next statement would be too deflating.

"Also, your handwriting."

Last month, Barbara had noticed the deterioration in her classic cursive writing and been bothered by it. She'd always been proud of her penmanship. Her panged expression told me this hit home. Barbara looked away from me, staring down the active street filled with tourists and locals, saying nothing and seemingly withdrawn into herself. Suddenly, she pointed.

"Look. The *mojigangas*. They're so big," she said.

The giant puppets of San Miguel de Allende had turned the corner, dancing back and forth in oversized traditional attire as they proceeded along the square to the corner where we were having lunch. I wanted to get wrapped up in the joy of the puppets, but Barbara was proving my point with her simple, matter-of-fact reporting. Normally, she would have burst into a belly laugh or a huge grin at such fantastical street art, then maybe even excitedly told me about their origin. In this moment, however, she was sitting still and making a simple observation. Another sign for my list: no more complex, fact-filled explanations from this English/ French double major.

I had to get Barbara to accept what I'd observed. I took her hand in mine and tried one more time.

"Most concerning," I said, "is your loss of interest in all your favorite activities—singing, gardening, cooking."

Barbara had continued reading voraciously and occasionally she picked up her knitting, but that was it. Her typical activity now was sitting on the couch watching endless episodes of HGTV, which was something she'd never done before. Barbara looked down and stared at our entwined hands for a few minutes.

"Yeah . . . but I don't know why," she finally replied in a quiet voice.

I squeezed her hand and responded in my gentlest voice.

"Well, let's make a neurology appointment when we get back home, okay? Let's find out what's going on with you."

Barbara nodded up and down several times while she continued to focus on our hands. Finally, she lifted her head and gave me a small smile. I leaned over and kissed her clasped hands in acknowledged agreement. I pulled her up and wrapped her in a tight embrace, oblivious to everyone around us and deeply relieved to no longer be carrying this burden alone.

With the difficult conversation behind us, Barbara and I were intent on enjoying the rest of our holiday. The next morning, we entered the living room of our hotel, coffees in hand, eager to sit by the roaring fire on this crisp December morning to plan our day's activities. A tall, attractive woman sat on one of the couches by the fire with a Jack Russell terrier nestled next to her. We all acknowledged one another with a nod as Barbara and I sat down on the couch opposite her. Barbara opened our travel guide, and we began conferring in hushed voices.

"Could I help you with anything?" the woman asked. "I live here, so I probably can answer any questions you have."

"That's kind of you," I commented with my faint introvert smile.

Barbara, by contrast, gave her a generous smile and opened a dialogue.

"I love your dog," she said.

We spent the next twenty minutes introducing ourselves and sharing our mutual love for San Miguel de Allende. As we talked, Barbara's usual enthusiasm and curiosity about new people came pouring out, and I was heartened by her excitement. She was engaged with this stranger like Barbara of old, with no indication of the apathy or disengagement characteristic of bvFTD, giving me a moment of hope. *Maybe I've been too hasty.* But much as I wanted to embrace that possibility, I knew that even advanced FTD patients often rallied to their old selves when meeting new people. My musings were interrupted by our new friend, Rebecca.

"Are you planning to look at real estate while you're here?" she asked.

"No," I stated, surprised by my quick, definitive response.

I usually jumped at the chance to look at houses every place we traveled. I inherited this tourist voyeurism from my mother, who took us driving through neighborhoods throughout my childhood, imagining what it would be like to live in those places. My quick rejection of Rebecca's kind offer was due to our recent purchase of a Creole cottage in the French Quarter of New Orleans, fulfilling our long-term retirement plan of spending wintertime enjoying the music and food of the city where I grew up.

"I'm a realtor here, is why I asked. But I understand if you're not interested."

"I want to," Barbara said with an eager tone I hadn't heard in a long time.

I whipped my head around to look at her, puzzled. Barbara's sudden enthusiasm for touring houses in San Miguel de Allende surprised me for two reasons. The first reason being her increasing generalized apathy. The second reason being because I typically had to drag Barbara kicking and screaming to look at real estate. Sometimes she simply dug in her heels. Once when we visited

Whidbey Island on a vacation through the Northwest United States and British Colombia, I wanted to check out housing options in this beautiful west coast paradise. Barbara refused, threatening to get back on the ferry if I did. And this was just one example.

I kept my feelings about her reaction to myself. Despite my surprise, I didn't want to dampen Barbara's excitement in any way. Still, not wanting to waste Rebecca's time, I felt the need to clarify our situation. I was the money manager in our family, and I always supported making big purchases when we could afford them and they enhanced our lives. While buying a second home became possible when we received the final payment from the sale of our consulting and training business, those funds were not endless.

"Normally, I would love to tour houses, but we just bought a second home this spring," I explained.

"That's okay. You don't have to buy anything," Rebecca said. "I'm having fun with you two, and I'd be happy to spend a day with you looking at houses. It's a great way to learn about a new place."

Barbara's eyes twinkled and her smile widened as Rebecca spoke. I didn't want to disappoint her, so I softened. I also believe unexpected encounters happen for a reason.

"I agree with you, on both counts," I relented. "So, if you're okay with us not buying anything, let's do it."

With that agreement, I allowed my enthusiasm to rise to match Barbara's. However, I never expected what would happen when we started house tours the next day. We pulled up in front of a bright pink house with multicolored bougainvillea draping down the front wall. The wall mosaic of hummingbirds in the small courtyard entrance was captivating, causing Barbara to coo with delight. A statue of Saint Francis was nestled among colorful Mexican shrimp plants, making me smile. Inside the front door, the grand entryway stairs led our eyes two floors up to a rooftop deck, leaving us both speechless. The balconies and courtyards overflowing with flora stole my flower-loving partner's heart. She exclaimed at every turn, expressing more pleasure than I'd heard from her in months.

"I want this house," Barbara proclaimed as we finished our tour of the place.

I reacted with disbelief and brushed her off with a flippant remark.

"Yeah, it's gorgeous. I'm glad we saw it. Can't wait to see what else this town has to offer."

We continued our real estate tour, and Barbara became more sullen as the day progressed. She showed no enthusiasm for a house with a lap pool, even though she was an accomplished competitive swimmer. At the end of the day, we both thanked Rebecca profusely and went to the bar at our hotel for a drink. Barbara jumped right in after we placed our order.

"You're not taking me seriously. I want that first house we saw."

"What?" I exclaimed. "Are you kidding me?"

I was unmoored and confused by Barbara's certainty. Buying in San Miguel would be a major twist in our plans, and Barbara had always been a pragmatic show-me-the-money kind of gal. I usually was the one upsetting our lives with new ideas and new adventures into the unexpected. But now was not the ideal time to change plans. We were retired, a phase we had long planned for and worked hard to achieve. And even though we were privileged to have choices, we had agreed on our retirement plans just a year ago. We planned to stay in our new condo in Portland, Maine, for the summer and early fall months, then spend winter and early spring months in New Orleans, where we could revel in the jazz scene and savor the incredible food and culture. In the shoulder seasons, we would travel. *How does a house in central Mexico fit into these plans? And why is Barbara so adamant about this house in San Miguel?* The second was the important question.

I searched Barbara's face in silence while I pondered this unexpected twist. She was serious. As a psychologist with strong intuition, I could usually spot the underlying causes of behavior, but I have never been able to figure out Barbara's position that evening. I had no clue what fed her strong desire for this house. Ultimately, I decided I didn't care. It was enough that Barbara still knew what she wanted and could express herself so strongly. And what she wanted, I wanted. We were compatible and adventurous in that way; when one of us had a clear desire, we followed it. I especially wanted to follow her lead now and give her whatever sparked her enthusiasm.

The next day we called Rebecca and put in an offer on the house. Though we would need to sell some investments, it would be worth it. I had no idea then what a fortuitous decision it was, but I believe Barbara did somehow. Three months later, we closed on our house in San Miguel and were awaiting close friends of ours arriving from Maine. Our friends Cheryl and Norine were chefs and restaurateurs with extensive ties to Mexico, especially the Yucatan and Oaxaca. We knew they would appreciate the excellent culinary options in our new town, as well as its prolific art scene.

However, their pending visit also made me anxious. I kept internally debating whether to share my concerns about Barbara with them. Being in such close quarters for an extended period, I imagined they may experience some of Barbara's changed behavior and be confused. I was especially worried she might say something off, potentially even insulting, as people with bvFTD often did.

Carrying my fear alone was harder by the day. I didn't want to violate any confidence between Barbara and me, though she hadn't directly asked me not to tell anyone about my suspicions. I needed to get my concerns out, but I didn't want to lay them on Barbara. If anything, I wanted Barbara to unload her fears on me, but this hadn't happened. Unlike me, Barbara didn't seem to have any concerns.

We still didn't have a firm diagnosis, of course. And although we called neurologists in both Maine and New Orleans during our time home after our winter holiday, we couldn't get an appointment for eight months. However, the appointment was made, and in the three months since then, Barbara had retreated into either denial or oblivion, I wasn't sure which.

I didn't share her ability to escape our pending discovery. If I told our friends, they could help me with my rising dread. My friends had been central to my well-being for as long as I could remember. Friends, including Barbara, were the relationships where I found unconditional love, and I desperately needed that love right now. I feared I would implode if I held my suspicions inside for five more months.

Our friends finally arrived, gushing over our new house and thrilled to see us in Mexico. I knew I would share the burden with them, just as I would want them to share theirs with me. The next morning, while Barbara slept in and we had our breakfast, I took a deep breath, preparing to reveal my fears.

"There's something happening to Barbara that I need y'all to know," I began.

I told them my belief Barbara was in the early stage of the same degenerative brain disorder that had taken her mother, a process they had heard about in the early years of our friendship. As I talked, Cheryl's eyes widened.

"Oh no!" she exclaimed.

Norine reached out to me, clasping my hand.

"What makes you think this?" she asked.

Due to our travels to Mexico and New Orleans, they had not been around Barbara for several months and had not yet spent enough time with her on this trip to observe any changes. I painstakingly described the numerous symptoms I had documented. I even told them I'd shared my suspicions with Barbara, who had acknowledged some of the changes I observed. Silence followed. The weight of the news created a heaviness in the air.

"We're here for you and Barbara. You know that, right?" Cheryl said. "Whatever you need. And even though y'all are planning to sell your place in Maine, we'll still see you often. You both mean the world to us."

I felt my neck muscles relax and my heart lighten.

"Don't carry this alone anymore," Norine added. "If you're right, this is going to be a difficult journey. We're your sisters. We're here through the joys and the sorrows."

The tears I'd been choking back every day streamed down my face. I was finally released from carrying this burden alone. I had true friends, and they would help me through this journey, no matter what came to be.

CHAPTER THREE

BRAINS AND BICYCLES

The smell of disinfectant and the bright white sterility of the neurologist's examination room overwhelmed me at first. Fortunately, we both had strong positive feelings for the neurologist when we first met with her in August. She was a kind, caring, competent woman with certifications in both genetics and neurology; she had ordered cognitive testing and a complete brain MRI for Barbara.

It was early November, and we were just getting Barbara's MRI results. I fidgeted with anticipation of the news we were likely to receive and the aftermath it would bring. Barbara had just emerged from a depressive state. Her cognitive testing results we got in early October showed deficiencies in her planning and decision-making capabilities, as well as some periodic short-term memory loss. I didn't know what would happen to her mental state after this visit.

We sat in the sterile exam room in mutual silence, an unspoken comfort born of almost forty years together. On the side wall, I caught sight of the poster with facial expressions used to help patients rate their pain from one to ten. My mental pain was already in high ascent, likely to fly way off this chart.

I turned my head away so Barbara wouldn't see me repeatedly trying to unlock my clenched jaw. I quashed the urge to leave her side and pace so I could release the tense muscles in my body. Instead, I stretched my legs out in front of me and flexed my toes. To stay connected to her, I caressed Barbara's back, feeling the coolness of her silk shirt on my palm. I'd been so certain a professional diagnosis was what I wanted, what I needed. Now I didn't want to hear the results. *I don't want to be right.* Being right this time wouldn't bring me accolades or a feeling of success. It would shatter me.

Get a grip! the self-reliant part of me responded, chastising myself for faltering in my conviction. Knowledge could yield power, especially medical knowledge. I'd experienced the power of understanding medical problems my whole life. With a concrete diagnosis, you could find a medical miracle. I learned this fact at age nine when my father was diagnosed with an autoimmune blood disease. He required numerous experimental treatments over the next thirty-four years of his life. If we hadn't gotten the diagnosis, these treatments would not have been possible. This lesson was further reinforced during my teenage years when my older sister was diagnosed with a bone tumor in her femur and her leg was saved by an experimental bone transplant. I had no doubt knowing everything possible about one's medical condition was best. However, right then, as I sat next to Barbara, I wished I could cover myself with a protective shield and hide from the truth forever.

Just as my desire for escape swelled, the neurologist opened the door. Her stark white coat stood in sharp contrast to the caring smile on her face. The strong cinnamon flavor from the Tic Tacs I had popped into my mouth earlier exploded. I suddenly became conscious that I had forgotten to put on deodorant, my attention having been focused on getting Barbara showered and ready this morning.

"I have your brain MRI scans now, Barbara. Do you and Susan want to see them?" asked the doctor.

"Yes," Barbara replied, a slight twinkle forming in her eyes.

That twinkle rarely made an appearance anymore unless she was looking at me. But Barbara liked and trusted this doctor. Also, she was expecting positive news. There could be multiple causes for the mild cognitive impairment her October testing had shown. We both hoped the doctor would identify a benign cause for the deficits, although I doubted it would happen.

I stood up and positioned myself behind the doctor so I could see the images she pulled up on her computer screen. The first brain image popped into view. I scanned the image, desperate to see a complete set of brain cells. I'd learned to read MRIs of the human brain in order to incorporate emerging neuroscience into our organizational psychology consultancy business.

I leaned in and focused my eyes like a telescope on Barbara's prefrontal cortex, which is the brain mass in the front of the head.

I was not prepared for what I saw. There was a black void where the gray matter in Barbara's right frontal lobe was supposed to be. Her brain had lost the cells that enabled her to pay attention, care about others, and make decisions; the ones that controlled her impulses and helped her anticipate and plan future events. There was simply nothing there, leaving a visible hole in the right front side of Barbara's brain. My list of her changed behaviors was explained in one stark image. Barbara's condition was more advanced than I imagined.

The empty space in Barbara's head was immediately seared into *my* brain, and I didn't know what to do with this unwanted knowledge. To stop the scream rising in my throat, I sucked in air through my nostrils and held my breath for what felt like an eternity. Slowly breathing out, I turned to see Barbara's sad eyes staring at the screen. She also had seen many healthy brain images in the training materials she'd edited for years. She knew the image in front of her was not a healthy one. *Is she also remembering the autopsy of her mother's shrunken brain, that horrible document we read together decades ago?*

I walked over to Barbara and locked eyes with her as fear rose in her beautiful blue-gray eyes. She grabbed my hand and squeezed. I gave her the most loving smile I could, desperate to share with her whatever inner strength I could muster. As I held her gaze, her fear started to diminish, and her grasp softened. When I felt her regain calm, I looked past Barbara at the doctor. She had been speaking to Barbara about the MRI, but her voice had only registered in my brain as background noise.

"Would you please repeat what you said?" I asked.

"From the MRI, it's clear Barbara has noticeable cell loss in her right frontal lobe, signifying FTD as you suspected from her family history."

There it was, out in the open, the dreaded diagnosis we'd hoped against hope would never come. It had been declared. There could be no escaping our reality anymore. Brain images didn't lie.

"Her grandmother, mother, maternal aunt, and oldest male cousin all died from this disease, right?" the neurologist added, consulting her notes.

We both nodded. The horrors of the past rushed into the room. I thought of when Barbara's mother wandered down the main road of their hometown in traffic; of her aunt wearing diapers and withering away in the nursing home; of her oldest first cousin, angry and acting out in bizarre ways. I looked at Barbara, now trapped by the same family disorder.

"Just to be sure, I recommend a genetic test," the doctor continued. "While the family pattern seems obvious, no one in your family has ever been tested to confirm that this is a genetic form of FTD."

Barbara stayed silent, head down.

"Okay," I responded, too tired to say more.

"We'll draw blood, run the test, and get back to you as soon as we have the results."

With that, the doctor rose and we followed suit. She hugged each of us in silence, her physical comfort more valuable than any words. We walked to the car in silence, holding hands, no words needed between us. We knew we were in this nightmare together.

Fortunately, there would be no debate about who drove. Barbara had declared a few months before that her reflexes weren't fast enough to drive, cognizant of her loss of anticipatory abilities. After we buckled in, Barbara whispered.

"Why do I need the genetic test? I clearly have FTD."

I touched her arm and mustered a weak smile. *Oh, my darling. I understand your reflex to stop here, not to dive deeper into this abyss.* Yet I had to tell her what I believed, so I spoke.

"Science has advanced greatly in the fourteen years since your cousin's diagnosis, and it's light years ahead of when your mother died, what, thirty years ago?"

We let that sad history have its own silent space for a moment. I already was convinced Barbara's brain disorder was genetic. I knew she was as well, so I continued.

"Now they know there are several genetic forms of FTD. When we find out which one you have, we might be able to find a treatment."

Was this false hope? And was the hope for her or for me? Maybe it was just for me, but it was what I needed in the moment.

"You know there's nothing to be done about it. There's no cure," Barbara replied with a faint hint of frustration.

I flashed to the *60 Minutes* program we'd seen last year. Reporter Bill Whitaker said FTD is "the cruelest disease you've never heard of . . . and it's always fatal." My throat tightened and my heart began to beat faster. I couldn't let this truth take root right now. I channeled my ever-optimistic mother instead.

"You never know. There's lots of brain research going on right now."

I silently pleaded with the universe to send a medical miracle our way. Barbara and I needed more time, more joy. I turned to make direct eye contact before I continued.

"There might be a clinical trial in the works that could help you. First, we have to know which genetic variant you have."

"Okay," she said, notes of fatigue evident in her voice. "If you think so, I'll do it."

She trusted me as she always had. I hoped I could deliver for both of our sakes. As I pulled out of the parking lot onto the city streets, Barbara began calling out words she saw on the billboards and businesses we passed on our drive home.

"Need a Roof?"

"Hot Donuts!"

"Need a Lawyer? Call Desiree Charbonnet."

When these verbal tics first started, I thought they were happening because billboards were a novelty to her, as there weren't any in Portland, and New Orleans had them in abundance. After seeing the MRI, I could no longer enjoy that fantasy. These repetitive vocalizations were evidence of Barbara's lack of impulse control caused by her missing brain cells.

To silence Barbara's verbal tic and the tension it was causing me, I took the long way home, driving through City Park and down Esplanade Avenue, hoping the majestic live oaks on this route would soothe her soul and mine. We parked and walked hand in hand down the block to our Creole cottage in silence, exchanging only weak smiles. We were still in shock from those stark images. I heard Barbara mumble behind me as we entered our cottage, and I turned, cocking my head.

"I'm taking a nap," she repeated, walking past me.

For once, her napping didn't worry me. Her desire for escape made complete sense.

"Do you need help with anything?" I queried.

"No, I can still fend for myself . . . for now anyway."

I caught Barbara's arm and pulled her to me in a deep embrace. She returned my hug, clinging longer than usual. Barbara dropped her arms first, looked up at me, and forced her lips upward in an attempt at a brave smile. I kissed her gently on her forehead, and she turned to walk into the bedroom.

My first instinct was to go to the TV room and numb myself, but I was too wound up to sit. Pacing, I moved from the TV room to the kitchen and back, not knowing what to do. I was glad Barbara decided to take a nap; I needed to sort out this news by myself first. My brain was a complete jumble. *How do I think about this? What do I do with this diagnosis?*

Heat rose up my neck and face; my palms began to sweat. I felt prickly sensations in my neck, shoulders, and arms. I had to get this rising pain and anxiety out of me. I had to scream . . . but I couldn't let Barbara hear me. I didn't want to make this about me.

I rushed out the door into our courtyard where Barbara couldn't hear my scream. As soon as I cleared the door, a piercing howl escaped from deep in my gut as I bent over, clasping my knees. My throat constricted. I gasped for air. The scream turned into a high-pitched wail. My mother's mantra, *What will the neighbors think*, flashed through my brain for a split second, but I didn't let it stop me. I couldn't. How could anything as trivial as neighbors' opinions matter now? And, besides, I had to get this ball of fear and anguish out of me to manage what was coming.

I stumbled to the patio table, wrenching the arm of a chair back so I could collapse into it. Our future was supposed to be fun and adventurous. We'd worked so hard with the intention of having a carefree retirement. *Now what? What is our life going to be like now?* I clutched my arms around my waist and doubled over as another screeching wail came pouring out of me. I tried to slow my breathing but couldn't. On the way home from the doctor, I had calculated where Barbara was on the typical FTD life span. She probably had five or six more years at most. Excruciating physical and psychic pain doubled me over.

Eventually, the disciplined part of me took charge.

Pull yourself together! You have to think. You have to plan.

Why? For what? the grieving part of me replied. *Our life as we intended it is over.*

Don't be overly dramatic. It doesn't help, disciplined me shot back.

With the many losses we would face weighing me down, my mind escaped back to our last overseas trip together in October 2019. We celebrated my retirement by traveling to Sicily and Puglia. This was our fourth trip to Italy but our first to these regions. I saw us standing in a street in Alberobello, delighted by the fairy-tale houses surrounding us.

"I'm so glad you wanted to come here!" Barbara exclaimed.

"These trulli houses are *so* unique. Pictures don't do them justice. They're so magical!"

"Magical, indeed," I responded, delighted at finally seeing these houses in person.

I'd been in a state of bliss that whole trip. Between the trulli and the large, ancient Ent-like olive trees in the village where we stayed, I had the full-on Hobbit experience of my dreams. It was something I'd wanted since college, when I devoured all J. R. R. Tolkien's books chronicling Middle Earth.

"This is why I'm so glad we're both free of work now," Barbara commented. "We can travel every year, maybe even twice in some years, exploring, and exploring, and exploring—what we've always loved doing together!"

Back in my new reality, I slumped forward and cradled my head, resting my elbows on my knees. Squinching my eyes tightly, I started to rock. The tears sitting in my eyes blurred the bright yellow clump of cosmos in front of me.

I felt myself rocking faster. *How am I going to manage this?* Barbara had always grounded me during stressful times. While I had strength and self-reliance, my emotions often rocketed me around before I charted a clear path forward. She was the one who maintained practical sensibility. Would I be steadfast enough to weather this hurricane of tumult in our lives?

I kept rocking until I exhausted myself and remembered Barbara wouldn't sleep forever. I stood, but couldn't unhunch my shoulders, rounded from the weight of my new reality. I walked inside and made my way to the guest bath, where my own swollen eyes and a red face stared back at me. I splashed water on my face and held my palms against my eyes. It was no use. Barbara was going to be able to see I'd been crying.

There were people I needed to call. Who should I call first? And what would I tell them? As I stared at my phone screen, numerous names flashed across my mind, but I didn't make a move. Everyone I told would be devastated. They'd all heard the stories of Barbara's mother and aunt. Most of our close circle had lived through those years with us. But the pain of others wasn't what stopped me. It was my own. I wasn't ready to give voice to this news. If I didn't tell anyone, maybe I could pretend it wasn't happening for a little while longer.

On the night of Barbara's official diagnosis, we had dinner delivered, as neither of us had the energy or inclination to cook. I placed the order while Barbara set the table, then pulled out the candles and candleholders as usual. When she lit the candles, the crystal wineglasses refracted the light, so the glow bounced off the ochre walls. We both watched, mesmerized. When the meal arrived, we savored Mediterranean lamb shanks, sautéed spinach, and saffron rice as though we hadn't eaten in days. I didn't have any words to lighten the mood, which wasn't possible anyway. Finishing our final bites, Barbara caught and held my gaze.

"I looked into my future and saw only a blank," she said. "I don't know how to think about this."

I struggled to stay calm, hoping my face wasn't turning visibly red from the stress of holding back the sobs in my chest.

"Forget about thinking, honey. What are you feeling?"

"Dread . . . fear," she replied.

I reached over and took her hand. I waited for her to say more, but she just looked at me with imploring eyes. I knew she wanted me to say this would all be okay, but I couldn't. We didn't lie to each other. I pulled in a deep breath, then slowly released it, letting the momentary calm settle in my chest before speaking.

"I feel the same way. And I think we're going to feel this way for a while. We're grieving," I said.

Barbara started drumming with her free hand. These impulsive motor movements were happening more frequently, and they increased my anxiety. I took this hand as well, gently, wanting to calm her as much as I could.

"It's important not to let our fears overwhelm us. Can you say more, so we can talk this through together?" I continued, trying not to think about how *reduced spontaneous speech* was another bvFTD symptom on my list.

I'd stopped expecting Barbara to volunteer her thoughts or feelings. Fortunately, she usually responded to my prompts. I could see Barbara searching for her answer, but then she replied with a question.

"Do you remember the first summer you met my family?"

That scene, with all its poignancy, had played itself out in my mind so many times. We had only been lovers for three months when Barbara asked me to go with her to Yardley and meet her whole family. That day, we were lying on chaise lounges next to each other at the deep end of her parents' pool. Both her brothers were there with their young families. I'd been staring at the youngest boy, just fourteen months old, in his stroller. I hadn't noticed Barbara's mother approaching until she sat down at the foot of my chaise.

Peggy's head swiveled back and forth between us, looking first at Barbara, then at me with an expressionless face. I braced myself, not knowing what was coming. I feared she was about to express the same disdain my parents did when I first came out to them.

"Barbara," she finally said, "there's something I need to tell you. Something's wrong with my brain."

Hearing this news for the first time from an older parent would have been difficult enough, but Peggy had just turned fifty-six. I turned to see Barbara's face crumble and her eyes lose their brightness. Her smile disappeared and a tightness pulled at the corners of her lips. Now, sitting across from me at the table decades later, Barbara was looking at me with the same fearful expression I saw that day.

"Yes, of course I remember," I replied, keeping my face as blank as possible, wanting her to continue.

Barbara's uncharacteristic stillness unnerved me. I almost jumped in to relieve my rising anxiety, but finally she spoke.

"That day turned my life, our lives, upside down. We were in a holding pattern for the next nine years, not really understanding what was happening with my mother."

She looked up at me, and I nodded, unable to respond to those raw memories. Barbara dropped her head again.

"Today was a day just like that one," she finished.

I reached over to pull her chin up gently, hoping the tears I felt sitting at the edges of my eyes wouldn't distract her. I dropped my hand from her chin and reached for her hand before responding with as much quiet strength as I could muster.

"Yes, it was. But we know more now than we did then. And we're in this together. Don't forget," I tried to reassure her.

Barbara gave me a weak smile, then looked down at our hands resting in her lap. I clasped her hand more tightly in mine.

"I don't want this to sound strange or heartless to you, but I've been thinking about those years too. And I believe we're really fortunate to have had the experience we had with your mother," I kept on.

Her head whipped up, her face forming a quizzical expression.

"How can you say that?"

"Because of that day, because of your mother's diagnosis and decline, we agreed we wouldn't . . . couldn't . . . wait to live our lives," I stammered.

I paused for a moment and gathered my strength.

"And, to our credit, we didn't. We've lived very intentionally since that day. We've done meaningful work. Explored many parts of the world. Experienced lots of live music. Shared so much."

I was an imaginative optimist while Barbara described herself as a grounded realist. I wasn't sure how she'd respond to my heartfelt take on our situation. The smile slowly forming and the twinkling in her blue-gray eyes looking back at me were all the affirmation I needed to continue.

"And you should congratulate yourself on all the work you've done since your mother's pronouncement that day. You've worked hard to keep your brain active. You've solved *The New York Times* Sunday crossword puzzle by yourself for years. And we've already had twelve more years than your mother did when she got her dementia diagnosis."

Barbara squeezed my hands and slowly nodded.

Anger was futile and regrets unnecessary.

||||||||||||||||||||||||

In the early months of Barbara's diagnosis, my usual forward-thinking brain never drifted into imagining life without Barbara. It simply wasn't possible. When Barbara and I met, I believed I'd never have a deep, lasting love. My fiancé had been killed in a senseless industrial accident when I was nineteen, and I'd guarded my soul carefully after his death. None of the relationships I had with men or women in my twenties lasted longer than a few years; I always found a reason to leave so I'd never be bereft again. But Barbara captured my heart and soul so quickly and so completely, I was all in before I could think about holding myself back from her. During the initial decade of our relationship, when both Barbara's mother and aunt fell victim to the same brain disorder, I didn't recoil from the genetic risk this presented for Barbara. I didn't care. Barbara was the person I wanted to spend my life with. Period.

Sitting in our TV room the morning after her MRI visit, I felt the same commitment I had the summer we learned about Peggy's brain problem. I would be here for the duration of Barbara's illness, no matter what path it took. I would take care of her and keep her out of a nursing home, which she desperately wanted.

My life up to that point gave me the confidence that I could handle Barbara's brain degeneration. From my training as a social worker and psychologist; my decades of project management; my family history of extensive medical problems and near deaths; my direct experience with Barbara's mother and aunt in their declining years; and, last but certainly not least, our financial resources and her long-term care insurance, I knew I was prepared to do this.

Furthermore, Barbara trusted me to be there for her to the end. She knew I wasn't going to find a new girlfriend, as both her father and uncle had done while their wives were in decline. Still, my confidence in providing Barbara's care didn't mean I was without questions. I had many. *What impact will Barbara's FTD journey have on my soul? My heart?* After having a true partner for so long now, my old pattern of withholding and running from commitment had been shed decades ago. I was wide open, vulnerable. *How will I function without Barbara by my side? Who will I be on the other side of this journey?*

When Barbara woke up the morning after the neurologist's visit, she was surprisingly cheery. Still in her sleep shirt, she came looking for me in the TV room where I'd been reminiscing. Glad to see Barbara's broad smile again, I stood up to hug her.

"What's got you so cheerful this morning?"

"I'm going to buy my ring," she declared.

I instantly knew what ring she meant. She'd fallen in love with an Alex Šepkus ring in a jewelry store on Royal Street a year and a half ago. The ring was Šepkus's original *Little Windows* design, made of 18 karat gold and adorned with thirteen small, natural, conflict-free diamonds, including yellow ones, which I'd never seen before. I had cautioned Barbara not to buy the ring when she first saw it. It was expensive, and she was living on savings as she waited for her Social Security payments to begin in 2021 when she turned seventy.

I couldn't believe Barbara still remembered that ring. She hadn't mentioned it since we first discussed the purchase outside the jewelry store, and I'd completely forgotten about it. But I didn't love things the way Barbara did, especially jewelry and clothes. She could spend hours contemplating an item she wanted, enjoying the consideration of it as much as the ultimate purchase and adornment. Barbara wasn't overly indulgent; she always bought a few high-quality items rather than loads of cheaper ones. She also had the money for this ring thanks to the final check we'd received from the sale of our business. Her desire for diamonds wasn't surprising considering she was an April baby, so diamond was her birthstone.

Then why wasn't I happy that she wanted to buy this beautiful ring? This purchase would have no impact on me. *Shouldn't I be glad she thought of something to lift her spirits? Has my mother's profound frugalness, which I hated, seeped into my heart without me realizing it?* No, I realized my response was grounded in memories of Barbara's mother. Her advancing, undiagnosed FTD led her to purchase so many things so quickly, she put her husband in significant debt before he realized what was happening.

Barbara noticed my silence.

"Aren't you happy for me?" she asked.

Her simple question shook me out of my head, turning my lips from a frown to a smile. I had always supported her when her desires were clear. I certainly wasn't going to change that now. I would just have to address the spending risk another day.

"Of course I am! It's just . . . you know how I am with big purchases."

"Yeah, but you don't hesitate to buy me expensive jewelry," she said, grabbing my hand. "You're not cheap. You just don't buy those kinds of things for yourself. I want to do this for myself . . . especially now. I want to spend whatever time I have left watching diamonds refract light. You know how I love that!"

I pulled Barbara close, hugging her for a long time. I smiled at her intentionality and her love of diamonds. *Whatever brings Barbara joy is welcomed by me.*

Three days after Barbara's diagnosis, we sat in our living room reading. Barbara hadn't turned a page in quite some time, nor had I. My brain wouldn't settle. I had woken that morning bombarded with more unsettling memories of the way Peggy's disease progressed. My chest tightened and I bit my lip as I reflected on the speed of Peggy's decline. Within two and a half years of her first neurology appointment, Barbara's father declared himself incapable of continuing her care and placed Peggy in a nursing home. I didn't know what Barbara's progression would be. I just knew it would be too fast for me. We needed to revise our lives in light of this new reality. We had no time to waste.

I'd spent the past few days giving Barbara space, waiting for her to make her wishes known. This diagnosis was hers and I wanted her to have control over it. I wanted her to tell me how she wanted to handle her life going forward. This morning, I began questioning my approach. *Does Barbara still have the capacity to guide her own life?*

Barbara had never been a planner. She viewed herself as grabbing life's opportunities when they presented, rather than creating opportunities herself. She hadn't planned to move to Connecticut where I met her; she simply had joined an old boyfriend when he wanted to leave New Mexico. She hadn't planned her career as an artist's agent; she just had seized the opportunity when her temporary job at a book production company evolved into that role.

"If I were alone, I'd just swim in the flow until something sparked my interest," Barbara had once told me, expressing her appreciation when I established retirement benefit plans for our business. Now with FTD, the brain cells that would have enabled her to plan her future no longer existed. *Do I need to step in and be more directive?*

I value autonomy fiercely. The agency we each have over our own lives if we dare to claim it is precious. I wanted it for myself, and I always wanted it for Barbara, who felt the same. Even now—or especially now—I didn't want to take anything away from Barbara she didn't willingly relinquish. We had worked hard to keep power dynamics from entering our relationship, and I wanted to maintain this even in the face of her diminishing capacity.

Still, time did not favor us, and I was not a patient person.

Although it had only been a few days since her diagnosis, Barbara's silence about the future was getting to me. My rising impatience was driven by fear that Barbara would soon lose her ability or willingness to speak, as her mother had within a year of her diagnosis. I couldn't imagine being without Barbara's soothing voice and pithy quips. It was hard enough that she had stopped singing. This precious gift was already lost. I couldn't keep waiting for her to speak to me about her future. Passivity wasn't my way in life.

Barbara sensed my growing restlessness. She looked up at me briefly, giving me a weak smile but saying nothing. I took a deep breath, trying to calm my agitation before I spoke. Quietly, I proceeded.

"Now that we have your diagnosis, there are several things we need to do."

She nodded and slowly raised her head, looking at me with that blank face that still unnerved me. I gripped my own thigh. I could hear the tautness in my voice. The still warm November air seeped under the front door of our 1880s cottage.

"We need to discuss some legal and financial matters right away. And we have to make some phone calls to family and friends. What do you want to do first?"

Barbara straightened her back, her shoulders rising.

"I was just thinking how glad I am that my father died this past summer, so I don't have to call and tell him my diagnosis."

I nodded. I'd thought the same two days before. I let silence follow even though I wanted to get back to the tasks we needed to face. Barbara picked up the conversation.

"I need to call my brother. I've been trying to think of how to tell him. The only words I can find are the ones my mother spoke to me: 'There's something wrong with my brain.'"

Salty tears blurred my vision. I scooted closer to Barbara on the couch and wrapped her in my arms. I didn't want to call her older brother either. He would take this news particularly hard, as he and Barbara had lost their younger brother to melanoma a decade before. Now his only remaining sibling was afflicted with the family curse, news that had implications for him as well. While I hugged Barbara, my mother's mantra, *Procrastinating doesn't make it easier*, popped into my mind. *Okay, girl*, I coached myself. *Gather your strength. If she's ready, you need to do this now.* I broke away from our embrace.

"Do you want to make the call alone or together? If it would help you, I could start the conversation," I asked.

Barbara looked up, smiling.

"That would help a lot."

I knew she'd take the lead once I opened the door, so I put the phone on speaker mode. When I heard the ringing sound, I realized I wasn't ready for this call. I hadn't rehearsed my lines. My palms became sweaty. *How am I going to tell her brother this horrendous news?*

"Hey, Barbie," he answered in the upbeat tone he always used with her. "Good to hear from you."

At the sound of his voice, I felt a stabbing pain in my chest. We were about to destroy her brother's world. Barbara smiled warmly as she leaned closer to the phone.

"Hey there," she replied as though this was just an ordinary sibling catch-up call.

"I'm on the phone too," I interjected.

"Oh, hi, good to hear from you. What's up?"

"Well . . ." I started, but no words came to me.

Don't leave him hanging, I admonished myself. *There's no going back now.* I swallowed and resumed.

"Barbara wanted you to know we met with a neurologist a few days ago. Her MRI showed that she's lost brain matter in her frontal lobe. The doctor told us she has FTD," I stated as simply as I could.

"Oh NO! Oh, God, NO! This wasn't supposed to happen again!" our sister-in-law's voice screamed through the phone. Her brother evidently had his phone on speaker mode too.

The scream unsettled me.

"I regret we have such bad news to share, but we knew you'd want to know," my words came out in a rush. "Barbara also has taken the genetic test. The doctor wanted to see what form of FTD she has. There's no doubt about the underlying diagnosis, though. We saw the MRI. We wanted y'all to know right away."

The silence was deafening; Barbara began to frown. I stayed quiet, giving her brother space to absorb this horrible news. An introvert like me, I knew he had to rehearse internally before he talked. After all, we had just upped the ante for him since Barbara's diagnosis meant his and his only child's risk of the disease had increased as well.

Barbara couldn't contain herself.

"Hey . . . did you hear what Susan said?"

"Yes . . . well. I'm glad you told us," he stammered before going silent again.

After a few moments, he spoke in a quiet voice.

"Barbie. I'm so sorry to hear this news."

"Yeah . . . me too," she replied in kind.

His voice struggled for normalcy.

"Uh, well . . . keep us informed about the rest of the tests, okay?"

I thought he wanted to end the call, but after a few seconds he continued.

"Are you going to call our son, or do you want us to do that?" he asked.

"We're going to call our niece and nephews ourselves," Barbara jumped in right away.

My heart soared hearing Barbara's emphatic response. We had built close, intentional relationships with the next generation, separate from their parents, and we knew they trusted us to discuss difficult matters. Even though those calls would be excruciating, we wanted to be the ones delivering the news. Barbara's diagnosis raised risks for them too. Familial bvFTD was caused by a defect in an autosomal-dominant *GRN* gene. With this type of genetic dominance, you had a 50 percent probability of carrying the defective gene when one of your biological parents was known to have it. Barbara having the defective gene meant her brothers and, as a result, their children, might have it as well. No one wanted this kind of news.

We spent the afternoon gearing up for the next three heart-wrenching calls we had to make. Each time we told the story of Barbara's diagnosis, it was like processing her death, except Barbara was alive. Yet, we knew this was a diagnosis of many small deaths to come before the final one. We survived those calls because of the clear messages of love and support we received from our millennial nephews and niece. Hanging up from the last of those calls, we slumped back on the sofa, thoroughly exhausted.

How many more times will we have to make calls like this? I didn't know if I had the strength. Finally, I spoke.

"I'm going to let the rest of our families and friends know through group emails, not phone calls. I know it's not a great way to convey such difficult news, but I'm not ready for the immediacy of everyone's reactions. I'm still dealing with my own."

"And mine," Barbara said, reaching over to hug me tightly.

I relished her body next to me.

"Do you mind writing the emails alone?" she asked. "I'm spent."

I agreed and drafted straightforward, detailed communications for each of the three audiences we still needed to reach: her extended family, my extended family, and our friends. Five minutes after pressing *Send* for the final time that day, support from thirty years' worth of friendships and deep family connections began flooding into my inbox. I was reminded how fortunate we were to have a large community of friends and family to help us. Even so, I knew how lonely a long disease could be. I had to find my own sustained strength to survive what was ahead.

I awoke the next day determined that we would have some fun. I needed to bring some normalcy back into our lives for as long as I could. Besides, it was a glorious, sunny day in the low seventies. November was usually delightful in New Orleans unless there was a late-season hurricane, which had been rare when I was growing up in this special city.

"How about going out to City Park with me?" I asked Barbara. "I feel like riding bikes or maybe the paddleboats. What do you say?"

"Yes, let's get out of the house," she responded with a hint of the happiness that always used to enrich her voice. "But I'm not comfortable riding a ten-speed bike anymore, especially with a crossbar. Not since I fell."

"Don't worry. The bikes at the park are the old-fashioned Schwinn Cruisers like we used to have as kids. You won't have that bar and we'll be riding on bike paths, not city streets," I reassured her.

Barbara jumped up from the chair with agility I thought she had lost.

"That's just what I need right now. Let's go," she said, heading for the door.

"Whoa, Speedy." I laughed as I caught her arm.

She gave me a sheepish grin, recognizing her own impulsivity. We didn't need to discuss it. We arrived at the cycle vendor with energy we hadn't felt in days.

"I want the red one!" Barbara exclaimed.

I picked one that was the same blue as my much-loved childhood Schwinn. Soon we were careening down the bike path, weaving and occasionally screeching in a way that would have embarrassed our younger selves. It suddenly registered with me that these bicycles didn't have the hand brakes of adult ten-speed bikes. Luckily, my memory kicked in before we reached the upcoming crossroad.

"Pedal backward when you want to stop," I called back to Barbara.

"Oh yeah," she chuckled. "I'd forgotten about that! Glad you remembered before we crashed!"

Suddenly I felt increasing wind coming from behind.

"Race you to the road!" Barbara cried out as she passed me, her competitive spirit emerging from nowhere.

"Hey, no fair!" I shouted, just as I had to friends in childhood bike races.

We sped along side by side under the live oak trees lining the pathway, giggling like ten-year-olds, grateful to forget our future for one sun-filled afternoon.

CHAPTER FOUR

LOSSES AND LATKES

was startled awake a few weeks later by a strong message already formed in my mind: *You have to talk to Barbara about her death.* I looked at her peacefully sleeping beside me. All I wanted was to cuddle her and cast a spell to regenerate her lost brain cells. The last thing I wanted was to invite death closer to us.

Yet, I knew the message was right. Barbara's diagnosis had been a death sentence with only the timing and terms unknown. I had to have the strength to face the truth we were now living, and to support her in doing the same. We'd stayed together by choosing intentional interdependence, which enabled us to be strong within ourselves and through one another. We had to rely on that mutual trust and strength to get us through the next phase of our lives together.

As I watched Barbara sleep, I reflected on the first time I had supported her deep well of inner strength. About four years into our relationship, I came home from a trip to the drugstore to find Barbara yelling into the phone. We'd been living together for three years, and I'd never heard her raise her voice, much less yell at anyone. I dropped the groceries on the counter and walked into the living room. She caught my eye and signaled me to come sit with her.

When the phone call ended, she wrapped her arms around me and began to sob. A wrenching, writhing cry escaped Barbara's lips, her body convulsing. I held her tightly, endeavoring to share her deep pain. Finally, the heaving subsided. She caught her breath and began to speak.

"My father . . . put my mother . . . on a feeding tube. She's having trouble swallowing. But he didn't . . . talk to us . . . her children. She wouldn't want this. I know it! Not a tube . . . prolonging her life. She wouldn't . . . and not in New Jersey," she got out haltingly.

Peggy was in a Jewish nursing home in New Jersey, the state that had denied Karen Ann Quinlan the right to be taken off life support. This decision by Barbara's father might have condemned Peggy to a similar fate. No wonder Barbara was distraught.

"We'll fight it," I responded. "If your brothers agree, I'll help you find a way to reverse this."

Barbara looked up at me as her face changed from despair to emerging hope.

"Can we do that?" she asked.

"It will be an uphill battle, and probably a long one, but it's worth fighting."

Barbara sat up tall and wiped her eyes.

"We can do it if we do it together," she declared.

Barbara was right. She and her brothers eventually persuaded their father he had made a mistake. With the help of New Jersey's ombudsman, they petitioned the state to have the tube removed. It took six years. Throughout the long fight, the pain of watching Peggy lying in a bed, her body slowly retracting into the fetal position, proved almost unbearable. But we won the battle and the war. When the feeding tube was removed, Barbara and I stayed at her mother's bedside and accompanied her to a peaceful end to her nine-year decline.

Reflecting on that struggle as Barbara lay next to me all these years later, sadness settled deep into my body. I watched the morning light dance on the ceiling as I considered the message I received in my dream. I'd never been afraid of death; I learned early in life to face it and talk about it. I'd long helped others to reconcile with it.

I credited this fearlessness in the face of death to my mother, who helped me understand death at a young age. Momma taught me the importance of feeling the immense sadness that accompanied the loss of a loved one while holding the gladness that your loved one wasn't suffering anymore. She always said we didn't make serious illnesses and pending death happen, but that didn't mean we were powerless in the face of them. Sometimes we could use the power of modern medicine to push off the timing of death; my family proved that possibility multiple times. At minimum, in most states, we had the power to determine the conditions of our death through advance directives. And we could always make choices about how we spent our remaining time, and with whom.

Fortunately, Barbara and I had done the hard work of defining our end-of-life terms decades ago. We'd both been strongly impacted by the Terry Schiavo debacle, which stretched on in the public eye as her husband and parents fought over Terry's end of life from 1998 to 2005. We never wanted such a battle to happen to one of us.

The difficult deterioration of Barbara's mother and aunt with their FTD battles had a deep influence on us as well. Both of them struggled with continuous bowel incontinence and mobility troubles for years before they died. Peggy was kept alive as her brain matter shriveled from the size of a cantaloupe to an apple. Similarly, Barbara's aunt was fed by a devoted nurse's aide while her brain and body deteriorated. Barbara had declared repeatedly she would never accept an end like her mother and aunt, and I didn't want that for her either. We vowed we would never lose power over our own deaths, but we were also humbled over the years watching friends and family die. The life force could be strong even in the face of previously declared end-of-life wishes.

My mind raced. Yes, we had advance directives, but Barbara's needed to be revised. Her recent brain diagnosis complicated her end-of-life choices. Her form of FTD, although classified as dementia, caused personality and behavior changes but rarely resulted in loss of core long-term memory like Alzheimer's, which was a much more common disease in this category. Sure, she might forget what day it was, but she wasn't likely to forget who I or others she loved were. She would forget how to count backward from one hundred, a standard memory test item, but she wasn't going to forget her strongly held beliefs and opinions.

Unfortunately, the law didn't make those distinctions. Even in states like Maine where death with dignity rights existed, laws typically restricted the options available for people diagnosed with dementia if they no longer spoke or were perceived as lacking the mental capacity to make their own decisions.

Since Barbara's genetic test results had confirmed her bvFTD diagnosis a few days earlier, I had become increasingly agitated by this fact. My heart raced and restlessness overtook my body as I thought about it. I jumped out of bed, trying not to wake Barbara. I needed to move.

As I showered, I reflected on the importance of Barbara controlling her end-of-life experience. I vowed to myself and to Barbara that I would fight for her to have as much personal power in the face of her disease as we could muster. To do that, I had to know exactly how Barbara felt about her end of life now that the genetic nature of her diagnosis was clear. The discussion was going to be harder for both of us now that her death was no longer theoretical.

Losing Barbara was beyond my comprehension. There was no death I had ever faced that would be as painful to me as hers, that I knew. Tears mixed with the water streaming from the showerhead as I absorbed Barbara's fate into my body. Then I wiped my tears and gave myself a pep talk. *Come on, girl. You have to do this. You have to hold yourself together to help Barbara.*

I dressed and went to my study to scour the internet for resources. I found dementia directives developed by End of Life Washington. It wasn't yet state law, but prior to this I didn't know any state had even tried to get dementia-specific language into their Medical Aid in Dying law. Studying the document, I gained strength. This could help Barbara define her end-of-life terms in detail. Then we could get a notary to certify she knew her own wishes, even with her bvFTD diagnosis.

After breakfast, I walked into the living room where I heard Barbara laughing over a passage from David Sedaris's *A Carnival of Snackery*. I paused. *Should I interrupt her fun? Is it cruel to start this end-of-life discussion now?* I weighed the timing and decided it would work well for me to bring this topic up when she wasn't sad or anxious. Her good mood would help carry us both through the impending emotional landmine.

I gently announced the need to revise her advance directives to cover all the legal issues raised by a dementia diagnosis. Barbara agreed the discussion was necessary, so I began with summarizing the actions we needed to take and why.

"I know you want a death with dignity option," I started, "but you have to be able to ask for that when the time comes. If you lose speech, like your mother did . . ."

I choked back tears as I named my greatest fear. I looked down to gather myself, then continued.

". . . you lose that option. So, we need to be as specific as possible about your end-of-life triggers. And after your advance directives are finalized, we need to make a video of you saying exactly what you want and get the statement notarized, so there's a clear record when the time comes."

"Yes, let's do that," Barbara said, sitting up straight on the sofa, trusting me without question. "I don't want to be kept alive past the time I'm functioning normally like my mother was. Quality of life is what matters to me . . . to us. We've always been aligned on that."

Before I could respond, she continued.

"I know you have the strength to do what I want done, but we also have to protect you. I don't want you to suffer any added grief or to have to fight with anyone while carrying out my wishes."

This was the most talking Barbara had done since her diagnosis, and from the fierceness in her eyes, I knew this mattered deeply to her. Heart-wrenching though this was for me in my tender state, I felt strengthened by Barbara's clarity and love for me.

"Okay," I responded, touched. "I have a really helpful guide of detailed dementia directives from End of Life Washington."

"Walk me through it. And, after we get the language right, I want to have a Zoom with my immediate family, niece and nephews included. They need to know directly from me what my end-of-life wishes are. I want all of them to look me in the eye and pledge to me that they will follow my wishes."

I was struck speechless by Barbara's intentionality, a strong personality trait she clearly still had. We touched foreheads and held hands, affirming our mutual commitment. Then, in a gentle voice, but still the focused taskmaster Barbara knew me to be, I asked a truly difficult question.

"What do you know right now about your preferences for end-of-life care and treatment?"

She answered without hesitation.

"I want to have care at home, not in a facility like my mother did. But I don't want you to do it. That's why we got long-term care insurance. When I start losing physical abilities, I want professional care. As kind and caring as you are, you're not a nurse. You shouldn't have to do that kind of care for me."

I paused my notetaking and looked directly into Barbara's eyes. She had responded today exactly as she had every other time we'd had this discussion. Only now, Barbara also included her intentions for me. Moved by her profound thoughtfulness, warmth surged through my chest. After a moment, I resumed writing down Barbara's words. When I looked up, she was staring out our oversized front window at the afternoon light illuminating the ochre building across the street. I knew she was formulating what she wanted to say next, so I waited. Barbara turned and looked directly at me, speaking slowly and emphatically.

"I know it may not be possible for me to stay at home until the end. I accept that. But, if I can't be at home with you, I want to be in hospice care where they'll accept my dying and treat me with the dignity I deserve, *not* a care home of any kind."

"I pledge to you, no nursing home," I responded, holding her gaze so she could see my fierceness.

We proceeded through the Washington guide, trading the lead back and forth, each looking after the other in this dance of awaited death. Finally, I asked the last question.

"What do you define as the end of your life?"

Barbara answered more succinctly than I expected. Her words revealed her strong desire not to lose the personal dignity and grace that had defined her whole life to this point.

"My life has been rich in quality and experiences. I consider it to be over when I no longer am able to feed myself or swallow my medicines; I have bowel incontinence and have to wear diapers; I'm noncommunicative/nonresponsive to my loved ones; or, no personality or spirit is evident in my eyes, whichever of these comes first. At that time, I don't want any assisted oral feeding or hydration. My preference is to have a physician-assisted death."

Hearing those powerful yet painful words, I burst into tears. We grabbed each other in a deep embrace. No more needed to be said. I knew then I would always be grateful for Barbara's strong character and unwavering intentionality about life. And now, death. She wasn't afraid. I needed to follow her lead.

||||||||||||||||||||||

A few weeks later, I was smiling as I walked up the three short steps to our front door after my three-month checkup for my knee replacement surgery. I couldn't wait to tell Barbara the good news. Bolstered by her daily encouragement, I had done all the painful, required physical therapy and it had paid off. The doctor had declared my knee to be perfect.

I unlocked the front door and was immediately confronted by an intense burning smell. Smell is the oldest and most sophisticated sensory system we have, and mine was setting off alarms. My nasal passages flared from the smoke hovering in our living room, and my throat closed around a stifled cough.

"What the f—!" I began to blurt out, but stopped before the third word escaped my mouth.

Barbara was standing in the doorway of the kitchen at the back of our cottage, her apron covered in splotches of red, tears streaming down her face. Her arms were hanging limply at her sides.

"I wanted to surprise you, but I ruined it!" she cried.

I rushed to the kitchen doorway, leaving the keys in the lock and the front door open to Saint Peter Street. Though not a safe move in the heart of the French Quarter, I wasn't thinking about external risks in that moment. I was consumed by Barbara's deep despair and my raw fear. When I reached Barbara, I hugged her close while peering over her head to see if there were any flames coming from the stove. Seeing none, I looked around the kitchen and spotted smoke rising from the cookware in the sink. Her trembling body hurt me to my core. I spoke with the false calm usually reserved for a scared child.

"Ruined what, honey? What's going on?"

"I wanted to make you eggplant rollatini," she sniffled. "But I burned the eggplant!"

I kissed her forehead and wrapped her tighter, rubbing her back in gentle strokes. I didn't say anything as I fought my reflex to be angry about ruined cookware.

"I can't cook anymore! I can't do it like I used to!" Barbara's sobs started up again as she buried her face in my shoulder.

My mind reeled as her vulnerability weakened my knees. I grabbed the door frame to steady myself. *It's not safe for Barbara to cook alone! It can't be!* Where I was merely adequate in the kitchen, Barbara had always been a master. Part of the "good life" we shared for years was due to Barbara's culinary skills. She delighted in making elaborate, tasty meals even when it was just the two of us. Her cooking was central to our social life as well.

This was a major blow I hadn't anticipated. Stress coursed through my body, tensing every muscle. I noticed the back rub I was giving Barbara quicken as I came to terms with the fact that I had to become the primary cook. *How can I handle this on top of everything else?* I wanted to scream at the top of my lungs at yet another, deeply impactful loss.

But I knew I couldn't scream; I didn't want to scare Barbara. Instead, I held her closer as I struggled to calm my racing thoughts and overcome my selfish reaction. I finally released Barbara and found my words.

"Oh, honey, I'm so sorry. Let's look closer. Maybe it's not as bad as you think."

Barbara turned and I followed her. I held my tongue as I surveyed the mess in our newly renovated kitchen. Red sauce was slopped all over the stove, counter, and floor. The burned pot festered in the sink, filled with water, disintegrated eggplant, and flaking metal. She had burned the hell out of it. I counseled myself in silence as I held Barbara's hand. *Don't show your disgust! Stay cool. You can always buy a new pot!*

"Wow, it looks like I was in the kitchen, not you," I quipped, trying to make light of the situation.

Barbara's lips turned up at the edges and her eyes brightened slightly.

"I appreciate you trying to make me feel better, but even you wouldn't make this big of a mess," she lamented.

She was right.

The scene in our kitchen reflected the real-world consequence of Barbara's diminishing ability to plan. Her brain simply didn't have the capacity to cook a multistep dish like eggplant rollatini anymore. If I'd known she had intended to try, I would have discouraged her or helped her. Her intended beautiful surprise for me turned into a harsh lesson about her current mental state. My heart ached for both of us.

Later that afternoon, I called some friends for help. I'd gone to high school with Gary, and he and his spouse Izzy had become dear friends since we bought our New Orleans French Quarter cottage eighteen months before. We even chose them as witnesses to Barbara's dementia directives taping the week before. They knew our situation well, and having their on-call support nearby meant everything to us.

"We need an outing," I declared when Izzy answered the phone.

"Sure, what do you have in mind?" he replied without hesitation.

"Something artistic, yet outdoors. Maybe the Besthoff Sculpture Garden out at City Park. Then we could have lunch at Café Degas afterward."

"Sounds wonderful. Does tomorrow work for y'all?"

Grateful our mutual retirement allowed us to make plans on the spur of the moment, I readily concurred.

"Yes, we can't wait!"

The next day, we emerged to a glorious day with low humidity, perfect weather for walking through the sculpture garden. This outing, with frequent pauses by the pond to watch the swans' antics, proved to be the relaxing yet engaging activity I needed to recharge. I was gradually figuring out what was necessary for me to maintain my sanity in the face of our ever-changing, ever-demanding situation.

||||||||||||||||||||||||

As dusk grew into darkness one early December day, Barbara set up the menorah for our nightly Hanukkah celebration. We loved this yearly ritual. I especially enjoyed seeing Barbara smile as she placed each of the candles in their respective holders. Five candles plus the *shamash* in the center. It was the fifth night of the eight-night ritual. In keeping with Barbara's flare for color, she always chose rainbow candles over the traditional blue or white ones. We sang the blessing in Hebrew as always, Barbara's voice strong as her muscle memory overcame her brain loss. I nearly lost my composure when her singing filled the room, but my joy triumphed over my sorrow. When the prayer concluded, we settled side by side on the couch to watch the candlelight dance.

While Barbara didn't attend synagogue and I wasn't Jewish, we always honored the Hanukkah miracle of light that had ensured the survival of the Jewish people. Throughout our relationship, we used this holiday to reflect on the meaningful events and people who graced our lives. This year was no different.

When the candles dwindled, I served roast chicken, carrots, potatoes, and broccoli. I wasn't a gourmet chef like Barbara, but I could manage basic meals. We ate in silence, both content to maintain the solemnity of the evening. After dinner, Barbara wanted to read more of her book, *The Carnival of Snackery*. She'd been rereading it for weeks, but it entertained her every time, eliciting chuckles and outright belly laughs, for which I was grateful.

After I finished cleaning the kitchen and checked on Barbara, I took my laptop to the dining room table to do something I'd been thinking about for days. I wanted to know if there were any clinical trials for treatment of Barbara's bvFTD. I'd learned about the value of clinical trials when my younger sister was suffering from hypertrophic obstructive cardiomyopathy, a condition that causes the heart muscle wall to thicken and stiffen, blocking or reducing blood flow from the heart to the rest of the body. She found a National Institutes of Health (NIH) clinical trial that saved her life. It would be a long shot in Barbara's case, so I mustered the courage to do my research while trying not to have any expectations. Given the rarity of bvFTD, finding a trial seemed unlikely, but it was the time of year for miracles.

I'd searched for clinical trials several times since my sister's success, so I knew what to do. I typed clinicaltrials.gov into my browser, followed by *GRN*-FTD in the Disease/Condition search bar. When I'd looked at this website over a year ago as I was researching Barbara's symptoms, the page listed only one observational study. There was nothing about treatment trials. But this time, my breath caught in my throat. I could hardly believe my eyes when three new clinical trials popped up on the page—and all three were for Barbara's genetic form of FTD. Blinking rapidly, I was afraid to move my hand for fear I'd somehow wipe the listings off the screen. *How can this be? A true Hanukkah miracle!*

I leaned forward and stared intently at the information on the screen, devouring every detail about the trials as my heart raced. The first required infusions every twenty-eight days. It was a phase 3 trial, meaning they already had proven the safety and efficacy of the medicine on a smaller test population but needed to prove effectiveness with a larger sample size to obtain FDA approval. The other two were described as phase 1/2 gene replacement trials, which meant no safety and efficacy had been established. Gene replacement was a promising scientific advancement I previously thought was only being tested for more common conditions like sickle cell anemia. Partly due to diagnostic deficiencies, Barbara's type of genetic brain disorder impacted fewer than twenty thousand people per year in the United States, so I never imagined such advanced medical technology would be available for bvFTD.

The gene replacement trials were the most intriguing to me because they were cutting-edge science. In these trials, the company sponsor and the medical community at large were investigating the effects of delivering a defunct virus carrying functional *GRN* gene copies directly into a patient's brain to replace the defective gene they had inherited. This experimental therapy looked promising to me, but it had risks. Phase 1 meant the companies were conducting the trial to assess the safety of this gene product for humans. No human had ever been exposed to a synthetic gene being shot directly into the brain before. Even with the extensive preclinical and animal studies, the outcome wasn't certain. There could be unwanted side effects in humans ranging from a negative immune system response to a misregulated gene expression.

I couldn't give up though. I devoured the profiles of the sponsors' boards of directors. Having provided consulting services to companies all over the world, I had extensive experience conducting analytical reviews of companies, examining factors like financial stability, training and experience of their leaders, and so forth. I certainly wasn't going to do any less due diligence about a company potentially offering my precious partner an experimental therapeutic agent. The profile for one of the companies offering the gene replacement trial impressed me. I examined everything I could find on the internet about this company and its leaders.

I could hardly sit still when I finished my research. It took everything I had to stop myself from shouting out in glee. But I had to do even more investigative work before I got Barbara's hopes up as high as mine were. I knew who I needed to contact to find out more: Dr. Murray Grossman at the University of Pennsylvania FTD Center. He was a giant in the field of FTD research, and he had treated Barbara's aunt over a decade before. He would know if these clinical trials were as promising as I felt they were. I would write him the next day. But for this Hanukkah night, I was content to hold on to the glimmer of hope that a medical miracle might really be possible.

RISING HOPE

Mid-December 2020
–
Mid-October 2021

We all know how loving ends. But I want to fall
in love with the world anyway, to let it crack me open.
I want to feel what there is to feel while I am here.

—John Green

CHAPTER FIVE

COURAGE AND CHOICES

We returned to San Miguel de Allende the week after Hanukkah. My spirits lifted the first mid-December morning when I entered our living room. The pink stone wall and colorful plants outside the glass doors to the courtyard excited my senses. A morning cup of tea, hot and milky-sweet like my beloved Irish grandmother drank, added to my joy. The air smelled fresh as I stepped into the courtyard. This day had dawned crisp and energizing, just the way I liked my mornings. At 6,234 feet above sea level, the climate here provided a welcome change from the relentless humidity and heat we had experienced in New Orleans since late July.

San Miguel would be our haven for the next three months. The beauty and friendliness all around us simultaneously calmed and revitalized me. Melodious church bells competed with the unpredictable bangs of firecrackers. The colors of this magic town exploded around me. Yellow, fuchsia, and orange blossoms sparked a smile in my soul. I returned to the living room and lit the gas fireplace, warmth instantly comforting me deep in my bones.

My tranquility proved fleeting as a question kept arising in my mind. *When will I hear from the Penn FTD Center?* Every day without an answer tested my limited patience and increased my anxiety, a feeling I tried hard to hide from Barbara.

The sudden pinging of metal on metal interrupted my worries. Barbara was coming down the staircase, her new ring rhythmically tapping the handrail as she descended. When she entered the room, I turned to embrace her with my eyes. I was startled to see her approaching with her phone held out to me. Her narrowed eyes and piercing look told me she was on a mission.

"Here, read this," she demanded. "It's my new mantra."

Every time Barbara expressed her feelings and intentions, I rejoiced and gave her my full attention. I took her phone and saw she was on Instagram. The post on her screen read: *If your path leads you to hell, walk through it like you own it!* I laughed aloud and Barbara joined me. Every time we looked at each other, we laughed louder and longer. I wasn't surprised at her claiming this statement. It captured Barbara's determination to function as normally as she could for as long as possible. She wasn't shying away from telling people her diagnosis, but she was determined not to let it define her. My laughing finally subsided into a beaming smile. I held her determined eyes with mine.

"Good for you! I admire your courage."

"Like I keep telling you, I don't experience the loss of planning and impulse control that you and the doctors tell me I have. So, I'm forging ahead as though it isn't happening. I can still read, even if I don't remember everything in detail like I used to. Enjoying the experience of reading is good enough for me," she stated.

Barbara had never been one to fret or second-guess what life presented to her. She stayed steady, confident, and capable, no matter what life threw her way. I valued this grounded, determined spirit of hers, and wanted to embrace it for myself. Lately, I'd been so alert to her changing behaviors—like asking me over and over what day it was, or her resistance to showering, or her saying no to everything before agreeing to it—I'd lost sight of her strengths, of her intention to embrace life head-on as she'd always done. Her sentiments were right on the nose, as usual. Difficult times called for heightened courage and love, not fear and withdrawal. Barbara plopped down on the couch next to me, and I pulled her close, planting a kiss on her forehead.

"I'm going to follow your lead and walk through this hell like I own it too."

We hugged, wearing our precious closeness like a warm blanket while we enjoyed the dancing flames in our fireplace. Nothing else mattered if we were together and on the same page. After a while, I broke the comforting silence.

"Owning your path, my dear, what do you want to do today?" I asked.

"Let's go look for some art to replace those depressing paintings we bought with this house."

It is common practice in San Miguel to buy a house along with all its contents. Most of the items in our new home had been tasteful and compatible with our style, but some of the large oil paintings in the bedroom and living room had been too dark for us, in both color and subject matter. Luckily, I found a place in town that had taken those pieces on consignment. This freed up both wall space and cash for us to purchase paintings we preferred.

Art had always been a shared passion of ours. While we were fortunate that most of the artwork we had was made by our many talented friends, we loved to go to galleries and find new work and discover new artists. Our art collection could be described as eclectic, including realistic photography, traditional Japanese drawings, and nature-centered oil and gouache paintings. Being in San Miguel had sparked a shift in our taste toward bright and lively nonrepresentational art. With more than one hundred fine art galleries, folk art galleries, and two world-famous art schools, this town offered numerous opportunities to expand our collection and make our new home reflect our broadening artistic preferences. We were both eager to take on this project.

Viewing art proved to be the perfect way to get my mind off my desperation for a response from Dr. Grossman. We purchased an inspiring modern art piece at the Fabrica la Aurora, a renovated textile mill that houses cafés, shops, and galleries. It had become one of our favorite places to go for an easy, inspiring outing.

Two weeks after we returned to San Miguel, Barbara and I set out on a walking mission. I had to keep her moving for her brain and general mobility. She'd always been physically active, playing tennis, gardening, bike riding, snowshoeing, hiking, and walking. Now she no longer initiated any physical activities, which left me puzzled and distressed. How had this self-starting, active woman suddenly stopped all physical movement unless prompted by me? I hadn't fully appreciated the link between brain-generated motivation and physical activity until I observed Barbara's motivation disappear like it never existed.

Halfway through our morning walk, we stopped to give Barbara a rest and enjoy a light breakfast at one of our favorite outdoor restaurants. Almost finished with my cappuccino and omelet, I smiled as I watched a bright orange guava fall from the tree in the middle of the courtyard, only to be caught in a net the proprietors had positioned just below the tree limbs. The peachy-pink guava jam on our table, surely made from fruits caught in that net, contrasted with the shimmering green hummingbirds swooping in to drink from feeders scattered around the patio. Barbara loved to watch the little birds' competitive antics. She giggled as she tracked their aerobatic maneuvers. I loved watching her joyous face; it was blank all too often these days.

Soon it was time to get back to our walk. Our goal that morning was to go to Parque Juarez, named after the first indigenous president of Mexico. The round-trip distance from our house was over a mile, and it included some low hills, so it was a good workout for two aging athletes. As I stood up and held out my hands to help Barbara out of her chair, an increasingly necessary action, she frowned and refused to grab my hands. She dropped her head to avoid my gaze.

"I don't want to walk anymore," she stated flatly.

I felt a sharp twinge in my heart, but I couldn't concede to her. Mobility was key to a high-quality life for both of us. Barbara had to keep moving; I couldn't accept anything less.

"Sorry, my love, but we agreed to walk to the park today. We both need the exercise," I coaxed.

"My back hurts," Barbara declared.

She pointed to her lower back and looked up at me. She had made this statement a few times now, starting just before we left New Orleans. I made a mental note to have her checked out by the local physical therapist I learned about yesterday. Even so, I wasn't going to be deterred from today's walking plan.

"Let me rub your back," I offered.

Stepping behind her, I massaged the muscles on both sides of her lower spine. Her shoulders relaxed as the pain seemed to subside. Walking around to face her, I extended my hands again. This time, Barbara reached out with both hands to let me pull her up to stand, giving me a weak smile as she stood. I didn't know if she actually felt better or forgot to resist, but I didn't ask. It was best to proceed with the task at hand anytime I didn't get resistance.

When Barbara had steadied herself, I dropped my hands and turned to walk out of the restaurant. Before I took my first step, I felt Barbara's hand reach for mine and entwine our fingers. This intentional connection delighted me, and I turned to smile at her, receiving a beaming grin in return. Her gestures of connection, previously commonplace, were less frequent now, which gave them even more meaning and value than before.

In Parque Juarez, Barbara and I strolled hand in hand along the wide pathways in the park with no fear of reprisal as lesbians from the kind, smiling Mexican families we passed. We were safe to enjoy the lushness of the trees and vegetation in the park, as well as the fresh air. When we got to the new basketball court, Barbara pulled me down on a bench to watch a group of young boys playing a pickup game.

Barbara had a soft spot in her heart for little boys. When her mother was suffering from postpartum depression, she had to mother her younger brother. He had been gone for ten years now, succumbing to melanoma, and Barbara still missed him deeply. I searched her face for any signs of sadness, but she was intensely focused with a contented smile on her face. Seeing her joy, I relaxed and focused on the game, feeling free to release my vigilance for a brief moment. Anyone watching us would have no clue about Barbara's brain or my constant stress. We were just two older women relaxing on a park bench under a robin's-egg blue sky as filtered sunlight dotted our faces.

IIIIIIIIIIIIIIIIIIIIIII

In many ways Barbara and I were unlikely life partners—a term we preferred to "spouse" and *definitely* more than "wife." As long-time second-wave feminists who fought for substantive equality, not just nondiscrimination, we were cognizant of the patriarchal history of marriage and the concomitant limitations it placed on wives. The term "life partners" worked for us because it expressed our daily intention of engaging together to build a meaningful life, one of conscious choice and mutuality. Still, we laughed a lot, and sometimes cried, about how different we were from each other.

Except for being introverts, and Barbara just barely, we didn't share one common trait on the Myers-Briggs personality scale. Barbara was an ISTP (fiercely independent; curious; pragmatic; and adaptable) and I was an INFJ (logical; intuitive; idealistic; overly empathic yet action-oriented). Barbara came from a northeast, Jewish, business-owning family whose grandparents were wealthier than her parents, while I came from a southern, libertarian, middle-class family with scientist parents who valued education as the best means of upward mobility. My nuclear family was emotionally enmeshed with a lineage of strong matriarchs on my mother's side, while hers functioned as separate orbs headed by multiple generations of failed patriarchs on her father's side.

When we first met I wore mostly browns and beiges, while she typically shined as the most colorful person in the room, pulling off orange with panache. Fortunately, I let Barbara take me shopping early on and discovered I'm a "jewel tone" gal. We started working together after just three years of living together, and it wasn't always easy. More than once, it almost derailed us. But we kept choosing to stay together in both the professional and personal arenas.

At the root, we respected, trusted, and genuinely liked each other. Most importantly, we shared the same core values—authenticity, personal integrity, and a commitment to truth and justice. Those values led us to join many protests, like the 1983 Seneca Women's Encampment for a Future of Peace and Justice, laughing in our tent as government helicopters buzzed overhead. Those shared values also led us to focus our consulting business on fostering health, safety, and error-free performance among front-line employees in twenty-four-hour industrial operations. We wanted to make a difference with our lives and our work.

Our shared values also helped us to build a love that bound us yet never constricted. With periodic counseling to assist us, we transformed our differences into an effective synergy. We served as guides for each other in good times and bad times. More than once, Barbara talked me down from my protective anger and tendency toward defensive retorts.

"Think about the outcome you want to achieve," she always said, never letting other people's behavior trigger hers.

Her support enabled me to finally come out to my parents, ending the torment that dishonesty had caused me for over a decade. My father disowned me when I told him my truth, but I had my integrity back in full, a precious intangible essential for my soul. For Barbara and me, the first duties of love were simple—help each other face the truth and encourage our partner to be her most authentic self, while not holding it against each other when we fell short. I benefited often from Barbara's deep wisdom in both personal and professional relationships just as she benefited from my guidance in many life challenges.

And now I was increasingly on my own. *How will I flourish without My Barbara?*

When I started up my laptop one cold morning in January 2021, a response from Dr. Murray Grossman, the director of the Penn FTD Center, had finally arrived. His message appeared in my inbox and my heart raced. This renowned FTD guru who cared deeply about FTD families was our best hope. If anyone knew the value of pending *GRN*-FTD clinical trials, it would be Dr. Grossman. I took a deep breath, releasing the air slowly and telling myself not to get my hopes up too high.

As I opened the email, my hopes rose despite my self-admonition. I wanted a medical miracle like the one my younger sister got from a clinical trial for her genetic heart disease. She had been at death's door when she drew the lucky straw and received an innovative treatment at the NIH called alcohol ablation—a direct shot of alcohol into the thickened part of her heart's septum. She had the perfect heart architecture, and the single shot of alcohol she was given killed the obstruction blocking her blood flow, instantly giving her body its required lifeblood. She emerged from this innovative treatment physically changed, back to her normal energetic self. That's what I dreamed about for Barbara: a treatment that would stop her brain degeneration in its tracks. I knew it was a long shot, but my family history proved it could happen.

I had become desperate to save the critical functions Barbara could lose without warning, such as her ability to speak coherently; to laugh and connect with friends; to show her love and care for me. Secretly, I even dreamed the brain's neuroplasticity—the incredible ability of the human brain to create new neural pathways to adapt to its needs—would enable Barbara to regain some of the capabilities she'd already lost, like motivation and empathy. The brain's powers of regeneration worked miracles every day for people with strokes and brain injuries. Why not for Barbara's brain disorder?

I began reading the email, simultaneously excited and afraid of what Dr. Grossman would say. He started with compassion, a good sign in a physician. *First, I am sorry to hear about Barbara's* GRN-*positive news,* he wrote. He continued with the clear message I was hoping to receive. *I would be happy to play a role in Barbara's care.*

With his assurance in hand, I leaned back in my chair and dropped my shoulders from their constant position of tension next to my ears. His simple yet meaningful words changed my life. I had an ally, an expert on my side. After savoring the relief Dr. Grossman's initial response brought me, I sat up again and focused on my screen. Two paragraphs down I saw the words I really wanted but didn't expect: *At the UPenn FTD Center, we currently are participating in three treatment trials for which* GRN-*positive mutation carriers are eligible.*

I'd never been so happy to think of Barbara as a mutation carrier. But the magic words in his message were "treatment trials." Dr. Grossman went on to say his nurse could arrange a time for us to speak, but I couldn't wait for her to initiate contact. I called immediately and left a message. Even that momentary disappointment couldn't quell my excitement. *Patience isn't your strong suit, Susan, but keep your eyes on the prize. He said treatments!*

Later that afternoon, Barbara looked at me strangely.

"Why are you grinning like a fool?"

Wait! Get more information before you share the news, said my wiser inner voice. I didn't listen. I'd always been transparent with Barbara, and I didn't want to change that now.

"You won't believe it!" I started, and quickly summarized my research about clinical trials, my email to Dr. Grossman, and his reply. With the caveat that I still had lots of questions, I described the three trials to Barbara. I tried to contain my excitement, but the pitch and speed of my voice gave me away. I repeated myself a few times to make sure Barbara grasped the medical concepts underlying each treatment.

Barbara finally cut me off.

"Let's apply for the gene replacement. Go big or go home!" she exclaimed, a smile springing to her lips.

I was simultaneously dumbstruck and ecstatic. Barbara understood perfectly. And this was the choice I wanted her to make because it held the greatest promise. Most impressive, she wasn't terrified by the idea of someone placing a new gene directly into her brain. If accepted into the trial, Barbara would be among the first humans to receive this experimental therapy. She would be a host for testing whether it was safe to have an external piece of DNA placed into a human brain, replacing her defunct gene, as a phase 1 trial was first and foremost a safety assessment.

But if it worked, it definitely would be my idea of a medical miracle. The new gene would provide instructions for making the progranulin* protein Barbara didn't receive from her mother's defective gene. If the replacement procedure worked, there was reasonable scientific evidence that the new gene would halt or slow Barbara's brain loss. My heart raced with the potential of it all.

Perhaps I should have been more cautious given the experimental aspect of gene replacement therapy, but I wasn't. I embraced the novelty of it, knowing it would take a scientific breakthrough to defeat Barbara's brain disorder. My hopes soared; my pipe dream might actually happen. This new year might not be as bad as I'd been fearing.

---

* The *GRN* gene in our brains provides instructions for making the protein progranulin, a protein essential for regulating the growth, division, and survival of nerve cells (neurons) in the brain as well as immune system cells. The gene replacement therapy would attempt to replace Barbara's defective *GRN* gene with a functional one.

CHAPTER SIX

BREAKTHROUGHS AND BIRTHDAYS

I n late January, I received confirmation of Barbara's initial acceptance into the screening phase for the gene replacement trial. This red-letter day was a welcome change from the three months of fear and despair I'd been carrying since she was diagnosed in November. It had only taken the University of Pennsylvania team two weeks to review all the required diagnostic records I submitted. The FTD Center's genetic counselor, Laynie Dratch, called me to convey their review results.

"We're first on the list for Barbara to take the qualifying tests. Is that what you said?" repeating back what she had told me.

I needed a double confirmation of the news she'd just given me before I could believe it.

"Yes, Barbara will be the first subject to be assessed at UPenn for this gene replacement trial, which is the first in the US, to see if she meets the final trial qualifications," Laynie repeated.

I reflexively sucked in air, holding my breath. Barbara had cleared the initial hurdle to be enrolled in a UPenn clinical trial. This was my dream for her and it felt like such serendipity. The University of Pennsylvania was also the hospital where, almost sixty years before, my father had received experimental surgery for the ITP autoimmune disorder that tried to kill him many times during my childhood. I still remembered the hospital lobby, as children weren't permitted in hospitals back then unless they were patients.

My father's doctors had given special permission for my sisters and me to visit while he recovered from his splenectomy. I immediately became enthralled by all the medical personnel hurrying past us in the lobby. They were saving my father's life, and I wanted to jump up and hug them all. This positive memory convinced me that enrolling Barbara in a trial at UPenn was a good omen for our future.

Laynie started speaking again and I tuned back in.

"But keep in mind, we still have to complete lots of trial start-up activities before we can schedule Barbara's screening visit," she said.

I barely registered her caution. The potential spurred me forward. This could mean everything for Barbara . . . and for me. Plus, we had a plan. I am always more relaxed with a plan in hand. After the call, I walked into the living room. Barbara's melodic laughter at *The New Yorker* cartoons filled the air. My spirit soared higher.

"Hey, sweetie, I have great news. You're first on the list of potential participants for the clinical trial at UPenn!"

Barbara's brows furrowed in confusion.

"What?" she asked.

My balloon burst a little as I looked at her blank face. I had told Barbara I'd be talking to the UPenn counselor today, but it appeared she didn't remember our conversation. Some days Barbara's short-term memory functioned perfectly; other days she didn't retain information for long at all. I didn't know if it was a true memory issue or a product of her growing apathy. Either way, I had to repeat information often. This time, I started the story from the beginning, slowly explaining how I had discovered the gene replacement trial and laying out the steps I'd taken the past several weeks to get her enrolled. Barbara seemed to track what I was telling her, but I knew she understood when I saw a twinkle emerging in her eyes.

"First on the list, huh? I might be making history!" she exclaimed.

I grinned back at her, chuckling as I leaned down to hug her. She definitely understood. Even I hadn't made the leap to this idea of making history, but that's exactly what Barbara would be doing if she entered into the clinical trial at UPenn.

Not too long after, the phone rang one morning with the worst news we could have heard at that time. It was Barbara's brother.

"Barbie, I got the results from my genetic test," he said into her ear.

Barbara activated speaker mode.

"I have a defective *GRN* gene too."

A simple statement yet one that changed so many lives forever.

Barbara's brother had decided to take the available genetic tests for FTD after our initial conversation with him about Barbara's diagnosis, and I had been hoping ever since that he would get a negative result. Barbara and I exchanged shocked expressions. Then we both spoke, one after the other.

"Oh, no. I had hoped this wouldn't happen," Barbara stated.

"I never wanted to hear you say this," I followed, anguish evident in my voice.

"Come join the gene therapy trial with me," Barbara entreated. "Maybe we'll both be cured."

Despite the difficult circumstances, hearing Barbara express such hope warmed my heart. She had told me she didn't expect the cure I was praying for; rather, she was doing this to improve the future for her niece and nephews. Yet, clearly she was entering into the clinical trial with a positive wish.

"We're still talking about next steps," her brother responded. "I'll let you know what we decide."

Ultimately, he and his wife opted for a phase 3 clinical trial involving a treatment and a placebo cohort because it was available closer to their Midwest home, and the treatment had shown some promise in its initial phase 1/2 study with presymptomatic patients. This clinical trial tested the efficacy of monthly infusions of a monoclonal antibody to elevate progranulin levels in the brain. It involved a larger population of people with confirmed *GRN*-FTD, but the treatment was not guaranteed for every participant. In this double-blind study, half of the participants would receive the antibody being studied and half would receive a harmless infusion with no therapeutic effect. This type of phase 3 trial has long been the standard procedure for the FDA to confirm a drug's impact before accepting it onto the open market. Although we were sad to learn her brother would not be in the same clinical trial with Barbara, we had hope for him in his choice of treatment. The future was shaky for all of us.

A few weeks later, I walked into our TV room one morning and saw Barbara sitting on the sofa, staring into the fireplace. When she sensed my movement, she turned to me and gave me one of her sparkling smiles. I responded in kind.

Barbara's smiles always sent my heart soaring, assuring me we were still deeply connected. I held on to each smile like it was a piece of gold because bvFTD usually caused the affected person to stop caring about their loved ones. It wasn't personal; it was due to a breakdown in the brain's salience network, the parts of the brain that enable human caring. Despite knowing the science, I knew it would feel personal if she showed no care for me. How could it not? This person you loved recognized you but no longer cared about you.

I'd been girding myself for this tragic turn in Barbara's behavior. For me, losing her caring energy would be worse than not being recognized by her. I considered myself fortunate to have been spared the deep pain of this behavior change so far. It made every day we still connected a gift.

"Come sit with me, Susan," Barbara implored.

This was the first time Barbara had made such an intentional request in several months, so I quickly complied. Before I could say anything, she touched my knee, and I almost burst into tears. She often reached for my hand when we walked or sat together, but I'd attributed that gesture more to her need for security than for intimacy. Barbara's hand on my knee, coupled with her direct eye contact, was a level of intimacy only I had been initiating lately.

"How are you doing?" she asked.

I couldn't believe Barbara's question, so simple yet so profound. She clearly hadn't lost her capacity to care for me. Energy pinged around in my brain as I searched for words to express myself. My amygdala responded before my mind; I broke down sobbing like a lost child. Barbara had reached into my soul with her question, finding the pain and loss I'd been trying to hide from her. She scooted closer to me and wrapped me in her arms, holding me tight like she'd done so often before bvFTD. Coming from Barbara now, this act of comforting was deeply powerful; it was the first time I'd received physical comfort from her in over six months.

Absorbing her embrace, I cried harder while Barbara held on tighter. I sorely missed receiving her love through physical connection, and I didn't want this embrace to end. Finally, my sobbing subsided enough that I could speak. She deserved the truth.

"I'm fine when I'm handling our finances and household chores," I started.

"Yep, you're the best at doing tasks."

I paused, not sure I was ready to speak my whole truth but knowing she wanted me to do so.

"I struggle when my brain starts pushing me into the future," I confessed.

"You've always thought months, if not years ahead," she remarked.

Looking upward in spontaneous gratitude, my whole body relaxed with the knowledge that Barbara still knew me so well.

"In fact, I can't fathom thinking about the future . . ."

More tears burst forth as I continued.

". . . without you," I sobbed.

"Well, I'm here now, and I'm determined not to leave you anytime soon."

We leaned closer. I never wanted to let her go.

|||||||||||||||||||||||

The glories of spring in San Miguel arrived in early March, especially the plethora of purple from the many jacaranda trees around town. Normally those purple sprays would have lifted my mood, but my spirits had been falling for the past month. I had tried to get more information from UPenn about the upcoming clinical trial but kept hitting roadblocks. Dr. Grossman had taken unexpected medical leave, and his return was unsure. Hiring a clinical coordinator was taking UPenn longer than expected, and the institutional review required for clinical trials was taking additional time because of the unique nature of gene replacement.

While these were all legitimate reasons for delays, I didn't care. I desperately wanted this trial to start. I wanted Barbara to receive her in-depth testing and officially qualify for the gene therapy before she lost more of her brain cells, more of herself. I wanted her cured. Waiting had never been easy for me, but this long wait was excruciating. It was like staring at a tree full of ripe fruit just out of my reach. No matter what I did, I couldn't touch the fruit, much less enjoy the taste.

Along with the stress of waiting, Barbara's slower responses and declining use of language were scaring me to my core. When I felt scared, I struggled to be my best self. In fact, I could be downright biting. Just the day before I had lost patience and snapped at Barbara.

"Why don't you answer me? You can still talk. I know you can!" I snapped.

Those words might sound benign, given the circumstances, but for me they represented both a significant failure as a partner and a lapse in my personal growth. When I snapped at her, my mind flashed back thirty years. I was at our therapist's office with Barbara seated beside me. We had made an appointment to address problems in our relationship as business partners, for which I was the cause. I had yelled at Barbara when one of her direct reports failed to do her job, a failure that caused us to be late with a client deliverable, which had never happened in the ten years we'd been in business at that time. The therapist reflected on what she'd heard from both of us, including my admission of undesirable behavior.

"Barbara knows you're under a lot of stress and that you're scared. She knows you're carrying the weight of the company's success and eight people's livelihoods on your shoulders. But that doesn't mean you can take your fears and stress out on her. You can't expect her to just accept and absorb your tirade."

The therapist's words sank in deeply that day, and I had no retort. As a child, I'd been expected to do exactly that with my father—absorb his emotional tirades—because he had understandable causes for his yelling. The stress, pain, and steroid medications he took for his autoimmune blood disease precipitated his rages. Still, I didn't want to be like him, unloading my fears and associated struggles on others, especially Barbara. Finally having a partner with whom I felt safe, I didn't want to drive her away.

Since that day with our therapist, Barbara and I had over two decades of working and living together with only minor disagreements. Now my old behavior had seeped back into our interactions. I thought I had mastered my fear triggers decades ago. Evidently nothing in those passing years had touched me as deeply as Barbara's continued brain degeneration did now.

My stomach constantly felt clenched, causing a growing ache right under my breasts. My perpetually tight jaw had started to cause tooth pain. I tried longer walks, nature photography, and structured breathing exercises to quell my tension. I began meditating again. Even so, I couldn't mitigate the rising alarms in my body. Getting the gene replacement trial underway was taking time we no longer had.

To qualify for the trial, Barbara had to have at least one measurable change in her cognition, behavior, or both. That criteria posed no problem, as her changes had been piling up fast. What I wanted was to stop those losses by getting her a new gene as quickly as possible. With every week that passed, I was afraid Barbara wouldn't get the trial dosing before too much degeneration occurred. Yet, I had no power to make anything happen. Having spent the last thirty years as an entrepreneur, largely in charge of my life's direction, this powerlessness disturbed me deeply. Something had to change, and fast.

As I attempted to manage my mounting fear, my mid-March birthday came around, and we decided to spend it in Morelia. I had hoped an outing exploring a new part of Mexico together would lighten my mood and improve my stress level. Instead, I found myself sitting alone in one of the city's famous ice cream parlors, medicating my sorrows with sugar. This day would be my saddest birthday ever. I was dining alone because Barbara had picked up a serious stomach bug and felt too weak to get out of bed. I should have been sympathetic, but I wasn't. I was feeling sorry for myself for being alone and without my beloved celebrating my special day. It was childish, yes, but I had dropped my self-protective armor so long ago, I only had the rawest of defensive responses available: self-pity.

I furiously licked my cone, locked in a battle inside my head.

You're being selfish!

Selfish! I've been doing nothing but giving for months! It's my birthday. I wanted just one day to be about me!

Oh, come on. You're stronger than that. It's just a birthday and not even a big one!

I don't want to be strong today! I want to be special! Barbara's always made my birthday special; I wanted that feeling one last time.

Suck it up! Remember what your mother always said: There's no use crying over spilled milk. Your life has changed . . . forever. From now on, you have to hold it together no matter what.

This harsh internal exchange brought me some much-needed insight. I had never doubted that I could manage all the tasks that now fell to me; I had long been a master of doing. I also knew I would succeed as Barbara's health-care advocate, as I was well-schooled in that role from an early age. What I didn't know was how I was going to maintain the emotional strength I needed to do it alone. I'd had Barbara helping me manage the adversities of life for decades, benefiting from her (sometimes infuriating) calmness and practicality. I wasn't used to managing all my feelings by myself anymore. *Can I do this alone? And how will I feel about myself if I can't?*

We flew back to New Orleans at the end of March, choosing to spend our thirty-eighth anniversary in the Big Easy. The morning before our April Fool's anniversary date, Barbara came out of the bedroom looking for me, wanting to hug and kiss me. My heart melted as usual until her breath overwhelmed me, and not in a good way.

"Have you brushed your teeth this morning?" I queried, holding her at arm's length.

"I don't know. I just want to kiss you."

"I want to kiss you too but let's brush your teeth first, okay?"

We went into our bathroom, and I watched while she brushed her teeth, if you could call it that. She put toothpaste on her toothbrush but barely passed it around her mouth before spitting out the toothpaste and reaching for her glass to rinse her mouth.

"Whoa, wait a minute," I said. "You haven't really brushed your teeth."

"Yes, I did. You just watched me."

And with that, I saw how lack of motivation and apathy impacted one's personal care. I'd been managing all our household affairs and Barbara's medical care, but I'd lost sight of this more intimate dimension of Barbara's needs. She'd always invested so much in self-care, much more than I ever had; it never occurred to me she would lose interest in her personal hygiene. Recognizing her poor oral care, I realized I had no idea whether she was bathing regularly either.

"Sweetie, when was the last time you had a shower?"

"I don't know, but I don't want one," she replied.

Barbara always said she couldn't start her day without a shower. When did this change? She didn't sweat no matter how hot it was, and she also never had body odor, so I had just been assuming she was showering. Clearly, I had been incorrect.

"Okay, let's take a shower together," I offered.

"Only if you don't hog the water," she replied, trying to suppress a grin.

We both knew who the water hog had always been in our family. I chuckled, happy to see her wry humor was still accessible. However, Barbara's increasing dependency started weighing on me.

As soon as she awakened each day, my focus turned exclusively to Barbara. In addition to making her meals throughout the day,

I now had to be involved in her entire morning routine. Never could I have imagined that I, a basic tailored-shirt-and-jeans person, would be cleaning and dressing this fashion-conscious woman who had always been impeccably groomed. I was coaching her while she showered, helping her brush her teeth, and even blow-drying her hair because she wouldn't. Her silky, stylish hair had long been a point of personal pride for Barbara, but now she couldn't be bothered. I even had to pick out her clothes each day to make sure Barbara was wearing seasonally appropriate attire.

Barbara's newly required level of physical caretaking proved to be a particular challenge for me. I easily could have helped her resolve any emotional difficulties she might be having with her disease, but I struggled mightily to put on her shoes. While I projected nonchalance, the growing extent and depth of her care triggered almost paralyzing emotions in me—fear, deep sorrow, protectiveness. To address those rising emotions, I reached inward for my deeply embedded self-reliance, determined to handle each new challenge by myself, never complaining, rarely asking for help.

I'm not sure why Barbara's declining self-care didn't cause me to activate her long-term care policy and bring in outside help when I could and clearly should have. Instead, her increasing needs caused me to envelop Barbara tighter, to protect her more than ever before. Barbara was my beloved, and it was my responsibility to care for her, so I did.

With all this, I embraced anything that gave me an experience of independence. Barbara had been sleeping late since we arrived back in New Orleans, so I was using that time to take long walks through the French Quarter. I enjoyed early mornings on those streets. The drunken tourists were still sleeping, so the Quarter belonged to the locals who called this neighborhood home. I exchanged friendly Hey-baby-how-ya-doings with street cleaners and garbagemen while photographing the endless details of French and Spanish architecture. When it rained, I contented myself with a good book.

I found myself caught between the two forces that had been dominant throughout my life: my need for personal freedom and my desire for intimacy. For nearly forty years, my relationship with Barbara had given me both. Now, the two were in conflict and I had to sort out which one mattered most to me. With Barbara's increasing need for care, I had to give one of them up.

Two weeks later, our longtime friend Karen arrived in New Orleans from Maine to celebrate Barbara's mid-April birthday. Karen had come to New Orleans to be with us soon after she learned of Barbara's diagnosis, despite the fact that she had limited time off from work. Though ten years younger than Barbara, they had bonded over a love for fashion and home decor, as well as Barbara's practicality and wisdom. Karen and I had bonded over politics and how we value deep friendships.

Karen had been my rock over the previous six months. This week, she had come to celebrate with Barbara, taking her out for fun activities and giving me a break from the increasing need for watchful care. Based on Barbara's frequent smiles, she was clearly benefiting from our dear friend's care and attention.

Karen, on the other hand, was alarmed at the changes she'd noticed in Barbara's behavior and personality.

"She still has her beautiful smile," Karen remarked, "but most of the time I can't tell what's going on with her. Barbara's face is mostly blank. I'm used to knowing exactly what she is experiencing by reading her face."

"This change in her facial expressions, or lack thereof, has been one of the hardest adjustments I've had to make," I concurred. "Barbara still feels things strongly, though, so we just have to work a little harder to know what she's experiencing and feeling."

Under normal circumstances, we would have celebrated Barbara's seventieth birthday in a new Asian or European capital. Such exotic adventures were no longer an option for us, so I arranged a birthday meal with three special friends at a Creole restaurant near City Park.

When I told Barbara about the plans the week before, she'd asked to have her hair cut and styled with blonde highlights. I'd been overjoyed. Her usual attention to her looks had returned, even if it would be short-lived. As a result, Barbara was in especially good spirits for her birthday. When our friends complimented her highlights, she flashed them a grin and quipped, "Blondes have more fun!"

Barbara's happiness permeated the celebration. She shrieked with delight when she saw the restaurant had printed up a special menu, highlighting her milestone birthday. We ordered drinks and took turns toasting Barbara—her singing voice, her dry humor, her youthful looks, her courage. Taking it all in with a delightful

grin, Barbara signaled she wanted to speak. Holding her prosecco high in the air, she made her gratitude for the celebration known.

"I appreciate every one of you who are here with me today. I appreciate you celebrating with me. Thank you for helping me enjoy my life. Let's party!"

As we clinked glasses, I didn't know whether to laugh with delight or cry with grief, knowing those might be the last statements of appreciation Barbara expressed to me and our friends. I couldn't stay in that possibility, though. I swallowed my sad thoughts with my whiskey.

"Here! Here!" I exclaimed, savoring the joy emanating from Barbara's eyes.

CHAPTER SEVEN

ADVOCACY AND ADVERSITY

Barbara and I returned to Belgrade Lakes in central Maine at the end of May for a long holiday weekend with Karen and her dear partner, Carol, also a close friend of ours. Coming to this place was the perfect gift for me. Belgrade Lakes held so many wonderful memories from the twenty-four years we owned a lake cottage there. From morning kayak trips around the islands in the lake and nearby mountain hikes to sunsets with wine and lots of laughs during Scrabble battles, those memories were almost countless.

When I walked out to the screened porch, the sound of water lapping the shore and loons calling helped my shoulders relax. My ever-vigilant brain could take a break here. Karen came out on the porch after me, closing the door behind her. I could see her brow was furrowed, signaling concern.

"Barbara's definitely declining more. Her attention span is shot, so I know why you're looking for a cure of some kind. But I need to know more about this clinical trial," Karen said as she sat down across from me.

"Sure. What do you want to know?"

"I'm scared thinking about something being injected directly into Barbara's brain. Is it really safe? Do you feel okay about her being a research subject like that?"

"You know I believe in science, and—"

"Yes, and it's *because* of your strong belief in medical science that I'm asking you these questions," Karen interrupted.

The higher pitch in her voice told me Karen was really scared about this trial, which is understandable when you don't know the details of the procedure. I wasn't intimidated by innovative medicine, though. It was hard to explain the effects on my psyche of years of hospital and medical exposure as a child and young woman, so I stayed silent and listened as Karen continued.

"Will you be okay if this clinical trial doesn't work? Or worse yet, if something goes wrong, if it makes her worse?"

"I don't think anything will go wrong—"

Again, she interrupted.

"I know you don't, but have you considered how you'll feel if it *does* go wrong? You need to think about this before you go through with the trial."

The loon bobbing in the water right in front of their cottage let out a piercing distress call, as though to punctuate Karen's point.

"You're right," I replied, scooting forward in my chair and giving Karen a quick smile of appreciation. "And yes, I have thought about it. We both have. And we've discussed it thoroughly."

Karen nodded, and her face began to soften.

"Without any intervention, everything that makes Barbara the woman we know and love—her compassion, her witty quips, her elegance, her personality—will disappear entirely. She might even lose the ability to talk," I said, clenching my jaw to prevent the flood of tears that always sat close to the surface these days.

I had no trouble crying in front of my friends, but I didn't want to upset Barbara. She worried when she saw me cry. I pulled in a deep breath to calm myself before speaking again.

"This clinical trial can't make anything worse."

Karen nodded slowly, her eyes holding mine. No more words were needed.

I awakened the next morning anxious that the clinical trial at UPenn still hadn't received the green light. An experimental brain intervention certainly deserved a cautious approach, yet I was prepared to throw caution to the proverbial wind if it meant stopping the loss of Barbara's brain cells. Needing to be proactive, I called the UPenn genetic counselor for an update.

"We've just hired our clinical coordinator, and the approvals are moving forward too," Laynie informed me.

I was convinced our lives could go forward in relative normalcy if only Barbara could get a new gene soon. This confidence kept me sane, while the waiting game threatened to pull me under. While I wanted to have a specific date for the trial to start, I let this news of forward motion suffice.

Once we were back in our Portland condo, more changes kept happening. Barbara no longer took initiative with anything except reading, which was a complete 180-degree turn from the highly engaged, proactive woman I'd known for decades. Most days she stayed in bed until I woke her.

However, when I opened our bedroom door one June morning, Barbara's blue-gray eyes greeted me. She was already awake, staring at the oil painting made by her closest high school friend hanging on the wall opposite our bed. The sun streaming through the window shades illuminated Barbara's face. As soon as she saw me, Barbara broke out in a light-up-the-room smile. She spoke, but I couldn't hear what she said; her morning voice was so soft it was nearly inaudible, despite my keen hearing. I moved closer to the bed.

"I didn't hear you. What did you say?"

"I said, will you marry me?"

This time her words came through strongly.

My eyebrows shot up, and my jaw dropped. I never expected to hear those words from Barbara. Where was this request coming from? Was FTD making her feel insecure and unsure of my commitment to her? I gave Barbara the most reassuring smile I could muster, trying to gather myself, but I was truly perplexed. As ardent feminists, we'd always agreed that marriage wasn't for us. Plus, we had never needed institutional approval for our love.

Maintaining eye contact, I sat down on the bed and cupped Barbara's face in my hands before speaking.

"I love you dearly, you know that, right?"

She nodded, still smiling broadly at me. She didn't look like she was doubting me. I dropped my hands and leaned closer to her.

"Do you know *why* you want to get married . . . *now*?" I asked in my gentlest voice.

Barbara replied without hesitation.

"I want to celebrate us!"

Her dancing eyes and direct gaze told me she meant it. She knew just what she was saying. Getting married was what she wanted. This did not come from fear or insecurity. She simply wanted to celebrate our love. And just that easily, Barbara persuaded me to accept her proposal, our previous viewpoint about marriage be damned. I smiled broadly.

"It would be my honor and my joy to marry you!"

Barbara sat up with energy I had not seen in months. We embraced, breaking only for kisses. While I monitored Barbara's shower later, my thoughts turned to the tasks ahead. My neck tensed and my mind began to race as I debated myself.

How am I going to make a wedding happen before we move away from Maine in mid-October?

Stop it, Susan! If you're doing this, you're doing it with joy, not anxiety.

I dropped my shoulders, grateful my internal wisdom came through stronger than my fears. I called our friend Karen with the news and asked her for help. She knew everyone in town. If a venue could be found with just four months' notice in this popular wedding destination, Karen would find it.

That afternoon, I asked Barbara who she wanted at our wedding. We'd celebrated our twenty-fifth anniversary with a big dance party—a live band, sit-down dinner, chocolate fountain, and over a hundred guests. I hoped this event would be smaller, more intimate.

"Just our closest friends and family," she replied.

Relieved to know we were still simpatico on important decisions, I hugged her close. Within a week, Karen had found a venue for us. It was the same hotel where we had stayed thirty-two years before when we first came to Portland from Connecticut to plan our move here. It was full circle. We could make this happen.

A few days later when we sat down to plan our wedding, I held my breath. Some days Barbara could express her preferences clearly, and some days I only got blank stares. I wanted this day to be one of the good ones.

"Who do you want to officiate our wedding?" I asked.

She immediately named a friend of ours who went to Harvard Divinity School and had been a longtime singing companion of hers. Shirsten was one of our most spiritual friends, so we quickly agreed she would lead the beginning of our wedding ceremony. I suggested having another dear friend of ours who was a Maine Superior Court judge oversee our vows and make the official marriage pronouncement. Barbara nodded vigorously in support of this idea.

Reaching those decisions together proved easy. Our eyes locked and my heart swelled. Barbara had been right about this wedding. We needed to celebrate *us* right now, not despite what was coming, but because of it. Even if the clinical trial didn't work, even if she died, Barbara had long been my soulmate; I would be tied to her in spirit for the rest of my life. I wanted the world to know.

I received a call from the new UPenn clinical coordinator, Dahlia, in mid-June. Dr. Grossman's leave was extended indefinitely, and a new principal investigator was being assigned to the trial study. She also informed me the trial sponsor had added another requirement—proof of Barbara's shingles vaccination. The shot had to be administered at least six months before the date of her gene dosing to avoid any potential complications with the transplant drugs she would receive to prevent rejection of the new gene.

Initially, I thought this would be an easy task to accomplish; Barbara had had the vaccine about two years before. Unfortunately, Barbara couldn't remember where she got the shot. I wasn't managing her life then, so I had no record of it. To make matters worse, I called all the pharmacies we had used in Portland to no avail; they didn't have a record of administering this shot to her. The final blow came when I called the office of our longtime doctor, who had retired from clinical practice the prior year. His front office staff said Barbara's file had no information about a shingles vaccine.

I wasn't about to accept defeat on a technicality. I drove to our former doctor's office to discuss the matter in person. It was critical. The receptionist stonewalled me, exhibiting no compassion for my plight. I asked to speak to the office manager and was told to wait for her to finish a meeting. I paced around the small waiting room with obvious impatience, oblivious to how my behavior was being received by other patients seated around me or the receptionist in her nearby cubicle. Tension gripped every muscle of my body. The sole thought in my head was, *They better find it, damn it!* I couldn't let something so minor stand in the way of Barbara getting her gene replacement therapy.

Finally, the manager approached, and I sprang before she could open her mouth. My eyes registered the startled expressions of other patients while my stressed voice bounced off the walls of the small waiting area.

"Please, I beg you. Y'all have to look through Barbara's records more carefully. There have to be notes you've overlooked from our previous doctor," I implored. "I knew this doctor for twenty-five years. He would have recorded his order for Barbara's vaccine."

"We've looked, and—"

"Not well enough," I broke in, gritting my teeth and raising my voice even louder. "You don't understand. Barbara's future depends on this. I'm not leaving here without a letter of verification from this office."

"But we can't just make it up."

Stay calm, girl. Remember Barbara's philosophy: You get what you want by being kind and understanding, not by getting upset and yelling.

My self-talk didn't work. My fear of failure had grown too strong. I simply didn't have the emotional fortitude I needed at this critical moment. I started crying and periodically raising my voice, struggling to catch my breath between sobs.

"I don't care what you have to do . . . BARBARA HAS TO GET INTO THIS CLINICAL TRIAL! You're not going to stand in her way, . . . not when I explicitly remember . . . our doctor wrote the order . . . AND BARBARA GOT THE VACCINE!"

"Let's go in this office here," the manager said calmly, leading me out of the waiting room.

I should have been embarrassed by my behavior, but I wasn't. I would have done anything to get Barbara enrolled in the gene replacement trial. I couldn't let this opportunity slip through my hands. I took a deep breath and tried again, this time from my more centered, reasonable self.

"Look, I'm sorry for being upset, but y'all aren't appreciating the stakes here," I said.

I slowly reviewed the situation, as calmly as possible, emphasizing why Barbara couldn't just go get another vaccine. I had to get this woman to care as much as I did about Barbara's vaccine record. Finally, her face softened slightly.

"Okay, wait here. Let me see what I can do."

As I paced around the room, my inner voice screamed at me.

Why did you fall apart? You know yelling isn't effective.

Yeah, but no one was listening to me. I had to make them listen!

As I waited, my initial hope and patience slowly dissipated. Too much time had passed. My face started to redden again, signaling my returning anger. I marched toward the door, planning my next approach, hoping I wouldn't explode again. Just before reaching the door, the manager turned the knob and entered with a frown on her face, holding a single piece of paper in her hand. Clearly, she didn't want to reward my previous outburst but had found something. She thrust the paper toward me.

"We found the order. I wrote up a verification letter," she said curtly.

My anger evaporated instantly. I held her gaze.

"Thank you. This means everything," I gushed. "And I'm really sorry for my behavior. I hope you can understand."

Her stone-like face showed no emotion at first. Then, slowly, her face muscles began to relax into the semblance of a smile.

"I'm just glad we found it for you . . . and for Barbara."

I rushed out to my car, grinning as I clutched the verification letter. *I know you wouldn't approve of my methods, Barbara, but I couldn't fail you. I just couldn't.*

With everything about the vaccine resolved, Barbara and I finally were headed to UPenn in early July, driving so we'd have transportation during the month we expected to be in Philadelphia. We had a scheduled screening time *and* a dosing date. If Barbara passed the screening, she would be the first person in the United States to receive an innovative gene replacement for FTD. Barbara called the dosing date "D-Day: the day I storm the beaches of neuroscience." I was amazed her brain came up with concepts like that despite the lost brain cells in her frontal lobe, but Barbara's language degrees still served her well. Her cleverness with words continued to entertain me. The human brain is such a mystery.

Barbara had fallen asleep in the passenger seat even though we'd only been on the road for one hour of our eight-hour drive. I stole glimpses of her as she slept, my heart aching each time. Barbara was my love, my core. The image of her disappearing brain suddenly slammed into my mind. Sweat formed at my temples and along the back of my neck, despite being in the air-conditioned car. I realized I was whizzing past cars in the right lane, and quickly released my foot from the gas, returning to a reasonable speed.

My mind flashed to a similar time in the midsummer of 1969 when I was a passenger in a car racing across the Louisiana state line with my entire nuclear family. We had a similar mission: to get my older sister to MD Anderson Hospital in Houston to assess her eligibility for a leg-saving medical procedure. That high-tension drive had been the climax of a yearlong family crisis that began the first week of my senior year in high school.

I came home from school one afternoon, innocently walking up the driveway and inhaling the sweet-smelling plumeria from my mother's garden. I opened the back door, and the piercing sound of my Momma wailing stopped me in my tracks. *What is going on?* I rushed into the den where I found my mother sprawled on the couch bawling. The only other time this had happened was when her mother, my beloved grandmother, had died.

"Momma . . . what happened?" I asked, afraid to hear her answer.

"Your sister . . . has a hole in her leg!" she finally cried out, struggling for air.

I was immediately alarmed and confused. My older sister had left for college eight days before, and my younger sister wasn't in the house.

"I don't understand. Which sister?"

"Your big sister!" she cried.

Now I was even more confused. We'd just talked to her two days ago, and she had been fine and excited to start college.

Momma's lips trembled as she continued.

"The university called me . . . an hour ago . . . your sister's in the infirmary . . . they did an X-ray."

Her wailing began again. I sat down on the couch and picked up my mother's limp hand from her lap. She gave me a weak smile, taking a deep breath before continuing.

"They found a hole . . . in her femur . . . right above her knee. Her leg's so fragile . . . they've put her on crutches . . . she can't put any weight on it."

The fear I felt that day pierced itself into the fabric of my being and stayed there throughout my sister's two-year medical ordeal. She had a serious medical problem I'd never heard of before: a tumor that created a bone hole. I'd learned all the important stuff of life from my older sister, like swear words, how Santa wasn't real, and that Daddy gave better presents than Momma.

As I drove, my mind skipped ahead to the day my parents had called me into the living room a year after my sister's initial diagnosis. I immediately knew they had something serious to tell me.

We only sat in the living room for important company visits; not even our relatives sat in this room.

"Your sister's surgery didn't work," my father explained in his sobering baritone voice.

The surgeon had removed her benign bone tumor and filled the hole with bone chips from her hip. It was supposed to cure the problem, but it hadn't. My parents' next words laid the foundation for my ardent advocacy for Barbara.

"Don't worry," my mother said, touching my shoulder. "We're going to look for another treatment. We're not going to let them amputate your sister's leg. We haven't exhausted all our options."

My parents always delivered medical news in a straightforward manner, but the word "amputate" hit me hard. Could she really lose her leg? What would I do if *I* couldn't play basketball, or pitch softball, or dance? Every night after I graduated from high school and throughout my first year of college, I prayed my sister wouldn't lose her leg.

Eventually, my parents found cutting-edge orthopedic surgeons at MD Anderson Hospital who offered an alternative to amputation. They were experimenting with bone transplants from cadavers and agreed to perform one of their earliest femur transplants on my sister. She had the bone of a young accident victim placed in her leg at a time when bone transplants were a medical innovation. The transplant worked and my sister earned a place in medical journals with this innovative surgery. More importantly, she has had a lifetime with her two legs. That groundbreaking experience embedded my confidence in medical science. Now I sought a similar miracle for Barbara—one that would stop the hole growing in her brain.

Hours later, as I drove across the Connecticut line, I looked over at Barbara again. She still slept, her head cocked against the passenger side window. The telltale down-turned mouth and sunken face had appeared again, screaming FTD. I looked up toward the bright blue sky as I navigated another internal debate.

Please don't let it be too late!

Don't get your hopes up too high. Remember, this trial is an experiment.

Yes, but medical miracles can happen, so why not now? Why not for Barbara?

To counter my fears, I focused my thoughts on the positive results of my sister's medical experience and the potential miracle awaiting us in Pennsylvania. My intuition told me Barbara would make history. We had the power of science on our side.

CHAPTER EIGHT

TRIALS AND TRIUMPHS

On Bastille Day, Barbara and I were at UPenn's Perelman Center for Advanced Medicine for her trial screening, approaching the fifth hour of a planned eight-hour visit. Barbara had chosen her new blue-and-white Alembika pants and matching tunic top to wear, along with the Ayala Bar earrings I'd bought her in Tzfat, Israel. She looked beautiful—the embodiment of the stylish woman I'd loved for over half my life. Anyone who saw her walking down the street would never have known her brain was slowly disappearing. But here, subjected to cognitive and neurological tests, her losses loomed large.

Barbara couldn't draw all the features of the complex geometric image the doctor had shown her just five minutes before. She could only remember three of the five words the doctor had given her ten minutes earlier. She couldn't follow instructions to connect a letter and then a number in sequence, such as A to 1, then

B to 2, and so on. She still could wow with words, though. When asked to say all the words she could think of that started with *f*, Barbara's answers were *fantastical, fortnight, frittata*, and *frivolous* rather than *fun, fast*, or *fit*.

The two clinical coordinators in attendance looked at me with their eyebrows raised as I grinned back at them with joy and relief. Thank the goddess that Barbara still had her language skills. I kept an eagle eye on her throughout this ordeal, checking to be sure her spirits didn't deflate as they did the first time she'd taken similar cognitive tests during her initial assessment in New Orleans. Her ego had been crushed that day.

"I've always done so well on tests, but I failed those miserably," Barbara had lamented. I didn't want that to happen again.

From what I could observe, Barbara actually seemed to be enjoying herself, not bothered by her inabilities at all. I'll never know whether her joy derived from the attention she was receiving, or she just was oblivious to her loss of cognitive abilities, or both. What mattered was that she wasn't held back by fear or poor self-esteem. She smiled broadly at everyone, delighted to be embarking on this clinical trial.

"I'm here to make history, so let's get going!" was the first thing she said to the team, instantly winning their hearts with her positive spirit.

After the testing concluded, Dr. David Irwin, co-director of the Penn FTD Center and the physician serving as the principal investigator for the trial, began walking us through the required paperwork. He engaged us in the painstaking review of a forty-page agreement we had to sign, with Barbara as the "study subject" and me as the "study partner." Dr. Irwin explained every possible risk in excruciating detail: how her brain could reject the new gene as a foreign body, how she might have an allergic reaction to the immune-suppression medicines she would have to take after the gene injection, and so forth. I was not deterred by anything he said, but then again, I wasn't the patient. Scouring Barbara's face for any signs of discomfort, I saw only the light of attention in her eyes. More focused than I'd seen her in over a year, Barbara remained committed to this trial.

When Dr. Irwin's explanations felt especially scientific, I restated the risks in shorter, simpler terms to be sure Barbara understood them. I particularly wanted her to comprehend how the gene would be placed into her brain, so I placed my finger to the back of Barbara's head as I reviewed the risks of this procedure.

"The neuro-interventional radiologist is going to insert into this soft spot at the back of your head a long needle with the new gene inside. Do you remember him telling you that when we met with him yesterday?"

Barbara nodded affirmatively, so I continued.

"His hand could slip when he inserts the needle. Do you understand that?"

"Yes. But that's not going to happen," Barbara stated with confidence. "Dr. P told us he's had lots of experience with children, and their brain passages are lots smaller than mine. I'm not worried about his hand slipping."

Barbara had clearly listened to and understood the neuroradiologist the day before. We listened to more risks being explained until Barbara finally leaned forward in her chair, making eye contact with Dr. Irwin.

"I'm not going to change my mind, you know. No matter what you tell me, I'm doing this. It's for my niece and nephews," she declared.

The otherwise stoic, tight-lipped physician broke into a sweet grin.

"Thank you for sharing this with me. Participation in medical research is meaningful, and you're a perfect candidate for this phase 1/2 trial. But I have to thoroughly explain *all* possible risks to you. We must have informed consent," he said.

"Okay, consider me informed," she quipped, sitting back in her chair as he continued his document review.

I beamed at Barbara, as did the clinical coordinators. A profile of grace and courage, she inspired everyone she encountered. I couldn't have been more certain of our decision.

When the screening visit neared its end, Dr. Irwin explained the timeline of activities for the trial. The dosing would be followed by three days of observation in the hospital, then weekly safety checks as an outpatient for the first month after the dosing. From there, we would follow up with the trial team every month for three months, after which the visits would shift to every three months for the remainder of the first year. During years two through five, the follow-up visits would be every six months, with the primary focus being on the safety of the patients. He cautioned us not to expect efficacy results until the first full cadre of patients had received the gene therapy, sometime during year two of Barbara's timeline. Then Dr. Irwin gave us the news I'd been desperate to hear: Barbara had met the screening criteria, and they could proceed with the gene replacement procedure the following week.

"You'll be Patient Number One in the US," he said before he gave us her four-digit patient number.

We locked eyes and burst out laughing when we heard Barbara's patient number was the same as the month and day of our relationship anniversary.

"This is so auspicious," we declared at the same time.

"I'm Number One!" Barbara exclaimed, thrusting her index finger in the air.

She looked as happy as if she'd just won the final round at Wimbledon, her childhood fantasy.

A week later, we were in the Hospital of the University of Pennsylvania (HUP) awaiting Barbara's trial dosing procedure. I leaned down to give her one last kiss and hug before letting her go into the treatment suite. Barbara kept her eyes on me as the nurse wheeled her gurney away, and I waved and smiled confidently back at her until she was out of sight.

My confidence wasn't an act; I wasn't worried. Perhaps I was being foolish. After all, I knew more than most about the number and type of medical errors that occurred in hospitals every day. My long professional career had been focused on understanding and preventing human errors in high-risk workplaces. But watching Barbara depart for this long-awaited miracle, I felt strong and assured. Barbara would be in the hands of the best in their field, and my intuition told me I wasn't going to lose her to a human error. Instead, I felt sure this medical breakthrough would succeed.

When I entered the nearby waiting room, an intense chlorine smell wafted toward me—so sterile, so dead. I was startled to find myself alone. Every other time I've waited for family members while they were in medical procedures, the waiting rooms had hummed with low, nervous chatter and intermittently ringing phones communicating the fate of loved ones. In the past, I'd always had at least one other family member with me. My solo status today came courtesy of the ongoing COVID-19 pandemic. But I couldn't complain. At least the hospitals now allowed one vaccinated family member to be with their patients, unlike the complete isolation that occurred during the peak of COVID infections. I couldn't imagine not being by Barbara's side for her dosing.

The quiet and aloneness of the room began to unnerve me. As I walked around, trying to release the tension building in my body, my confidence and previous assurances to friends and family quickly abandoned me.

What if something goes wrong?

No! This is a happy day!

But something could go wrong.

Stop thinking that! Positive energy only!

I sat down and began the yogic breathing Barbara had taught me years earlier when the stresses of our business had caused me deep anxiety. With the steady rhythm of my breathing, calmness seeped into my chest. Ever since Barbara's diagnosis, emotions moved through me like a roller coaster, fear and sadness always ready to drop me into a fast descent. But not today. I refused to let negativity take hold of me.

Distract yourself! Think of a fun adventure you've shared with Barbara.

Our most exotic adventure popped into my mind first: the time we rode the high-altitude train across the "roof of the world" in the Himalayas from Lhasa, Tibet, to Xining, China. The air had been so thin even on the train that we had to connect to the oxygen hoses in our cabin while savoring the view of the jagged Tanggula Mountains, snow-capped even in summer. I recalled Barbara's glowing face and her periodic cries of delight as we spotted Tibetan antelopes running, prayer flags whipping in the wind, and yaks grazing undisturbed on the grasses beside the train tracks. My whole body reveled in this sweet memory and my surety returned. I believed deep in my bones this treatment was going to work. I trusted science; it had come through for me before.

As the minutes passed, I continued to be of two minds, confident and wary. When I tried to read, black letters blurred as my positivity faded. The reality of what was going on across the hall began to unnerve me again. A neuroradiologist was injecting a new gene directly into the back of Barbara's head. She was only the second person in the world to undergo this gene replacement procedure. The first person had a reaction to some of the accompanying medicines. Even though they had modified the medicines being used with Barbara, how could I not be a little worried?

Hey, calm down. You've researched this. It's going to be okay.

I tried to grab onto these reassuring messages from my inner self, but in this sterile, isolated waiting room, my self-trust weakened. Barbara had agreed to a brand-new, experimental procedure, and the more I thought about it, the more it felt like science fiction than science. Researchers had wrapped a synthetic gene inside a defanged virus, using the virus like a Trojan horse with a warrior gene inside instead of soldiers. They hoped to trick Barbara's brain and body into accepting a man-made gene as though it had been inside her brain since she was a viable embryo. Sweat formed in the middle of my back. Cutting-edge science had been what I wanted. But my courage was faltering.

I instantly felt ungrateful for doubting this procedure and tried to reset my mind in a positive direction. I recalled the confidence the neuroradiologist performing Barbara's procedure had shown when he told us Barbara had the perfect brain architecture for the gene injection.

"A straight shot, with nothing obstructive in my path," he'd said. "I can get this gene right where it needs to go in your brain."

My younger sister had her successful ablation treatment for hypertrophic obstructive cardiomyopathy because she had the right heart architecture. I knew from her experience how important the right anatomy was in high-stakes medical experiments.

Recalling the radiologist's words calmed me. I stopped pacing and slowly stretched my neck, releasing the tension I'd been holding.

Right then the clinical coordinator, Dahlia, walked into the waiting room.

"It's done! Barbara's asking for you."

I looked at my watch. Had it really been only twenty-four minutes? I jumped up, grabbed my book, and followed quickly. Walking into the recovery area, the first face I saw was the neuroradiologist who performed the procedure. At six feet eight inches tall, he stood out like my father always had, who was only two inches shorter. I let out my breath when I saw him grinning at me.

"The first thing Barbara said to us when she came to was 'Where's Susan?' Yesterday she said *I* was 'the man' and now she only wants you," he chuckled. "I guess I'm just chopped liver now!"

I grinned in response and gave him a heartfelt hug.

"How did it go?"

"It couldn't have been better. Her brain gave me the straight shot I needed!"

I felt the *thud, thud, thud* of my quickened heart. I knew not to expect an instantaneous change in Barbara's brain, but we were on our way. The experiment had begun. I walked over to Barbara's recovery bay, where she greeted me with a woozy grin.

"There you are. I've been asking for you," Barbara slurred.

Her sweet face evaporated all my fears and loneliness. I broke into a broader smile—for her and for all the medical experts and support people helping us. There was no question we had made the right choice for our future.

Following Barbara's dosing procedure, they took us to the hospital room where the clinical team would monitor Barbara's safety for the next three days, keeping watch for any signs of infection or rejection, just like they would a transplant patient. Because of the steroids she had received, Barbara kept talking and moving her legs under the stiff sheets of her single bed. I tried to hold up my side of the conversation from my nearby bed, but I was completely exhausted and fell fast asleep around 10:00 p.m.

I startled awake at 3:00 a.m. when the sudden infusion of bright fluorescent light from the hallway hit my brain like an alarm. I saw one of the floor nurses leading Barbara back into our room. I shot up.

"What . . . what's going on?"

"Oh, Barbara just took a little walk," the nurse said in a kind, gentle voice. "We found her wandering down the hall, looking in other rooms."

"I couldn't find you," Barbara whimpered, coming over to sit on my bed.

I smiled at the nurse as I wrapped my arm around Barbara's shoulder.

"Honey, I'm right here in the bed next to yours. I told you last night I'd be as close to you as I could get with these single beds."

She leaned into me more.

"I forgot. I knew you wouldn't leave me alone in a hospital . . . but I couldn't find you."

My whole body tensed as I struggled to hide my alarm. Barbara's mother had started wandering just before her decline accelerated. Is that what this was? Did Barbara get the replacement therapy too late?

Calm down. She's just disoriented on drugs. It's a new place.

I accepted the wisdom of my inner voice. Yesterday's joy returned to my body. I moved over and pulled Barbara into my small bed, enveloping her tightly. Everything would be fine.

We stayed at an inn across from the hospital for a month, making it easy to attend the weekly safety checks required for the first month after Barbara's dosing. When the first follow-up visit proceeded positively with no signs of infection or rejection, we got the team's approval to take some trips around town. Since both of us had been to Philly many times in our lives, we had done the usual tourist activities like the Liberty Bell, Independence Hall, the Betsy Ross House, and my favorite, Elfreth's Alley. The three-hundred-year-old houses adorned with colorful, geranium-filled window boxes were stunning.

Still, we needed an outing to a new place. We drove out to Fairmount Park, the largest landscaped urban park in the world, to explore the 1.2-acre Shofuso Japanese Cultural Center. Barbara and I loved Asian gardens; the yin and yang of their designs were inspiring, energizing, and quieting all at once. Of all the Asian gardens we'd visited, my favorites so far were the Garden of the Humble Administrator in Suzhou, China, and the Dr. Sun Yat-Sen Garden in Vancouver, British Columbia. I anticipated the Shofuso grounds would not be as elaborate as either of those, but they would be serene. Nature and serenity were what I craved after several weeks spent in a hospital.

The day we drove to Shofuso, it was sunny and in the high eighties. We strolled along the paths admiring the flowers and the Japanese artifacts without sweating. Barbara stopped by an intricately carved stone lantern sculpture almost as tall as her five-foot-three-inch frame.

"Take my picture," she directed.

I turned back toward her, and a warm, tingly feeling pulsed through my neck and ears. Her familiar blue fabric hat shaded her face, but Barbara's bright yellow socks, red sneakers, and royal blue pants spoke loudly. She felt good about herself.

After the photo, we continued our slow meander along the gravel path until we came to a midsize pond. Barbara was captivated by the large, multicolored koi in the pond. We sat on a bench to watch their graceful, swirling antics. Silent minutes passed. The trill of birds in a nearby bamboo grove kept us company as we relaxed into the tranquility of this pond and surrounding gardens. Barbara reached for my left hand, which was lying on the bench next to hers, and held it up.

"You need to get a ring . . . for our wedding."

Our wedding day in early October was fast approaching. I turned to face her, my eyes sparkling with delight.

"What do you suggest?" I asked.

She held up her left hand where she wore her prized Alex Šepkus ring.

"You need to get a ring like mine; different jewels but the same design."

I had only ever bought expensive jewelry once before when

we were traveling in Greece; I couldn't resist their beautiful gold laurel leaf designs. Now, in this intimate moment, Barbara's strong sense of style and symmetry spoke to me. A warm smile spread across my face as I imagined how easily people would spot our connectedness through our matching rings.

"Yes, honey, that's just what I need to do."

A week later, we visited a jewelry store on the outskirts of Philadelphia that carried Alex Šepkus rings. Thrilled to be on this outing, Barbara walked from the car to the store with a bouncing step I hadn't seen in years. Thrusting her arm forward as we entered the store, Barbara instructed the jeweler.

"Susan needs a ring like mine."

Her long, slender piano-playing fingers displayed rings better than anyone I knew. The jeweler took her hand and smiled.

"You have good taste. The *Little Windows* design is one of Alex's best. I have three in the store with different combinations of stones."

I examined all three, instantly selecting the design with ethically sourced Montana sapphires and white diamonds. The ring would have to be sized for me at the Šepkus studio, but the jeweler assured me I could pick it up during our return trip to Philly in late September for Barbara's next safety check, which left plenty of time before our wedding. With that assurance, I bought the ring and relaxed with the knowledge that the last task for our wedding preparation was complete.

Barbara's weekly safety checks went well, but they weren't easy. She was subjected to everything from basic vitals and blood draws to an ECG, brain MRI, and cognitive testing. At certain points, lumbar punctures also were performed to extract spinal fluid. All this testing was focused on monitoring Barbara's body for any negative side effects of the gene replacement therapy. As important as the lumbar punctures were, each time they happened I wished I could spare her, but I couldn't. They were the most important assessments for detecting systemic infections. The extracted viscous spinal fluid also contained the progranulin they wanted to measure to determine whether the new gene in her brain had started working. Still, they disturbed me.

By contrast, Barbara's attitude during the three hours of testing each week amazed and impressed me, as it did the clinical team. Each visit for those initial four weeks, Barbara greeted the research team with a huge grin and her forefinger raised in the air.

"I'm Number One!" she said every time.

She rode high on this mantra, giving herself the credit she deserved for her bravery in undergoing an experimental brain procedure. The team reciprocated her positivity.

"She's been our best research participant," they told me, and I knew this was true.

Two days before the final weekly safety check, I asked Barbara how she felt about these visits. I wanted assurance that the high spirits she exhibited for the team reflected her real feelings. I knew she'd be honest with me, if she could, though self-reflection was a cognitive function that bvFTD often stripped away. Sometimes I got blank stares when I asked Barbara questions like this.

"I feel good," she answered, no emotion showing on her face.

Then she lit up with an impish grin and continued. "I get to be the center of attention. And they're pleased with me."

The childlike nature of Barbara's glee and her desire to please others brought tears to my eyes. Not wanting to reveal my honest emotions to her, I gave Barbara a hug so she couldn't study me too closely. Although grateful she felt positively about these visits, I couldn't deny the sadness her words engendered in me. Seeking attention and pleasing others had never been personality traits of My Barbara. She never looked outside herself for validation, which was a primary reason I'd fallen in love with her. Barbara's self-esteem didn't depend on others. It came from deep within her, so I could trust it—trust her. I wasn't sure how to process Barbara's new desire for attention and approval.

Lighten up, girl! I admonished myself. *Be glad she's absorbing all the good will coming her way. She deserves it.*

The morning of our last weekly testing visit, I woke up feeling fidgety. I instantly realized this irritation coursing through my body stemmed from a lack of information. I had no idea what the tests were telling the team about Barbara's post-replacement condition. I'd been floating along, content that Barbara had gotten the gene replacement and no side effects were evident. But these preliminary wins didn't satisfy me anymore. Even though we'd been cautioned not to expect results for at least a year, four weeks post-injection, I felt like I needed to know whether Barbara's gene therapy had worked.

I doubted whether anyone would answer my outcome questions. In a clinical trial, you never learned what impact the treatment you're receiving is having on others and sometimes not even on yourself. And principal investigators especially didn't like to talk about results in a phase 1 research study where the patient's safety was the primary focus. Moreover, they never liked to draw conclusions about treatment effects from a sample size of one. But I wasn't asking to learn about the science of it all, even though I liked to know such things. I needed information on Barbara's progranulin levels purely for my peace of mind. I'd gone to the last safety check determined to get my question answered.

"So, how's Barbara doing? Are you seeing any changes in her brain since the gene replacement?" I asked in as relaxed a tone as I could manage during my study partner interview later that day.

"The good news continues to be Barbara's tolerance of the procedure. She isn't showing any signs of rejection, any elevated kidney enzymes, or any of the other issues we would be concerned about. We're very encouraged," Dr. Irwin replied.

"That's wonderful!" I responded.

I was genuinely grateful Barbara had no patient safety issues. Still, not deterred from my mission, I peppered Dr. Irwin with more questions.

"And what about her progranulin levels? Are you seeing any changes there? Is the new gene working?"

He smiled indulgently and cocked his head to the side.

"You know the first few months are only about safety. We need more data before we can answer any functional questions."

Feeling some remorse, I hung my head for a brief minute. Then I gathered my strength and looked Dr. Irwin in the eye.

"I thought you might say that. But it's so hard not to know. Everyone keeps asking me what you're finding. What do I tell them?"

"Tell them Barbara's making history. And she's so brave. They should be proud of her," he said kindly.

I nodded slowly to signal I understood and appreciated his response. He had honed in on what mattered: Barbara's reason for joining this trial. She had accepted the fate of her bvFTD diagnosis from the beginning. She wasn't looking for or expecting a miracle; her practical nature wouldn't have had that outcome in mind.

Barbara had joined the trial for the sole purpose of contributing to a future cure for FTD, not to save herself. *I* wanted her saved. *I* was the one seeking a medical breakthrough, a promise Barbara wouldn't die anytime soon. *I* needed more time with her. But that need wasn't in my power to fulfill. Barbara's joy in contributing to a better future for others with familial *GRN*-FTD had to be enough to keep me going for now.

September promised to be an intense month of activity and travel for us. We had to make final preparations for our wedding, as well as pack up our condo and move our furniture and art to Mexico now that we had finally sold our Maine condo. Never wanting to maintain three properties at once, this condo sale had been our intention since we decided to buy our San Miguel house. Later in the month, we also had another trip to UPenn scheduled for Barbara's month two assessment. Each follow-up visit got us closer to finding out how the experimental gene replacement impacted her disease.

I felt grateful when I awakened this morning, knowing we had a day of fun decisions ahead of us starting with what cake we would serve at our wedding. The baker recommended by our chef friends had just arrived to share his portfolio. Barbara became animated, eyes opening wide when he showed us photos of his creative concoctions, which integrated flowers and cake into edible masterpieces.

"What kind of cake do you like best?" he asked.

"I want carrot cake," Barbara responded immediately.

Carrot cake would not have been my choice, as I'm a moist chocolate cake aficionado. But did I want to negotiate with Barbara on this? Did I really care what kind of cake we had at our wedding? Barbara's joy in this moment and on our wedding day mattered more. I conceded to the carrot cake on one condition: no raisins. Barbara's belly laugh indicated she had expected my terms of acceptance.

Later in the afternoon we met with the florist. I hadn't thought about it when I made the appointment, but afternoons could be tricky for Barbara. Her energy level tended to wane, and her apathy often increased as the day progressed. I needed to have realistic expectations before we went to this meeting. After parking the car in front of the shop, I broached the subject.

"Flowers are your area of expertise, honey, so I want to follow your lead when we meet with the florist. Are you feeling you can select the flowers for our wedding?"

"Of course," she said, giving me a look that said, *What's your problem?*

You fool! Stop second-guessing everything.

Barbara knew her plants, even their Latin names. She had planted beautiful, cross-seasonal perennial gardens in both houses we'd shared. In fact, we'd gotten a better price when we sold our Victorian townhouse in Portland years before because of the beautiful landscape Barbara had created over the twenty-five years we lived there. Why had I been nervous about her ability to pick the right flowers for our wedding?

When we walked into the florist shop, the smells and colors of dianthus, asters, Japanese anemone, roses, and zinnias notified our senses. Barbara's face flowered too; being surrounded by plants had always been her happy place. I felt my neck relax, knowing Barbara would be comfortable in this milieu. I didn't have to be on guard. I asked the receptionist to notify the owner we'd arrived. We had known him for years; he was an artist who used living plants as his brushes.

Dan gave us a friendly smile and warm hugs as he greeted us.

"Do you want me to show you what we can get for your wedding, or do you already have ideas in mind, Barbara?"

He always appreciated her knowledge of flowers.

"We want flair," Barbara replied, grinning broadly.

"Of course you do!" Dan chuckled. "Are you thinking ceramic planters in the front where you'll be standing, with tall arrangements like gladiolus?"

I knew gladiolus represented faithfulness and integrity, so I responded right away.

"Yes, let's use those."

"But no pinks," Barbara directed. "I want purples. And let's mix them with other flowers in orange and green hues."

I wasn't surprised by Barbara's response, since purple had always been my favorite color and orange hers. In no time, we completed the design for the large vases.

"What do you want in the bouquets you'll be carrying?" Dan inquired.

Again, Barbara had her answer ready.

"I want to carry a stem of orchids."

Was it my imagination or did Barbara seem sharper and more energetic than usual? Was it the stimulating circumstance sparking her neurons, as can happen with FTD brains, or had the gene replacement caused this change in attention and interest? I wanted to believe the latter, so I did.

My focus returned to the task at hand just as Dan pulled out a long stem of small orchids—ten cymbidium apple green flowers topped off with a deep-red center lip—and draped them across his extended forearm. I knew Barbara would want that orchid as soon as I saw it on his arm. She loved the shade of green in this flower. I didn't. Sure enough, Barbara's face lit up when she saw the orchid stem he held.

"Yes, exactly! That's what I had in mind," she said and turned to me. "What do you think?"

My eyebrows shot up. As a result of her growing apathy, Barbara rarely sought my opinion anymore. Pleased she had asked, I hesitated for the first time to speak honestly to her. So, I started slowly while I thought about how to express my truth.

"It's the perfect color for you, my sweet. The kimono-style jacket you're wearing even has some of that color on the back. It'll look great!"

Thankfully, Dan took my cue.

"What about you, Susan? What colors are you wearing?"

"My silk jacket has several shades of purple, some dark and some lighter. That color green would look fine with it . . . but . . . to be honest . . . it's just not my favorite color."

"No," Barbara said, truthful as always. "She really doesn't like that color."

"Well, what about the cymbidium lamplighter Aladdin for you?" he asked.

"Perfect," Barbara replied.

She knew the plant and knew it would work. My face must have telegraphed confusion because Dan spoke up.

"It's an orange-toned color with the same red lip of Barbara's orchid. Your baker can use the two together in his cake design. It will show a clear connection between you two while also displaying your individuality. A perfect flower metaphor for your relationship."

The day before our wedding in early October, we eagerly awaited the arrival of our nieces and nephews. I was about to check on Barbara's readiness to greet them when my phone rang. I froze when I saw the caller's name. It was Dr. Irwin from UPenn. He'd never called me before.

Oh no! I can't take any bad news today.

Answer it! If he leaves a message and you can't ask him any questions, it will haunt you.

I hit the answer button and greeted Dr. Irwin as calmly as I could.

"Susan, good to hear your voice. I was afraid I wasn't going to get you in person. I have good news to share," he said.

I could hear real joy in his usually steady, pleasant, no-nonsense voice. I couldn't believe my ears. *And to think I almost didn't answer.*

"What is it?" I asked, daring to hope.

"We just got the results from Barbara's last lumbar draw, and her spinal fluid shows normal levels of progranulin, which is double what she had before the gene therapy. The whole team wanted to give you the good news . . . as your wedding present."

Normal. Did he say normal? That meant the new gene had worked! I could barely speak.

"Oh . . . my . . . God. Thank you! I can't believe it. I'd given up knowing anything definitive for a year, at least," I practically sputtered.

"I know. I pushed you off because we weren't sure when to expect the progranulin to start showing up. This actually is Barbara's second positive reading, and that's a really good sign."

His news flabbergasted me. Two months of normal levels. The new gene had worked right away! No wonder Barbara seemed more engaged recently.

"I still have to caution you," he continued. "All of this is experimental. We don't know if Barbara will continue to get those positive readings."

I heard him but threw caution to the wind. *We have our miracle!* I raced into the living room and pulled Barbara into my arms, twirling her around in a spontaneous dance.

"What's gotten into you?" she asked as she sat down to catch her breath.

I held on to her hand, flushed and grinning broadly as I repeated several times.

"Your gene therapy is working!"

"I know. I've been feeling it. I just didn't want to say anything, in case my brain was playing tricks on me," Barbara chuckled.

I pulled her up to me, and we hugged tighter and longer than we had for months.

The next day, I awakened with a big smile already on my lips. It was our wedding day! I would be making a public declaration of love and commitment to Barbara, my best friend and lifelong partner, and I couldn't be more thrilled. Perhaps given her brain disorder, I should have been feeling the bittersweet timing of our marriage, but I wasn't. Barbara and I already had had almost forty years of fun, growth, and deep connection. With the great news from UPenn, we looked forward to many more adventure-filled years together. Sure, Barbara had lost parts of her personality and some abilities that I loved. Certain aspects of her social behavior also had changed. But her essence remained intact. I could happily live with her for a long time just as she was that day.

As the ceremony unfolded, we felt blessed to have our dearest friends and family members with us to celebrate our decades-long relationship and the future before us. We were especially pleased with our ring warming, an Irish tradition we had modified to include our oldest siblings. My sister held Barbara's ring throughout the ceremony while her brother held mine, infusing the love and blessings from our family lineages into the rings we would place on each other's fingers after our vows. In many LGBTQIA+

weddings, families are not always supportive. While we were fortunate to have most of our family members give us their support, this ring warming would draw in all their positive blessings, countering any remaining ill will lingering around our union.

We reveled in the tenderness and intentionality of the wedding program we had written. Barbara and I were each known as wordsmiths. In fact, most of the people in the room had lost multiple games of Scrabble to one or both of us, so everyone listened intently to our specially crafted words.

The mood in the room shifted briefly as our guests collectively held their breath ahead of our exchange of vows, anticipating the poignancy of traditional sentiments. But we didn't talk about sickness or health or death parting us that day. This was not because of superstition or avoidance; we simply didn't need to say those words because we were living them. Instead, we wanted to make clear to everyone that the depth of our connection would transcend death, whenever it came. So, we spoke our own words to each other. Barbara's presence and intention on our wedding day rang as loudly as mine when she said:

I choose you to be my beloved spouse, the companion of my heart, the partner on my path, the matching piece of my soul, and I promise to honor and cherish you forever.

We had believed and lived the truth of this declaration since the beginning of our relationship, and nothing that happened in the preceding two years had changed this.

Though it is hard to pick, the best part of our wedding day came when Barbara and I danced during the finale of our ceremony. The opening chords of "This Will Be (an Everlasting Love)" by Natalie Cole cued us. We locked eyes, clasped hands, and rose in unison. We swayed for a minute to synchronize our bodies to the rhythm, then began moving our feet and dipping our hips in the steps of The Stroll, a dance from the late 1950s. We both loved the synchronicity of this walking dance. It allowed us to keep direct eye contact, and on this day of all days, we didn't want to stop looking at each other.

When we got halfway down the aisle of chairs, we added twirls to our rhythmic moves. Our friends and family jumped to their feet, clapping and cheering. Soon the whole room was swaying. We put on a show. And though we may have been less nimble than in our early days, we were in greater harmony than we'd ever been.

ACT THREE

UNRAVELING TRUTH

Late October 2021
–
Late June 2022

You need power only when you want to
do something harmful; otherwise,
love is enough to get everything done.

—Charlie Chaplin

CHAPTER NINE

FESTIVITIES AND FRIGHTS

We arrived back in San Miguel in late October, just in time for Día de los Muertos, the Day of the Dead. Our magical town was awash in large orange, double-globular marigolds, some in pots and many lining the door frames of houses and shops throughout town. *Tagetes erecta*, Barbara called them. Locally, they're known as *cempasúchil*, Aztec marigolds, a plant native to Mexico and Central America. They brightened up the town even more than usual, as did the roving musicians heralding the coming of the spirits. Barbara loved the Catrina skeletons everywhere in town. Every time we saw one, she wanted her picture taken, so I obliged. I hadn't seen her so carefree in a long time.

On Halloween, Barbara and I went to lunch at one of our favorite restaurants near the town center. While we waited for

our food, Barbara wandered over to the large wall of plants in the courtyard. I watched her move methodically down the wall and imagined her testing her knowledge of the plants she saw. I reveled in her new levels of energy and engagement since her gene replacement. When she finished, Barbara came back to the table and joined me to watch the comings and goings all around us. A minute later, she grabbed my hand and squeezed it. I looked toward her as Barbara flashed me a million-dollar smile.

"I'm not afraid of death, you know," she said.

My eyebrows popped to attention. Those were the last words I expected to hear from Barbara on this vibrant, sun-filled day. *What brought this on? How did she go so quickly from plants and people-watching to death?* I chose to believe Barbara simply got caught up in the celebratory atmosphere of death as Day of the Dead celebrations approached, and I encouraged her in this vein.

"I'm glad! I love that the Mexican people don't avoid death."

"They celebrate it!" she emphasized.

For three millennia, Mexicans and their indigenous Aztec ancestors had honored death as a natural part of the cycle of life and looked forward to their loved ones returning every year in spirit form. Día de Los Muertos celebrations were their way of never forgetting them. Barbara squeezed my hand again.

"Remember me the same way the Mexicans remember their loved ones every year," she said, eyes intent on me while still smiling.

Speechless, I silently thanked the waiter for delivering our food right then. With the renewal Barbara seemed to be having from her gene therapy, I had begun to believe her death would be far in the future. I wanted to stay in that belief bubble as long as possible.

Two days later, Barbara and I went out to the Día de Los Muertos parade passing near our house. Snobbish about parades after so many Mardi Gras celebrations, I reminded myself there wouldn't be any of the large, syncopated brass bands I loved. Still, we both wanted to participate in this important holiday. Seeing all the townspeople and tourists marching in the parade dressed in La Catrina and Catrin costumes with skeletal face paint they had clearly invested in with both time and money proved delightful. This parade was culture personified and gave me a deepening sense of belonging to our new town. I could see myself in future years donning La Catrina makeup and dancing down the street with the spirits of my loved ones.

Two weeks later on a bright November morning, my spirits were flying high.

"Let's renovate our kitchen," I said excitedly at breakfast.

Barbara paused her fork midair and cocked her head.

"Another kitchen? Really?"

In the previous five places we had lived together over the past thirty-nine years, we had renovated all five kitchens. Barbara shouldn't have been surprised that I wanted to renovate the one in our new San Miguel home. It was the only part of the house I hadn't liked from the beginning.

"We don't know the first thing about doing renovations in another country," Barbara cautioned, ever the practical one.

"How much different can it be?" I replied.

With that simple exchange, we began another renovation project together. Unlike lots of couples, we always had fun when we renovated—maybe because we never did the work ourselves. Instead, we focused our energy on design and materials selections. Often, we started with very different ideas, yet those differences never caused us any angst. We enjoyed discussing each other's solutions and never struggled to agree in the end. The act of creating something together enlivened both of us. I wanted that experience with Barbara again.

I gathered contractor recommendations from neighbors and two realtors we knew, which was a research task Barbara normally would have done. The choice became clear to me after the initial interviews because we needed an experienced, trustworthy partner. The work would be done in the first seven months of 2022 while we lived in our condo in New Orleans. We had to be in the States during that extended time so we could travel to Philadelphia for safety checks every three months. We counted ourselves fortunate to have a second home.

Before we left for the States, the contractor we selected advised us to go to the town of Dolores Hidalgo to pick out authentic tiles for our kitchen backsplash. We learned from one of our guidebooks that Father Miguel Hidalgo, a key figure in the Mexican independence movement, had taught indigenous populations in central Mexico the craft of ceramic making to escape poverty in the early 1800s. The intricate hand-painted patterns of the Talavera de Dolores, as their tiles came to be known, had been modeled after the tiles imported by the Moors to Toledo, Spain, in the early eighth century. We loved this history, so we made a day trip to one of the recommended ceramic factories.

Barbara and I both felt at home in factories. In fact, we loved them. During my professional years, I consulted in every type of factory one could imagine, from car manufacturing and food processing to papermaking, pharmaceutical production, chemical plants, and more. Barbara had grown up in the factory her family owned. They made lithographed tin toys until their business had to evolve to making housewares after the invention of the plastic Hula-Hoop supplanted their metal toys business.

The layers of dust we encountered in the Dolores factory surprised us initially but also assured us this place produced authentic Talavera tiles. We found so many optional designs, I became overwhelmed. By contrast, Barbara felt energized by the choices, diving right into the acres of colorful tiles available to us. I knew from experience she would point out all the colors and patterns that excited her, and there would be many, but she wouldn't make any decisions. This was not because of her FTD; this had always been her shopping style. My job was to narrow the options to a reasonable few, so I followed behind and picked up the samples I liked from the ones she identified. When we finished this first selection round, we had four tiles we both liked.

I had brought samples of the other materials we selected for our kitchen—naturally stained mesquite wood for our cabinets, and black quartz with veins of rust and white for our countertops. We placed the four selected tiles next to these other materials. Without hesitation, Barbara pointed to the one she wanted, and I chuckled. As we'd done so many times in past renovations, Barbara and I agreed right away.

The ease of our decision-making process felt especially sweet at this moment. Barbara's level of interest and focus on our renovation project was as strong as before she had lost any brain cells. I wanted to shout out my joy, but settled on giving Barbara a quick, tight hug so I didn't startle anyone. *My plea for a miracle is being answered!*

Over the next two months in San Miguel, Barbara and I embraced our renewed hope. We walked through town and ate lunch out most days, continuously finding new restaurants and taquerias. Several times per week we went to Parque Juarez to inhale the clean air. We visited galleries to absorb the colorful local artwork. We were finally living our retirement life in San Miguel, carefree and unworried now that Barbara's gene therapy was working.

Then, one night we walked to a local restaurant and music venue to meet friends for dinner and listen to a local group with a terrific female vocalist Barbara wanted to hear. Just after our food arrived, Barbara leaned toward me.

"I'm really hot," she said.

Her face had become flushed and I reached for my water glass. Before I could hand her the water, Barbara's eyes rolled into the back of her head, and she began to slip off her chair. One of our friends grabbed her before she fell and the other one jumped up to call an ambulance. I put ice from my cocktail on Barbara's forehead, and she slowly recovered but looked disoriented. When we learned the ambulance would take thirty minutes to arrive, our friends suggested they drive us to the hospital instead. Two of us half carried Barbara to the car, adrenaline pumping so we did so with ease.

I called our local doctor en route, and she arranged for the head of the emergency department to meet us at the hospital. Over the years, Barbara and I had experienced a few harrowing ED visits. I knew she hated emergency rooms, especially the long waits typically required in cities. Amazingly, and despite my limited Spanish, we were whisked right into the treatment area upon arrival. Everything up to that point happened so fast, neither of us had time to be overwhelmed.

Over the ninety minutes of testing that followed our arrival, my emotions rose to the surface. Feeling like a taut string on a violin, I worried Barbara would be scared and disoriented by this ordeal when it actually was me who had become unnerved. My thoughts pinged around relentlessly as my foot tapped nonstop. Barbara reached over to put her hand on mine.

"Honey, calm down. I'm going to be okay," she said to me like I was the patient.

I grabbed my head and leaned forward in the chair I'd pulled up next to her bedside. Never having seen anyone's eyes literally roll back in their head, I struggled to get that image out of my brain. Gripped by fear of the unknown, I couldn't fathom what Barbara's fainting could mean. My mind raced as I felt the heat of my reddening face.

What could be happening? Do I need to call the doctors at Penn?

I took three deep breaths, exhaling as slowly as I could manage. We were getting methodical, focused care here and I needed to stay calm. On my third inhale and exhale, I could feel the calm I desired washing over me. After two more slow breaths, I raised my head and gave Barbara a faint smile.

"I'm okay," I told her. "I'm sure the doctor will figure this out."

She smiled back and nodded affirmatively. True to her old self, she remained calm the whole time. She stayed fully engaged with the doctor and nurses throughout the multihour testing required to identify her problem. I took my cue from her, relieved that this experience had not impacted her in a negative way.

Around 11:00 p.m. we found out Barbara had a serious urinary tract infection, a problem unrelated to her brain disorder. I responded with a mixture of panic and guilt. *Why haven't I noticed how much her energy was flagging?* Before I could speak, the doctor told us older women often had asymptomatic infections that advanced quickly without any pain symptoms. I'd never heard of silent UTIs. Grateful to learn I hadn't been negligent in Barbara's care, my anxiety began to dissipate.

That night, Barbara stayed in the hospital to receive needed IV fluids. Once she settled in her room, she told me to go home, insisting she would fall asleep quickly and be fine alone. Though thrilled with her confidence and independence, I wasn't about to let her out of my sight. I needed to see her recovery for myself.

Ironically, this emergency room experience gave me the assurance I'd been seeking that Barbara's gene replacement had made a positive impact on her functioning. If she could handle this challenging episode with such presence, I was confident other positive changes would follow. I couldn't wait to see what the team at UPenn thought at her six-month checkup.

Two weeks later, we arrived in Terminal F at the Philadelphia airport, which felt like coming home. We had traveled to Philly so often over our forty years together. On past trips, we would race off the plane and make our way to baggage without thinking. But our arrival this January night was not like the others. Mindful of Barbara's continued back pain when walking, I had arranged for her to have a wheelchair upon arrival with an attendant to wheel her to baggage claim. It had been an expeditious decision, so I wasn't prepared for my reaction when I saw Barbara in a wheelchair. My left hand involuntarily went to my chest and my breathing halted. I had spent the last three months reveling in Barbara's renewed engagement and alertness, but now I had to confront her increasing physical vulnerability.

Get a grip, Susan. She can still walk.

Yes, but what if this is just the beginning?

Don't go there! Stay positive.

And with that internal admonishment, I signaled the attendant to head for baggage claim. When we arrived, I asked Barbara if she needed the bathroom. I'd taken her to the toilet on the plane, but these days I asked her often because she'd had some recent incidents of urinary incontinence. I wanted to spare both of us that experience in a public setting if I could. Barbara said no quite emphatically, so I had the attendant wheel her to the carousel. We stopped a few steps away from the carousel where we could see the bags drop down onto the belt. I briefly considered asking the attendant to wait with us while I retrieved our checked bags but talked myself out of it. It took so long for luggage to arrive at this terminal, he'd be losing out on too many tips if I did.

Barbara stayed seated in the wheelchair while I listened for the signal that bags from our flight were arriving. I gently rubbed her back and hoped the frenzy of the airport wouldn't overwhelm her. Our life in San Miguel was so tranquil compared to travel days, which were so chaotic.

Finally, the buzzing sound and the rotating red light announced the imminent arrival of our luggage. Since I had special status on the airline, I knew our luggage would come out early. I squatted in front of Barbara to get her attention, making eye contact so she'd know I was telling her something important.

"Honey, I have to get our suitcases from the carousel."

I broke eye contact, twisting slightly and pointing in the direction of the chute, then looked back into her eyes.

"I'm just walking over there; you can see me from here the whole time. Please stay in your wheelchair and guard my rolling bag. I'll be back in a jiff, okay?"

Barbara nodded affirmatively, indicating she'd heard me.

"It'll just take me a minute," I repeated for emphasis. "Guard my carry-on. Keep it safe, okay?"

She wrapped her fingers around the handle and gave me a big smile. She understood her job. I turned around, walked to the edge of the carousel, and saw our two bags drop down the chute. The belt moved slowly, but I waited for our bags to come to me because I didn't want Barbara to lose sight of my back. When they came within reach, I hoisted each bag onto the floor, pulled up both handles, turned, and started rolling them toward Barbara. But there was no Barbara, just an empty chair. *How did she disappear so fast?* I couldn't fathom it, but I had no time to waste. My carry-on that held our checkbooks, laptops, medicines, and Barbara's medical records stood unattended. Yelling Barbara's name as I ran, my head swiveled in every direction. My heart pounded as I grabbed the handle. *One concern resolved! Now where the hell is Barbara?*

I threw our suitcases onto the wheelchair and set my briefcase on top. I pushed the chair to the backside of the second carousel, but there was no Barbara to be found. *Where IS she?* I kept swiveling my head, but she had disappeared from the baggage claim area.

Maybe she headed to the taxi stand on her own. I raced out the exit door and described Barbara's appearance to the taxi attendant. They hadn't seen her, so I ran back inside and headed to the glass-enclosed baggage claim office. I described my predicament, hysteria evident in my voice.

"Oh, yeah, she walked past here a few minutes ago," the attendant said. "She must have gone to the bathroom. Up there."

He pointed to his left and agreed to watch my belongings while I looked for her. I even left my carry-on behind. I had to move quickly. I raced to the bathroom and called out Barbara's name repeatedly. No response. To be sure, I dropped my head down and awkwardly walked across the row of stalls, searching for Barbara's orange-red sneakers. Not finding any, I screamed out to the empty room, "Where the hell *is* she?!"

I didn't have time to break down. I sprinted back out the door. As I exited, I noticed the escalator we always used in the past. *Surely, she didn't walk back to the terminal on her own!* But I couldn't think of anywhere else to look, so I took the escalator up and ran across the bridgeway. Descending on the other side, I spotted a TSA agent and breathlessly gave him Barbara's description. He said he hadn't seen her. My heart sank; it was his job to be observant.

What do I do now?

Don't give up. Show him a picture!

I engaged the agent again.

"Are you sure? Please look at this photo."

He glanced at it and shook his head again.

I couldn't waste time wringing my hands. I jogged to the bathrooms around the corner and did another search. No red-orange sneakers. I felt dizzy and grabbed the wall. My throat tightened. I walked shakily to the sinks and applied a wet paper towel to the back of my neck.

You can't fall apart now, Susan. You have to find her!

But where else could she be?

Stay calm and think!

Maybe she'd taken the elevator, not the escalator, and got lost in that strange warren of halls. Her sense of direction had always been bad. Maybe she was still wandering around there. A semblance of hope returning, I sprinted back across the bridgeway, propelled by adrenaline.

My whole body froze when I saw a small gray sign next to the elevators: Parking Garage Levels 3–12. *Oh, shit! She could be lost in the parking garage.* I flashed to the time in our early forties when Barbara and I had visited a market town in France with some friends, and Barbara had wandered off on her own and gotten lost. By the time I found her, her body was shaking violently from fear; she had been sure her inability to find her way back to us meant she had FTD like her mother. If she had gotten lost in this airport parking garage, her fear would be off the charts.

I leaned my head against the wall. Abject terror that I might never find her drained my energy for a moment. My mind wouldn't accept that outcome. *You can't give in! Go get help.* Not able to move, I invoked the spirits I've always known looked out for me. *Please . . . I need you like never before. Help me find her!* I stood tall, pulled air and energy into my diaphragm, and ran down to the baggage claim office to ask the attendant to call the airport police.

"I have no idea where she could be," I told him.

And with that admission, I slid to the floor, unable to hold myself upright any longer. He'd obviously had to contend with people who'd lost their luggage. But this was a lost person, *my* person! He quickly made the call to the police and came from around the counter to help me stand.

"They'll find her," he assured me.

I couldn't just sit and wait.

"I'm going to check those bathrooms again," I said.

He gave a quick upward jerk of his head in reply.

As I walked up the handicap ramp again, I almost laughed out loud at the irony of my situation. Barbara's gene replacement made her more independent, which I desperately wished for, but now I wanted the opposite. I desperately wished she had remained in the wheelchair like I told her to do.

Finding no Barbara in my second search of the nearby bathroom, I headed back to the luggage office to wait for the police. Just outside the door, my phone rang. I pulled it out of my pocket and saw Barbara's number. I blinked in confusion; I thought her phone had been in my bag; otherwise, I would have called her already.

"Barbara, is that you? Where are you?" I asked.

An unfamiliar voice responded.

"No, I'm an agent at the American ticket counter. I have Barbara here with me. Are you Susan?"

I confirmed my identity and told her I was in Terminal F baggage claim.

"Stay right there. I'll bring Barbara over to you."

"Thank you!" I choked out.

My knees wanted to buckle again, but I pressed them into action. I had to cancel the police search. I gathered my belongings and headed back into the baggage area to wait for Barbara. I found a seat, too exhausted and emotionally spent to stand. I glanced at my watch, alarmed that twenty-five minutes had passed since I saw the empty wheelchair. My mind revisited all the horrors that could have happened. Barbara wandering alone in the parking garage. Barbara getting into a cab by herself. A stranger taking her. My anxiety and anger rose with each thought.

Then I spotted Barbara coming into view. Her face lit up when she saw me while my head nearly exploded. I tried to contain my emotions so I didn't scare her, but I couldn't.

"Where did you go?" I asked more gruffly than I intended.

"The bathroom," Barbara explained.

I struggled to control the impulse to dump my pent-up fear in her lap and was only partially successful.

"Don't you understand? I thought I'd lost you!" I blurted out.

Barbara ignored my tone completely. She reached for my hand.

"I knew you'd find me," she said with childlike confidence.

Stunned, I wanted to scream, *It's not that simple!* I couldn't fully fathom the implications of Barbara wandering off by herself at that moment, but I knew this day represented a fundamental shift in my world. The hope I'd wrapped myself in was in tatters, riddled with swirling questions and barely contained terror. For months I'd relaxed into the belief that Barbara's behavior would no longer decline and could even improve, returning My Barbara to me. Now I found myself back in a wary state of existence. Spent and daunted, I kept quiet as we exited the terminal to catch a taxi.

CHAPTER TEN

DISTRESS AND DEPENDENCE

I was sitting alone in the living room of our New Orleans cottage with filtered streetlight seeping through the shutter slats. The rare quiet of the French Quarter on this night in early February was a welcome reprieve to my weary, confused soul. My emotions were like a yo-yo these days, alternating from excitement and joy to defeat and sadness multiple times within a single day.

I'd been riding high from Barbara's success at her six-month checkup a week ago. She had improved greatly in her ability to recall and draw the many facets of an abstract image she'd seen for only a minute. She'd gotten further in the process of counting backward by sevens than ever before. Her vocabulary continued to impress, and her sparkling attitude further endeared her to the UPenn team.

Then, this morning, a completely new bvFTD symptom emerged. We had gone to a clothing boutique on Magazine Street to buy Barbara some new clothes due to the weight she had gained from her increasingly compulsive eating. After helping her pick out options and settling her in the tiny dressing room, I sat down next to the register where the young male clerk stood refolding tops. We chatted about why he'd moved to New Orleans from rural Alabama, as if it hadn't been obvious from his pink hair and flamboyance.

Barbara came out to show me her first outfit, and we both told her how great she looked. The clerk said she could find more pants in the next room, and Barbara went to look. I'd been giving her more independence when we were within contained spaces. Still traumatized by the Philly airport incident, I held on to her tightly when outside or in large indoor spaces. A few minutes later, Barbara walked back into the front room in her underwear, slacks across her arm.

"This fabric is itchy," she noted as she passed us, unphased by being in her underwear in front of a stranger.

I didn't know whether to laugh or cry. I wanted to chuckle and say, "I didn't think you could still shock me, but you did!" At the same time, I wanted to jump up and cover her, saying, "This world is a cruel place for people with brain disorders." I did neither, and simply watched Barbara pass by with my mouth agape. When she reentered the dressing room, I explained the source of Barbara's social disinhibition to the young clerk and thanked him for his kindness in an awkward situation.

Replaying the incident in my mind that evening, I had so many questions. *Why* were Barbara's impulsivity and social disinhibition getting worse while her attentiveness and mental comprehension improved? During my family's prior medical challenges, I could always count on science to supply the answers I needed. But Barbara's brain disorder was rare and her gene replacement experimental. No one fully understood all the ins and outs of bvFTD, including its progression.

So much of the FTD journey was individual. No two people progressed in the same way or at the same speed. Each person's brain degeneration was idiosyncratic, taking unique twists and turns. Some, like Barbara, lost foresight as well as planning and decision-making capabilities. Others spent their families into bankruptcy or became highly sexual. Many bvFTD patients lost their judgment and social graces, creating awkward exchanges with strangers as well as their own friends and family. Until today, Barbara hadn't previously ventured into any dangerous or socially awkward actions.

Sitting alone, I desperately wanted to know what to expect from Barbara in the future. The UPenn team couldn't give me all the answers I sought, and none of my research helped me either. *How can I manage with so many unknowns?* Lack of information unnerved me; it always had. I needed information to maintain calm and control in crises. Without it, I became untethered, which was a deeply uncomfortable place for me to live.

The next morning, I finished cleaning up the kitchen after breakfast and walked into the TV room to enjoy quiet time with

Barbara. My plans shattered as soon as I saw her. Barbara had been aggressively picking at a mole on her arm, making it bleed. My mind became consumed with the thought, *I need to protect My Barbara from FTD Barbara.*

"Stop that!" I screamed, and leaped to grab Barbara's wrist, wrenching her bleeding arm toward me and out of her own reach.

"I can't let you hurt yourself!" I felt my lips curl as I screamed in her face.

I immediately recoiled from my actions, dropped her wrist, and stepped back. I'd never had the impulse to attack Barbara like that, much less done so. And no matter what she had been doing, I couldn't justify berating her for it. *What was I thinking?* Every part of this woman was My Barbara.

Barbara immediately started picking the same mole again. Blood trickled down her arm, and I responded to the red color like a bull in a bullfight. I grabbed her wrist and yanked her arm away again, giving her a glaring look. Trying not to hurt her, I had to be sure the mole was out of her reach. Barbara responded by thrusting her chin up at me and tightening her hand into a fist.

We had become engaged in a battle of wills I didn't want. And I didn't know what to do next. Ignoring her self-harm couldn't be the solution, yet this physical tug-of-war couldn't continue either. I tried to reason with her.

"Honey, we don't want to fight with each other. I know we don't. If I let go, will you stop attacking your wound?"

Barbara nodded affirmatively.

"Yes," she said quietly.

I released her arm and she instantly began picking at herself again. My heart sank like a rock as I reflexively jerked her arm away a third time. I couldn't trust her word anymore, a breach of faith that caused multiple emotions to surge through my body—sadness, anger, surrender all jumbled together. Anger won.

"What is wrong with you?" I growled.

"I don't know," Barbara replied with no discernible expression on her face, still trying to pull her arm away from me.

Her authenticity pierced my heart. My question answered itself and my anger melted away. Barbara had not been in control here. The perseveration devil had overtaken her brain. Loosely holding her wrist, I collapsed into a nearby chair. The cry of an injured animal escaped my lips. Barbara stared in silence at my hand on her wrist before she spoke.

"I'm sorry," she said, with no evidence of regret in her voice at all. "I don't know why I'm doing this."

The truthful yet toneless, matter-of-fact way she named her reality tore my soul apart. I dropped my hold on her and shook my head in dismay. Barbara reached both arms toward me.

"Here, tie my wrists," she insisted.

My whole body snapped to attention.

"What? What are you telling me?"

"Tie my wrists," she repeated. "I can't stop myself, so you have to tie my wrists."

"You can't be serious. I can't do that!"

The power of Barbara's disease to cleave us apart became frighteningly palpable. I turned on myself.

Don't ever manhandle her again!

Agreed, but what do I do? I can't let her harm herself!

Stay calm. Distract her. Or hold her close.

I didn't think any of those options would work. Barbara's words, *I can't stop myself*, kept repeating on an endless loop in my mind. She had named the situation in such simple terms. Her disinhibition in the boutique and her perseverating actions crossed a critical line. My life no longer had predictability. I couldn't anticipate Barbara's FTD-driven behavior or stop it once it started.

How can I ever have peace of mind again? I stared out the French doors to our flower-laden courtyard, a space of beauty and calm so opposite to my life right now. I couldn't compute my future. I had to learn how to live with the unknown, the unpredictable. *Can I do it? Do I have the personality to do it?* I had only questions, no answers.

That afternoon, I approached Barbara's side of the bed to awaken her from her nap. My chin quivered as I reached out and gently touched her shoulder.

"Barbara, time to get up," I said in a voice so quiet I didn't even recognize it as mine.

I gently tapped her shoulder.

"Honey," I called louder this time.

Barbara's eyes opened and she blinked twice, trying to bring my face into focus. A smile instantly sprang to her lips as she recognized me. Her eyes brightened.

"Hey," she said, love filling her voice.

I dropped my chin, ashamed.

"I'm sorry I got upset with you this morning."

Barbara cocked her head on the pillow.

"You did?"

I felt my eyes widen. She didn't remember any part of the difficult exchange we had over her wound picking. Was that willful forgetting or a true failure of memory? Except for frequent *What day is it* questions, Barbara had still exhibited powerful long-term memory and only occasional lapses in short-term memory throughout the past two years. I couldn't fathom how our highly charged interaction today hadn't embedded in her memory bank.

A surge of heat suddenly coursed through my body. *I don't want the power her disease is giving me!* Our commitment to mutuality and my definition of love demanded that I refrain from seizing Barbara's personal power or taking advantage of her disease state in any way, even if she seemed willing to relinquish her power to me. More than ever, I became determined to help Barbara maintain personal agency in every possible situation. I swallowed to dissolve the lump in my throat, then quickly recapped what happened between us that morning.

"I lost my temper with you when you wouldn't stop hurting yourself."

Keeping her eyes on me, Barbara pulled me into a hug.

"It's okay. We're okay."

I couldn't let Barbara's need to be connected with me absolve me of my anger-driven actions. I resolved to manage my emotional responses better. Somehow. Some way.

In the evening, after putting Barbara to bed, I wandered into the TV room and plopped into an armchair. The darkness in the room suited my mood. *How am I going to manage our constantly changing circumstances? Where am I going to get the emotional support I need?*

I considered myself fortunate to have multiple people who loved me and often offered to help. Lack of loving support wasn't my problem; I was. Not having Barbara as my reliable emotional rock, I had fallen back on my old pattern of self-reliance and self-protectiveness. I feared reaching out, knowing I wouldn't be able to handle rejection should I feel it in even the slightest form. Too emotionally fragile, I knew an unanswered call or a delayed reply to a text or email would send me into a tailspin. *Best to go it alone*, I told myself. That had worked for me before I had opened myself fully to Barbara. I needed it to work again.

A tear trickled down my cheek as I mulled this over. Too tired to scream or cry out in anguish, I intuitively recognized I wouldn't make it if I reverted to self-protective mode to avoid the psychic pain consuming me. The slow loss I was experiencing with Barbara had become too huge to avoid. It seemed I could experience the hurt of this renewed loss only in consumable doses. Otherwise, my emotions would come out sideways, as they did that morning. *I've got to lean on my friends more.* The truth of this realization enabled me to release the breath I hadn't even noticed I was holding. Leaning back in the chair, I used yogic breathing to relax the tension racking my body. *Will people really be there for me or will I be too much for them?*

I had learned when I was eleven and my beloved maternal grandmother died unexpectedly that I couldn't always count on my loved ones to console me. My mother's own loss left her overwhelmed with grief after my grandmother's death; she had no strength for or interest in comforting me, creating a double loss I struggled to manage. This longstanding fear of emotional abandonment didn't go away easily. I needed support, but I knew my emotions could be too much for people sometimes. It was probably best to engage my friends and family more often when I was at least partially grounded. That way I could share my pain without overwhelming them. If I was unable to meter my agony, I would release my feelings in private where I wouldn't scare anyone away.

A few weeks later, darkness and the fierce cold of winter draped our French Quarter street in late February, contrasting sharply with the excitement and warmth of our neighbors standing on the sidewalk with me. We waited together for the Krewe of Bohème parade to pass in front of our cottages. Having inherited my mother's infectious joy of Mardi Gras parades, I spontaneously jumped up and down with pent-up energy.

My excitement soared for Barbara to have her first Mardi Gras experience. This Krewe would be a small walking parade, not one of the super-Krewes that rolled with thirty floats and ten or more large marching bands. We planned to attend one of those extravaganzas next week—the women-only Krewe of Muses—but I wanted Barbara's first experience of Mardi Gras festivities to be a little tamer. The Krewe of Bohème called themselves "a social club for artistic and adventuresome people." Headed by the Supreme Green Fairy rather than a king or queen, this Krewe gave a nod to the absinthe highs sought by the bohemian class throughout New Orleans's long history.

I heard the music of the revelers approaching and turned to Barbara sitting patiently on our steps for once. As soon as I saw her, I started laughing. She wore a flashing set of pipe-cleaner cat's ears I'd never seen before and grinned like the Cheshire Cat.

"Where did you get that headband?" I asked.

"A woman just walked by and gave it to me right off her head."

That's a New Orleanian for you, especially during Mardi Gras.

"Come stand with me," I urged. "The parade has reached our block."

The sub-Krewe *Les Rebelles* came into view first, dressed in cabaret costumes straight out of Moulin Rouge. Cold be damned. Before I knew it, Barbara started walking off with the dancers, joining in the parade like she was joining the second line of a jazz funeral—a fun time she'd had with me many times before. I caught her hand and explained this parade involved watching, not walking.

Next came dancers wearing headdresses and decorative tutus lit with phosphorescent bulbs, their colorful lights brightening the night. A six-piece brass band followed them, setting the perfect dancing rhythm for the Bayou Babes prancing behind. Barbara squealed with delight at this sub-Krewe's winged fairy costumes when they came into view. She wanted to join the dancing women, but I wasn't going to let her wandering impulse ruin our night. I entwined my fingers with hers so I couldn't lose her and began dancing in place to the band's jivy tunes. Barbara immediately joined me, forgetting about the marchers pulling away.

The parade finale included a tractor float carrying the Supreme Green Fairy clad in a chartreuse gown with glowing headdress, waving and throwing handmade green fairy earrings and green-wrapped sugar cubes. Barbara reached out in the traditional throw-me-something-mister pose of New Orleans parade watchers, grinning more broadly than I'd seen in months. I loved my city at that moment; it always delivered the fun. We'd stepped out our front door and entered a fantasy land, giving us the reprieve we needed. *Laissez les bon temps rouler!* I thought. *Let the good times roll!*

Ten days later, Barbara's young cousin Rachel came to town from Washington, DC. The sun provided enough warmth that day for us to sit in our courtyard in the dappled shade of the sweet-gum tree. Birds chirped in the background while we chatted, and Barbara napped inside. We discussed many topics, including the unique architecture of our Creole cottage, a style she knew well from her years attending Tulane University. And while our discussions interested me, we both knew we were avoiding the real conversation we needed to have. I waited for her to take the lead. Finally, Rachel dropped her head and sat quietly for a moment, the mood turning somber like the dark-edged cloud blocking the sun.

"I can't believe the family curse is taking Barbie too," she lamented, using the diminutive name all Barbara's family members used. "I'd hoped my dad would be the only one in their generation."

I reached for her hand and nodded in agreement. Her father, Barbara's oldest first cousin, had passed away from bvFTD at the age of sixty-one. He experienced dramatic personality changes and strange behaviors like setting up an online dating account, which caused his wife and children a great deal of pain.

"Now Mom tells me Barbara's brother has been diagnosed with this brain disorder as well," Rachel continued.

I had no words. I felt the same gut punch that hit me when we'd received her brother's news the year before, but I didn't want my silence to end our conversation. I knew from Rachel's younger brother that these cousins had just discovered their own 50 percent risk for the familial brain disease. They originally had received incorrect information, having been told the type of FTD hitting their family was only transmitted through the female line, a scientific fallacy. Learning the truth had understandably unsettled them.

I squeezed Rachel's hand before speaking.

"Are you worried for yourself now?"

Rachel's head whipped up, and she held my gaze.

"Yes, for me and my brother. To make it worse, Mom keeps pressuring us to get a genetic test. We're not sure we want to do that," she said.

I knew from years of discussing this testing choice with Barbara how difficult a decision Rachel was facing. If you learned you had the defective *GRN* gene, as Barbara and her older brother had, you knew you were doomed to a difficult but sure death in the all-too-near future. It turned into a matter of when, not if.

"What do you think I should do about testing?" she asked, her eyes begging me for the answer.

I proceeded cautiously but directly.

"You have to decide for yourself. If it were me, I would take the genetic test."

Not wanting to sound cavalier, I hastened to add more context.

"Barbara never wanted to take a genetic test, though. She always said there was nothing to be done anyway, which had been true when the testing first became available. Thankfully, things have changed. This clinical trial Barbara is in holds some real promise for preventing the onset of bvFTD symptoms. It's a game changer," I explained.

"That's a good point. I had been thinking more like Barbara."

Chances were Rachel would debate this decision endlessly without some professional assistance, so I offered more guidance.

"Like I told your brother, talk this over with a genetic counselor. They can guide you, so you don't get stuck in your fear," I encouraged.

"As a social worker, I know that's the right approach. But when it's about your own future, it's hard to be brave," she mused. "Keeping your head in the sand seems far easier."

I hugged her.

"I get it. I really do. But pretending isn't a solution."

The soft cooing sounds of a nearby dove accompanied our breathing as we sat with the magnitude of the situation and her understandable desire to hide from it as long as possible. Every person had to make this difficult decision about genetic testing for themselves. Before we went back inside, I chose to make one last point.

"Only do what *you're* comfortable doing, Rachel, and only *when* you're comfortable doing it."

|||||||||||||||||||||||||

Walking in the early light of a mid-March morning a few weeks later while Barbara slept, I relished the rare quiet of the Quarter. The joy of Mardi Gras and the fun times we had with our dear friends recently visiting from Maine had dissipated. Thankfully, our friends had found Barbara to be more like her previous enthusiastic self, and their feedback had bolstered me.

Now, though, the challenging routine of my life had begun

weighing on me again. I'd never liked repetitive chores—making the bed, cooking, cleaning—and now I held the sole responsibility for those tasks. I needed some stimulation, which walking in the Quarter provided any time of the day or night. While I needed these walks, every time I left our cottage I worried about Barbara waking up and wandering off to find me. *How can I take care of myself and Barbara at the same time?* This was the continuous quandary I struggled to resolve.

Barbara's increasing dependence had begun to unnerve me again. Since I was young, I'd been my own person and done my own thing, so much so that my mother often cried about my independence. I had no time to myself anymore. While Barbara and I always had been strongly connected on a psychic level, we'd had physical freedom from each other due to my work travels and her myriad interests. This new level of physical tethering represented a major change in our relationship, and a deeply uncomfortable one for me. I longed for freedom but didn't want to abandon Barbara to someone else's care.

As I walked, I pondered my growing dissatisfaction. Physical dependency wasn't the only issue. I missed the stimulation and deep engagement that always had defined my life. Barbara had met these daily needs of mine for decades, and now she no longer could. Recognizing this truth stopped me dead in my tracks. I'd been hanging on so strongly to our good times since the gene therapy, I hadn't admitted this fact to myself before. Sadness clutched my insides and I almost doubled over with pain in front of the Saint Louis Basilica. I wasn't comfortable falling apart in public, though, so I stood up to my full height and continued my walk through the park to the river, my source of strength and wonder since childhood.

I climbed the steps to the Moon Walk overlooking the Mississippi River just as the rising sun hit the steel of the twin-span bridge, making it glow. I walked to the edge of the concrete. In front of me, ferries made their way across the river; their strange V-shaped dance across the water was necessitated by the strong currents of the Mighty Muddy, as we called the river. As always, I became mesmerized by the width and power of this rapidly moving river. I tried to hold my focus on the massive tankers plying the waters in front of me, but I lost the battle. The sight of this river usually restored my Piscean soul, but today my inner despair took hold, weakening me until I collapsed on a nearby bench. I could only think of how trapped I was in the strong current of my present life, barely able to stay afloat, at risk of being pulled under by an unseen eddy.

My shoulders slumped as I replayed yesterday's heart-wrenching conversation with Barbara in the courtyard under the dappled shade of our only tree.

"When are we going to Paris?" she had asked, her face lit with a rare expression of excitement.

"What are you talking about?" I responded, incredulity evident in my voice.

"We said we'd go to Paris in the spring . . . for our honeymoon," Barbara stated with innocence and clarity, hitting me in the gut like a fist.

Her long-term memory was definitely functioning. We had

indeed said many times last fall we would go to Paris in spring. And if I'd been in a more balanced state of mind, I would have figured out a way to make this happen, but I hadn't been. Our lives had changed so much in the last five months. Initially the changes were positive, but now they were increasingly for the worse. There were so many obvious barriers to a trip like this, especially Barbara's pain when walking and her new tendency to wander. I'd dismissed the possibility of Paris from my mind when I lost her in the Philadelphia airport, and assumed she wouldn't remember. Unfortunately, she did.

Before replying, I reflected on our previous visits to Paris—our walks down Boulevard Saint-Germain, the exhibits in the Musée d'Orsay, the coffee and croissants at Café de Flore. I desperately wanted all that and more with Barbara again, and I briefly let myself imagine the possibility. Then more realistic images came to mind: Barbara sitting down on the streets of Paris due to pain in her back and feet; me unable to lift her due to my own shoulder pain; Barbara struggling to eat *moules frites* in our favorite Belgian-style restaurant and me having to help her while my meal got cold; me at Musée L'Orangerie, lost in the beauty of Monet's *Water Lilies*, only to discover that Barbara had wandered off and I couldn't find her.

We had rekindled our desire for more travel adventures following Barbara's gene replacement, but the emerging reality of our post-therapy lives had dashed those short-lived dreams. I had to burst Barbara's hope bubble, and it ripped my heart out.

"I'm sorry, my love. We can't go to Paris," I said.

"Why not?"

"You're having too much trouble walking, and Paris is best experienced on foot. You know that."

Barbara thrust her chin toward me.

"I can walk!"

"Every time we go walking these days, you complain about your back or your feet before we get a block from home. We can't walk around Paris that way."

"I can do it. I can!"

Barbara's determination had always been one of her most admirable traits. Now I just wanted her to be realistic. I gently caught her hand in mine, and she didn't pull away. I placed my other hand on her cheek.

"I know you desperately want to believe you can, and I wish with all my heart that you could. But we have to face facts."

Barbara's hand went limp, and she hung her head. No more pleading. She knew I spoke the truth. I'd never had to deny Barbara anything, and to deny her Paris, the place she loved most in the world, pained me deeply. It was a hollow victory.

As I replayed that wrenching conversation, a shiver coursed through my body. Despite the pleasant temperature and the sun streaming down on me, I felt only deep cold inside. For over two years, I'd been living in the *if only* times. *If only* I could find a miracle treatment for Barbara's diagnosis, I'd be able to relax. *If only* Barbara's gene replacement prevented any further decline, we would resume our fulfilling lives. *If only* we could have a few more months to travel before Barbara's decline limited us, we would be happy. But none of these *If onlys* had been real.

Barbara's cognition had improved after the gene therapy, yes. Unfortunately, too much behavioral and physical degeneration already had begun before her dosing. FTD had the power in our lives now, not us.

Not too long after, I sat in our courtyard reflecting on the importance of being in New Orleans during this heartbreaking time. While not a native New Orleanian, I'd moved here at age ten and still considered this unique place My City. My worldview had been shaped in this city where strangers turned into friends while sitting in adjacent chairs at a music festival, or sharing the anticipation of a Mardi Gras parade, or joining a second line at a jazz funeral. With its culture of community and friendliness, New Orleans constantly wrapped me in a hug. I desperately needed that community embrace right now.

I absorbed every "Hey, darlin'" I received from street cleaners, buskers, and waiters across the Quarter. These greetings made me feel seen. My high school friends here, people I'd first met as a gawky fourteen-year-old, often invited Barbara and me on outings. They anticipated my needs without being asked and frequently let me know I didn't have to handle my life alone. I needed all this caring energy around me now more than ever. I even drew comfort from knowing my parents were laid to rest only a few miles from our French Quarter cottage. The lessons I learned from them propped me up when I faltered.

The hope that had sustained me for the past fourteen months began to fray. I had begun slipping, and others had caught me with their love and energy so I could keep going. Warmth permeated my chest as I breathed out gratitude for all the support sustaining me amid my new reality.

This was a day set aside for us to have fun, providing a welcome relief from my growing angst. We planned to attend the Tremé Creole Gumbo and Congo Square Rhythms Fest in Louis Armstrong Park, a short walk from our place. I awakened Barbara and tended to her bathing and dressing, both of us grinning in anticipation of the music and food awaiting us.

Stepping out our door, a warm blue sky perfect for a music festival greeted us. Leaving home always presented risks these days, but I refused to relegate us to the roles of jailer and prisoner. I vowed we would seek out fun adventures for as long as Barbara could physically manage them. I wouldn't give up our life together before I had to. Birds of all varieties sang their appreciation of spring as we walked together down the sidewalk holding hands.

We walked through the park enjoying the colorful clothing adorning the lively crowd. Among the grand live oaks in this park, I spotted a smaller tree with a large canopy and good sightlines to the stage. Tree shade would be essential when the midday sun hit, so I claimed our spot close to its trunk. We'd come mostly to hear Charmaine Neville, sister of the famous Neville Brothers, but we also loved rocking to the Tremé Brass Band and the Rebirth Brass Band playing on either side of her set. Barbara and I both favored brass instruments, especially horns and saxophones, and these two bands lit them up in style.

We had come hungry, so we started with breakfast. Barbara had selected the bacon maple beignets advertised on one of the many booths we passed in the food court. I was a beignet traditionalist, wanting only a light coating of powdered sugar on the flash-fried dough. As we walked to our selected tree, we identified our lunch choices for later: Cajun seafood eggrolls and dark-roux chicken and andouille gumbo. Only in New Orleans could you have food and music this stellar in the same place.

We finished our beignets as the Tremé Brass Band started to play. Their opening song was "I'll Fly Away," a 1920s hymn every New Orleanian knew because the song featured at most funerals in this city. The irony of this tune starting off our morning wasn't lost on me. The slow dirge tempo at the start of the song, which pays homage to the person's passing, gripped my soul. Ever since I'd admitted to myself that no miracle cure would save us, I'd been battling tears and unwanted notions about Barbara's death. Each time this painful thought rose up, I quieted my anxiety by repeating the words Barbara had long used with me anytime I anticipated a negative turn in our lives.

"Don't paint the devil on the wall!" she always said.

Just then, the band shifted into the faster-paced part of the song, which signifies the community's joy for the dead person's "coming home," which was southern for going to heaven. I jumped to my feet, as did most of the people around us. New Orleanians had to dance when they heard up-tempo music. It was core to our culture. That mood shift turned me back to the purpose of the day being fun.

When the band switched seamlessly to "The Treme Song," used as the theme music for the streaming series *Treme*, I felt a tug on my shirt. Barbara wanted help getting out of her chair so she could dance too. We gyrated and sang together throughout that song and several more. When the band swung into "Treme Second Line," one of our favorites, Barbara almost lost her balance. My breath caught as I grabbed her around the waist to stop her falling, then relaxed when she laughed and wrapped her arms around me. When she lost her balance a second time, I became unnerved. Barbara had always been the most coordinated person I knew.

"Do you want to rest?" I asked.

"Why? I'm having fun," she responded, her glistening face reinforcing her enjoyment.

I put my worries aside and followed Barbara's lead. After all, her rhythm was still impeccable, and that was what counted in dancing. We fell back into our chairs several minutes later with sweat on our brows and our bodies still pulsing. I was surprised and delighted Barbara had danced so long without resting. Then I remembered her stumbles. I pushed the pain of Barbara's physical struggles down, wanting to stay in the joy. Still holding her hand, a sudden chill passed through my body. *This could be our last time dancing together.*

My lips trembled and I struggled to catch my breath.

"I'll be right back," I whispered as I jumped up and moved quickly away, stumbling to the edge of the crowd. Alone, I struggled to breathe. I brought my hands to my hips and inhaled deeply, to no avail. I tried a second time.

You're having a panic attack. Try to relax.

How can I?

You're jumping way ahead. Stop it.

At this internal admonition, my breathing evened out. A weak smile formed as I recognized my longstanding tendency to get ahead in my mind rather than live in the present. I forced my attention to shift back to the music and excitement of the festival. Finding Barbara's flowered shirt amid the crowd, I instantly felt grounded again. I shook my arms and body for a minute, releasing my fears of the future and vowing to focus on the positive aspects of my life, which were numerous. I made my way back to Barbara, the woman I could still hug and sway with, even if we couldn't gyrate for hours like we'd long loved to do. Our lives together had so much love and joy to celebrate; I didn't want to miss a minute more.

CHAPTER ELEVEN

WANDERINGS AND WORRIES

It was April 1, our relationship anniversary. We'd come to DC to visit family before heading to Barbara's spring checkup at UPenn. Since we couldn't go to Paris, I'd splurged on a five-star hotel in the Penn Quarter area of the city with excellent restaurants and museums, including the National Portrait Gallery.

As I finished my morning latte in the hotel's well-appointed café, I revisited Barbara's wandering incident before we left home the day before. She'd been reading in the living room of our New Orleans cottage when I walked in to announce I wanted to go out for lunch. She nodded in agreement, and I went into the bedroom to get my wallet and brush my hair. From our bathroom, I heard the front door close. I rushed back into the living room to find Barbara gone. Running out the front door, I spotted her halfway down the block, heading toward Bourbon Street and moving faster than usual. In Barbara's brain, she had somewhere to go, even though we hadn't discussed a specific lunch spot. Impulsivity drove her forward; nothing else mattered. I had to come to terms with her wandering not being a one-off.

Does Barbara need someone attending to her at all times? Should we move to a gated location to keep Barbara safe? I didn't want to darken this celebratory day with troubling concerns, yet I couldn't ignore them either.

I paid my bill and picked up a cappuccino for Barbara before taking the elevator back to our room. As I approached our door, I told myself to stay focused on the present and count my blessings. At least I didn't have to worry about Barbara in the mornings, as she typically slept at least two hours longer than me. Walking into our suite, buoyed by thoughts of the wonderful dinner celebration I had planned for our anniversary, my positive mood returned. My voice almost sang as I called out to Barbara.

"Rise and shine, my darling!"

Hearing no reply, I walked into the bedroom to rouse her, a regular morning routine. Still coaching her in sing-song tones as I entered the room, my eyes saw only thrown-back bed covers. No Barbara. *Stay calm! Check the bathroom.* I yanked open the door. No one. *Surely . . . she can't be wandering around the hotel . . . in her pajamas!* But I knew she could be. Anything was possible these days.

I dropped my head to my chest even as I recognized I couldn't give in to my exhaustion or the emotions churning in my body.

I had to find her. I ran to the other hallway on our floor, hoping Barbara hadn't gone far. Not seeing her, I pressed the elevator button and jumped in, punching the *L* button four times. I raced into reception, almost knocking down a bellhop carrying two large suitcases. I found the clerk who helped us check in the previous day.

"I've lost my spouse and she's in her pajamas!"

I explained her brain disorder and pleaded with him to help me. His standard customer-service smile evaporated as I was speaking.

"Let me check the security feed," he said. "I'll be right back."

I couldn't just stand there waiting. I ran outside, hoping I wouldn't see silk pajamas moving slowly down the street. Fortunately, only tailored suits and stylish high heels were in my line of sight. I rushed back to the front desk as the clerk emerged from the back room.

"She came down the stairs next to your room in a white hotel bathrobe," he reported. "Those stairs end up near the dining room."

I stared at him, dumbstruck. I'd been on the elevator, bringing Barbara a cappuccino, while she had been trudging down fifteen flights of stairs. My mind couldn't compute this. I raced across the hall and found her in the dining room sitting at a table drinking coffee. In a bathrobe. *I can't believe they served her dressed like this!* Barbara's face lit up when she saw me walking toward her table. I slowed my pace to appear more composed than I felt.

"Susan. Where have you been? I've been looking for you!" Barbara said as though I was the errant one, and having coffee in a hotel restaurant in a bathrobe was the most natural thing in the world.

Still reeling from the panic of losing her, I waited before responding. I didn't want to speak sharply to her. I planted a smile on my face and reached for her water glass, buying time with a long drink.

"I came down earlier to get coffee for you, like I always do in hotels. Why did you leave the room?" I asked.

"I wanted to find you! It's our anniversary."

Her pure love, innocence, and sharp memory melted my heart. It was the damn brain disease that made my life miserable, not her. I had to hold firmly to that difference if my love for Barbara had any chance of surviving this ordeal. Before I could speak, the waiter delivered a plate with salmon eggs Benedict and a side of hash brown potatoes. My mouth dropped open as Barbara dug in immediately, eating at the rapid rate you would expect from a person deprived of food for weeks. Only she hadn't been. Her impulsivity drove her actions now.

Did she really order this food herself? How was that possible?

Barbara hadn't been fending for herself for months, not even where food was involved. She never even went into the kitchen, except to pass through it on her way to the courtyard. Had I been infantilizing her? Was she capable of doing more than I thought? I cautioned myself not to draw any conclusions from what I was seeing. Her brain disorder caused inexplicable and unreliable behaviors, including positive ones like her ordering breakfast for herself.

Shaking my head in amazement and watching Barbara enjoy her meal, the final remnants of my fear dissolved. I wasn't even embarrassed to be with this disheveled woman in her standard-issue white bathrobe in the middle of a five-star hotel restaurant. I basked in Barbara's triumph of independence and persistence. I received it as an anniversary gift.

A few days later, Barbara's April safety check at UPenn went relatively well. She scored positively on the cognitive testing as she had done in January. Her physical exam proved more worrisome. She didn't have the usual robust reflexes in her knees, and the hand tremor I'd seen on occasion had been worse that day. No one on the trial team expressed alarm to me, though, so I dismissed my concerns about her physical challenges as unwarranted anxiety. And while the team commiserated with me about the impact of Barbara's wanderings, they registered this behavior as normal for bvFTD.

Home in New Orleans now from our twelve-day trip, I felt exhausted. I needed rest but couldn't afford that luxury. I decided we had to move from our lovingly restored French Quarter cottage to a more secure place for Barbara—a condo where she couldn't easily disappear onto a tourist-packed street. I needed to arrange everything, and soon.

Last October, when we moved our household items from Maine to San Miguel, I declared I'd never move again. But we had to do this. Worrying about Barbara's safety had become much more nerve-wracking than the thought of packing and moving one more time.

How am I going to manage this workload?

Don't gripe. Just square your shoulders and do it!

Doing what had to be done had long been my modus operandi, regardless of the effects on me physically or mentally. I'd internalized the mantra my grandmother used when she sent us off to school in the morning: Don't fall down. True to her instructions, I'd always handled whatever life threw at me without "falling down." *Can I pull it off this time?* I wasn't so sure. My soul was weary.

|||||||||||||||||||||

As I cleaned up the kitchen one morning, I had the space and time to ponder my current fatigue level. Was it my age? I had hit the big 7-0 a month earlier. No, my level of weariness resulted from new changes in Barbara's behavior and my certainty that more were to come.

The previous evening, Barbara's impulsivity had moved to our dinner table. I ordered shrimp fried rice through a delivery service, and as soon as I set the plate down, her eating sprint began. Throughout our relationship we'd laughed about how fast Barbara ate (or how slow I did, depending on your perspective). Last night's eating pace reached another level of speed. My stomach churned in disgust at the sight of my sophisticated, cultured spouse shoveling food in so fast it filled her mouth to the point of falling back on the plate while she kept shoveling.

I had laid my hand gently on Barbara's left forearm to stop her fork action, but she wouldn't be deterred. Without skipping a beat, she had picked up the serving spoon with her right hand and shoveled an enormous bite into her mouth. Instantly, she gasped, either choking from the volume or from inhaling some unchewed food. Her face turned beet-red so quickly I thought I would lose her. I jumped up but hesitated to use the Heimlich; I didn't trust my skill with this technique. Instead, I hit her hard on her back as I simultaneously dug the bulk of the food out with my fingers, then gave her water to swallow, all in the space of seconds. She started breathing again, and I fell back into my chair, spent.

A week later, the challenges kept mounting. One night, Barbara couldn't settle down in bed. Lying next to her, I tried to relax and read my book before turning out my light, but she was in constant motion. Multiple times, Barbara pulled her knees up and down, sometimes alternating with thrashing her legs from side to side. I recognized her actions as signs of agitation, so I stopped reading and tried to calm her.

"What's bothering you, my love?"

I waited for her emotions to form into thoughts, for those thoughts to find words, and for those words to find the motor function needed to get them out of her mouth. This word journey had been taking longer of late, but I'd learned to be patient. Eventually Barbara would tell me what I needed to know. Meanwhile, I rubbed her arm to soothe her.

Finally, Barbara spoke.

"Uh . . . uh . . . there's ghosts . . . ghosts flying around the ceiling."

Barbara had started having illusions* about two weeks before

---

* FTD can cause illusions, misperceptions of sensory input, which are not the same as the hallucinations caused by Parkinson's disease or Alzheimer's disease, which involve perceptions of something not actually present.

she had her April checkup. She'd been prescribed medication to quell the agitation they caused her, but the medication didn't prevent the illusions from forming. Since we returned to New Orleans, the frequency of her illusions had escalated. She'd begun reacting to the gnarly tree roots all over town like they were alligators. She saw monster faces in the scraggly vines crossing the stone wall in our courtyard and didn't want to go out there anymore. But this was the first time she'd mentioned ghosts. Living in an early nineteenth-century home in New Orleans, for all I knew, there might be ghosts, but I wasn't about to confirm that to Barbara.

"I'm sorry your brain is tricking you again," I said in my calmest voice. "There are no ghosts. Those moving white images you see on the wall are car lights. They come through the shutter slats when a car passes down the street."

"No, they're ghosts. I see them," she said adamantly.

"No, my sweet, they're car lights. Your brain turned them into ghosts, but they're not really ghosts," I reassured her.

"My brain is tricking me," Barbara said, repeating the phrase I used with her every time an illusion surfaced.

"How about wearing your eye mask?" I urged. "That'll block out the moving lights and help you relax, so you can fall asleep."

Barbara agreed, so I got up to find the mask in her bedside table drawer. I stroked her cheeks before I slipped the mask over her head and returned to my side of the bed.

"You're okay. You're safe. I'm right here, so just relax and go to sleep."

I picked up my book again, desperately needing to relax so I could fall asleep. When I finished a chapter, I turned out the light, nestled under the covers, and fell instantly to sleep. Ten minutes later, Barbara's leg thrashing awakened me. I sat straight up in bed, my heart racing. I pressed my hand down on her leg to stop the motion.

"What's going on now?" I asked in a clipped tone.

"I don't know," she finally said.

I stroked her leg as I tried reasoning.

"We only have a queen-sized bed here, so when you move your legs around, it wakes me up. Do you think you can stop?"

"Okay," she said, wanting to do as I'd asked.

Barbara's body grew still. I rolled over and fell asleep again. Fifteen minutes later, I awakened a second time, this time due to the noise of her nail biting, something Barbara had never done before bvFTD took over her brain and body.

"Barbara! Please stop that," I said loudly, my exasperation evident.

Her quiet voice came back to me in the dark.

"Sorry."

The biting stopped. I closed my eyes and drifted off again.

The hiatus short-lived, Barbara's leg thrashing returned in intervals of ten to twenty minutes, chipping away at my kindness. Awakened for the eighth time that night, I let out a primal, bloodcurdling scream as I flailed my arms and legs. My fists were so tight, pounding the mattress on both sides of my body, that I wasn't sure I could ever unfold them into individual fingers again. No longer a loving spouse or a kind caregiver, I wasn't even a sane person. I had become a trapped animal.

"You have to let me sleep!" I wailed. "It's two o'clock in the fucking morning!"

My flailing fist landed on Barbara's thigh, but I didn't stop. I wanted to hurt FTD Barbara. No, I wanted to beat FTD out of My Barbara.

"Ow!" Barbara cried after the second hit. "You're hurting me!"

I stopped immediately, arm in the air ready to land another blow. I jumped out of bed and fled to the living room. Shame seeped from my pores as justifications crowded my brain. *I tried so many times to be loving. I can't take it anymore! I need my sleep!*

My chin quivered as I warred with myself. I couldn't— wouldn't—justify my actions. There could be no acceptable excuse for my frustration boiling over like that. After all, I wasn't the victim here. I slept with Barbara by choice in case she needed me and because I wanted to be near her as always. Still, I could have slept on the couch this one night. I chose not to.

With that understanding, I walked back into our bedroom. Approaching Barbara's side of the bed intent on apologizing, I heard her soft snoring. I clamped a hand over my mouth to stop the simultaneous laughter and scream in my throat.

Now she's asleep? I threw my hands up in the air and walked back into the living room. *My caring words didn't relax her. My cajoling had no effect. My anger erupted and she relaxed into sleep? Someone, please explain this to me!* But there could be no explanation for the bizarre behavior emanating from a bvFTD brain.

The next evening, after I'd gotten Barbara into bed, I sat in the living room thinking about the words several friends and family members had spoken to me over the last year. "Barbara's lucky to have you," they kept saying. While grateful for their heartfelt appreciation, I had my doubts about the truth of their sentiment. As Barbara's needs had become more physical in nature, I recognized my inadequacy as a caregiver. Managing Barbara's finances, handling her appointments, keeping her in contact with friends and family, and ensuring her I still loved her all came as second nature to me. Managing her toileting and bathing continued to be more difficult for me, both physically and energetically.

I always had lived mostly in my head, or in a cloud, as my mother used to say; not in the physical world. One night during my high school years, Momma arrived home from a PTA meeting with a large brown bag. She thrust it at me.

"These are the clothes you wore to school this morning. Your gym teacher couldn't believe how absent-minded you are. I've always known it," she said.

I had driven back home in the blue bloomers I'd worn for my after-school basketball game, oblivious to the fact my clothes remained in my locker. I'm sure I'd been thinking about something more important than clothes.

Caretaking my own physical needs had never been a high priority of mine. The mundane nature of life on the physical plane drained my energy. No wonder I had become exhausted by the attention I now had to give to Barbara's physical care, everything from bathing and dressing her to toilet care and teeth brushing. I found it tedious and even repugnant at times. I needed to hire someone to help me with her physical care. Still, I resisted. But the question was *Why?*

Did I think asking for help meant I failed as Barbara's caregiver? The immediate response in my head came as a resounding *No!* but I forced myself to probe the question further until the truth emerged. Deciding to hire someone else to care for Barbara felt like a personal failure on my part. I believed I should be able to deliver whatever Barbara needed. She had been my beloved for decades and she needed my care. Shouldn't that be the end of it? Besides, caring for my friends and family when they needed my support always had been a vital part of who I was and who I strived to be. Being a caregiver was an essential part of my self-image.

So why did I need outside help for Barbara? My mother never did. In my mid-teen years, my father had brought his ninety-two-year-old mother with dementia to live with us. My mother took over her care with no complaints. When I left for college as a freshman, my father brought his older sister with advanced-stage breast cancer to New Orleans for better medical care and my mother didn't blink an eye. She just added Aunt T's care to the care she already had been giving my older sister who was home recovering from her bone tumor surgery.

"That's what families do," she had said. "We take care of our own."

Of course, as a child and young adult, I may not have been privy to my mother's whole story. Maybe she did struggle and I just didn't know it. But my experience of my mother's caregiving abilities had been the bar I set for myself throughout my life. I measured myself against it now. *Why am I failing to care for Barbara's physical needs with patience and love? What do I lack that my mother had?* These questions plagued me.

I couldn't deny my limitations as a physical caregiver. Toileting care had always been difficult for me, even as a teenager babysitting for infants in diapers. Barbara had known this about me for a long time. It's why she never wanted me to be the one delivering her physical care. She had made that clear in her advance directives. Still, I felt like I should be able to do everything she needed, including wiping her butt when the need arose.

She deserved care from a person who loved her as much as I did. She deserved quality care from me. How could I be comfortable leaving her care to someone who didn't know her or love her as I did? I'd been going round and round this dilemma for months. Unresolved, I walked into the bathroom to start my bedtime routine. Picking up my toothbrush, I focused on the person in the mirror and let my internal dialogue unfold.

You need to rethink Barbara's care.

I know, but it makes me sad and ashamed.

This is taking a toll on you. And coming out sideways on her.

Continuing to look at myself, my eyes narrowed. There was more to my resistance than a fear of failure or shame. I had to admit there was a selfish piece too.

I didn't want strangers around me all the time.

I didn't want to give up my privacy.

As an extreme introvert, I needed a lot of time alone. While I no longer had the independence I craved, at least I could be in another part of the house from Barbara, undisturbed and unobserved for parts of each day while she read or watched TV. Having home care aides in our small condo with us would mean having to give some of my attention to that person as well. Worse, it meant having their attention on me throughout the day. I had to admit to my reluctance to relinquish what modicum of privacy I still had.

Recalling an exchange with my mother two decades earlier, a chuckle of self-irony escaped my lips. My mother and I had faced off in her bedroom, my neck and jaw locked tight while she shot daggers at me.

"Momma, your privacy isn't as important as your safety!" I had said, sure of my logic. "If you want to keep living at home, you have to get help during the day."

"No . . . I . . . don't," she declared for the second time, my arguments failing to penetrate her stubbornness.

"You're eighty-six years old! You need someone with you for your children's peace of mind if not your own."

"You don't understand. Some day you will!" she retorted.

That day had arrived. But I couldn't let my pride or my privacy desires stand in the way of what Barbara and I needed to manage our current ordeal. I needed to look into home care for Barbara. We had invested in long-term care insurance when she turned fifty just in case familial FTD raised its ugly head. The day we'd anticipated, but never wanted, had arrived.

|||||||||||||||||||||||

The social worker from the home care agency I'd selected was scheduled for an initial site visit this morning. Still unsettled by the decision, I kept reminding myself Barbara had wanted an outside, trained person to handle her physical needs. She'd explicitly requested a home health-care person, not a family member, to do her bathing, dressing, and toileting when she no longer could do it on her own. The intimacy involved in such care tasks didn't deter Barbara from having a stranger do them; she'd never been body shy. And she knew, from years of watching her mother and aunt decline, how difficult the daily care for a person with bvFTD could be. She wanted to spare her loved ones, especially me, this struggle.

Barbara often had been wiser than me, and she definitely proved to be right about professional care. She hadn't wanted me to grow weary of her, something I never imagined could happen. But bvFTD, not Barbara—never Barbara—had worn me down. It had slowly been consuming her and challenging me to my core.

The antique bell rang on our front door, startling me. I jumped off the couch. Barbara looked up from the book she'd been reading, unaware of my tortured thoughts. I gave her a big smile of assurance.

"That's the social worker we're meeting with today," I reported.

Barbara nodded affirmatively, telling me she remembered.

This seasoned professional immediately put both of us at ease. I felt her genuine warmth and let go of my trepidations. We exchanged information on Barbara's condition, her care needs, and our time requirements—five hours a day, starting at 9:00 a.m., for five days a week. The social worker turned to Barbara.

"What qualities would you like in your home health aide?" she queried. "What's most important to you?"

I appreciated the respect she showed Barbara while I wondered what her response would be. They maintained eye contact as Barbara formed her answer.

"I want someone kind."

We waited to see if there was more to come, but true to form, Barbara had defined her essential needs in a pithy way. Kindness—the quality of being friendly, generous, and considerate—was exactly what she, and really anyone, needed in a caretaker. And with that, the social worker assured us she would find the right person to care for Barbara. I felt the weight lift from my shoulders knowing we'd have help in a week's time.

After the social worker left, I turned back to Barbara. She already had returned to her book, unconcerned by this major change in our lives. I chuckled to myself. The practical Barbara I'd always known still existed behind her disease. *I guess I can accept this change in our lives if she can.*

I had to acknowledge the facts. My well-honed tendency toward self-reliance had not served me well. I simply couldn't deliver the daily degree of quality care Barbara required by myself. Trying to do so had put significant stress on my body and self-doubt in my psyche. We needed this change.

Two days later, I sat at the dining room table paying our bills when Barbara came into the adjacent living room to put on her socks and shoes. She grinned at me, and I flashed her a quick smile in return before continuing with my task. I'd always had immense powers of concentration, so I had no idea how much time passed before I looked at Barbara again. Bent over, holding a sock partway on her foot, Barbara's face had become beet-red from keeping her head down for an extended period. I jumped up and reached the couch in three quick steps. Her right foot already shod, Barbara had been struggling to fit the sock over the toes on her left foot.

"What's going on, my love?" I asked, keeping my voice as calm as I could manage.

"I . . . I can't pick up my foot," she said.

"Sit up please," I requested. "Let me help you."

Assuming she had experienced a coordination issue, I leaned down with one hand to pick up Barbara's foot. I couldn't lift it. It was dead weight.

I tried again but couldn't flex her foot up from the toes or heel. A whimper formed in my throat. I clamped my lips shut to hold it back. Using both hands this time, I reached down and lifted Barbara's leg, resting it on my knee. Working the sock onto Barbara's foot, I felt the cold in her extremity as I went.

With difficulty, I worked her sneaker onto her foot, wiggling it back and forth. My anxiety rose as I struggled with this inflexible foot. *What is happening? What if she can't walk anymore?* I couldn't entertain that possibility. Pushing harder, I got her foot into the sneaker and quickly tied my famous slip knot to complete the job.

Giving Barbara a weak smile, I pulled her up from the couch, terrified I would cause permanent damage to my increasingly painful left shoulder. I'd been told two years before I needed total shoulder replacement surgery, but Barbara's bvFTD had made that impossible. The only thought circulating in my brain was, *I have to keep Barbara mobile.* Her back pain had been attributed to a pinched nerve. She'd finally received a nerve block to reduce that pain. I couldn't let any other movement problems destroy our quality of life now. Still holding Barbara's hands, I gently guided her.

"Walk with me," I instructed as I took a step backward with my left foot.

It took a minute before Barbara caught on to my instruction and matched my movement by stepping forward with her right foot. Stepping back next with my right foot, I held my breath to see if Barbara could follow. Keeping her eyes on our feet, Barbara lifted her left foot and stepped forward. I let out a long breath and tried this foot dance again. When I stepped back with my left foot, Barbara matched me with her right, less tentatively this time.

We repeated our mirrored motions, my right, her left, my left, her right, across the living room and into the dining room. As I increased the pace, Barbara kept up with me. Eventually I added a slight sway in my hips, and she responded until we were dancing together. When she recognized our dance movements, Barbara looked up at me and burst out laughing. I laughed in response and pulled her to me in a bear hug.

Immediate crisis averted. I could only pray it wouldn't happen again.

CHAPTER TWELVE

ASSISTANCE AND ANSWERS

We had survived our move to a three-story condo building with a locked gate located in the back of the Quarter on Esplanade Avenue. Fortunately, Barbara seemed unphased by the move. In fact, she was enthralled by our balcony. She said she felt like she was in a treehouse surrounded by the live oak trees lining the median down the center of the street.

However, this May morning would be the real test of her ability to handle change, as her new caregiver, Jada, had arrived at 9:00 a.m. sharp. Jada had been a home health aide for a decade, caring for two Alzheimer's patients during those years. Since Barbara remained asleep when she arrived, I sat Jada down in our living room to give her background information on Barbara and her brain condition before I introduced them. I explained how different bvFTD was from Alzheimer's, especially with regard to memory.

As I described Barbara's loss of frontal lobe brain cells and the consequences of this loss, my heart broke for the umpteenth time. I emphasized Barbara's remaining attributes and abilities, encouraging Jada to talk to Barbara normally and be patient for her answers. I stressed the importance of keeping Barbara moving every day, while acknowledging her lack of motivation and periodic back pain. The agency had briefed Jada, I knew, but I wanted her to hear it all from me. We had to be on the same page with Barbara's care. Finally, I asked Jada if she had any questions.

"No," Jada replied. "You've given me a good understanding of Barbara's situation."

Clarity achieved, we went upstairs to the bedroom and found Barbara under her pile of covers with her eyes open.

"Good morning, sweetie. This is Jada, your new caregiver."

Barbara turned her head toward Jada. As soon as they made eye contact, Barbara broke into her most inviting smile.

"Hi," she said, offering a simple welcome to this new person in our lives.

Relieved, I continued.

"I'll let you wake up a little more while I show Jada around the bathroom. She's going to give you a shower this morning."

"No," Barbara responded, the smile still on her face.

Jada looked at me, eyebrows raised.

"Yes, honey. It's Monday. Monday is always a shower day," I stated in my most matter-of-fact tone.

Making eye contact with Jada, I explained.

"Barbara's response has nothing to do with you. 'No' has become her first response to everything, so just keep going. She won't resist."

As I said these words, I recognized how much information I held about Barbara, the subtle nuances of her disease and how to manage it. *How can I impart all of this to another person?* I proceeded with the bathroom tour, emphasizing what needed to be done to keep Barbara from falling. We walked back into the bedroom.

"Okay, let's get you up, Barbara, and then I'll leave y'all to it," I said.

I wanted to stay and observe Jada's toileting and bathing skills, along with her interactions with Barbara, but I didn't want to insult her. A caregiver with a decade of experience and strong references surely knew what she was doing. I did stand at the bottom of the stairs, though, my ears on high alert like the mother of a newborn. While I couldn't hear every word, I appreciated Jada's tone—gentle yet firm. I reminded myself I had served Barbara's needs best by hiring a trained caregiver. I had to let them manage together from here.

I walked into the dining room and sat at the table to prepare a timeline of activities for Barbara's day. I also made a list of breakfast and lunch items Barbara liked and indicated where Jada could find them in the kitchen. By the time they came into the room, smiling and seemingly relaxed after their morning hygiene tasks, I had completed my list making. Seeing Barbara comfortable and well-coiffed relieved my initial tension. Confident and ready to leave them alone, I quickly explained my lists to Jada, kissed Barbara on the forehead, and left to do my errands.

While I only had a couple hours of chores, I had decided to stay away for at least four hours, giving Barbara and Jada uninterrupted bonding time. That meant having lunch out by myself for the first time in several years. The novelty overwhelmed me. Where did I want to eat? What did I want to eat? All this time I'd only been making decisions based on Barbara's needs. Now I had a chance to follow my own desires. I felt stymied. For years now, I'd pushed my own wants so far back it took a while to bring them to the forefront.

I finally settled on Acme Oyster House, a well-known tourist spot in the Quarter that was also popular with locals. Their food was reliably delicious, and there was always a line outside. Due to Barbara's difficulty standing, I hadn't been to Acme in years. Waiting outside, I reviewed the menu from memory. A cup of seafood gumbo was a given appetizer. The next question was harder to answer—fried shrimp or hot roast beef po'boy for the main course? I felt almost giddy in anticipation of this food. Then, out of nowhere, uninvited tears formed at the rim of my eyes.

It's only fun anticipating these good eats with Barbara.

I'd traveled so much for business, I wasn't bothered by eating alone in a restaurant. But, on those trips, it was more of a utilitarian act. Half the fun of waiting outside Acme's was talking about what you were going to order once you got inside. I'd never come here alone.

I left the line and walked half a block over to Hotel Monteleone. Their restaurant also had great food, but more importantly for me now, it was a hotel. Barbara's absence didn't sting so harshly in this functional hotel milieu. Throughout the meal, my mind kept drifting to Barbara. Was she worried by my absence? Did she even register it?

Then I pondered the more important question: Did Barbara feel well-treated? Surfacing this thought caused me instant discomfort. My freedom immediately felt frivolous. I had to know how Barbara felt. I asked for the check and hurried home.

As soon as Jada left for the day, I eagerly investigated Barbara's feelings about her new caregiver.

"How was your day?" I asked, squatting next to her chair.

"Good," she replied, not taking her eyes off the home remodeling show she had been watching.

I put the TV on mute and sought her attention.

"I want to talk with you about your day. Can you look at me, please?"

Barbara turned to me with the same exasperated face she'd given me for decades every time I wanted to talk about feelings and she wanted to continue with the task at hand. I almost laughed when I recognized this familiar dynamic. As usual, I plowed ahead anyway.

"How was it to have Jada with you today?"

"Good."

"Are you okay if she keeps coming?"

"Yeah," she replied, then smiled. "She showed me pictures of her kids on her phone. And she showed me people dancing."

"That sounds like fun." I hesitated but asked my most important question. "Do you feel safe with Jada?"

Barbara cocked her head, indicating her puzzlement at my question. I immediately regretted asking, concerned I'd planted an undesirable thought in her head.

"Yeah. She's kind," Barbara finally replied, no worry evident.

Relax, girl. A competent caregiver is what you both need.

A few weeks later, Karen and Carol arrived from Maine. Their visit was a welcome interlude in our otherwise monotonous lives. I'd warned them the week before that they probably would notice Barbara's lack of physical fluidity. They hadn't seen us since last October when we were dancing at our wedding. However, I wasn't prepared for the alarming shock I saw in their eyes as we walked to breakfast. For no obvious reason, this morning I couldn't get Barbara to walk with a normal gait. Her movements were more disturbing than usual, and we stopped twice in the first block to rest on people's stoops.

When we started walking again, Barbara's body was bent almost in half, her posture propelling her body forward at a faster and faster pace. I stopped her out of fear she would fall and gently adjusted her posture so she stood upright. Never in my wildest dreams had I thought I'd have to attend to Barbara's posture. As the daughter of a West Point graduate, she'd always prided herself in her ramrod straight back. Now her torso kept returning to a seventy-degree angle, my adjustments holding for less than two minutes at a time.

On the fourth stop, I tried a different tactic. I linked Barbara's arm in mine to give me leverage in controlling her pace. It wasn't a wise move; Barbara's body weight felt like it was pulling my arm out of its socket. Without prompting, Karen moved to Barbara's other side and linked arms with her, relieving the strain on my deteriorating left shoulder. I caught Karen's eye and gave her a smile of thanks, but her brow remained furrowed. No smile came in return. Her stark response prompted me to reflect on our situation.

Maybe you shouldn't be taking Barbara out for walks anymore.

Immobility isn't an option.

I lived in fear of Barbara losing her ability to walk. This change would restrict us more than all the other changes we had faced combined. And it would signal the end game. We couldn't be at that stage already. We just couldn't be. My attention snapped back to the present when Barbara stumbled over the uneven sidewalk characteristic of every neighborhood in New Orleans.

"You have to slow down and walk upright to keep your balance," I reminded Barbara, exasperation in my voice.

Another stumble and near fall. I tried a different message.

"Please slow down! You're going to fall flat on your face if you don't."

"I can't slow down," Barbara blurted as she continued pulling forward.

Her truthfulness nearly broke me. So much of what Barbara

did these days she did fast. Fast drinking, fast eating, fast walking. Was it her lack of impulse control causing these speedy actions? If so, she couldn't stop her impulsivity. But what was the source of this physical imbalance she was showing? Whatever it was, we had a high-risk situation on our hands.

Yet, I didn't call a ride share to get us to the restaurant, which was still several blocks away. I was trapped in tunnel vision about Barbara's situation and my own. My usual problem-solving abilities were paralyzed by my deepening concern over the inadequacy of my caregiving skills. I no longer had a handle on the big picture. I was reduced to small and immediate firefighting.

"Let's sit for a minute," I said as I eased Barbara onto yet another of the many stoops available in the French Quarter and Marigny districts. I rubbed her back and shoulders to help her relax and slow her breathing while I considered what to do. Barbara's voice broke through my thoughts.

"Let's get going. I'm hungry."

I knew she wasn't actually hungry. Her drivers were impatience and impulsivity.

"Here's what we're gonna do," I said. "We're going to stand up straight, wrap our arms around each other's waist, and walk heel to toe. You match the pace of my feet, like we're dancing together, only side by side."

"Okay, but no slow dancing," she said, her ironic humor still intact.

Thankfully, dancing side by side finally got us where we needed to go.

Later that evening, after I'd gotten Barbara into bed, Karen and Carol asked me what was happening with Barbara's posture and walking difficulties. I had no satisfactory answers for them or myself.

"What you witnessed is not an everyday occurrence," I explained. "In fact, she's never struggled to hold herself upright like she did today."

Karen sensed my fear rising and sought to comfort me.

"The walking was troublesome, but Barbara seems so much more present and connected. Maybe there's a simple explanation for her struggles today, and you can get it fixed like you did her back pain."

I assured her I would follow up with Barbara's orthopedist and with UPenn to get this movement issue resolved.

Unfortunately, by mid-June I still had no answers on Barbara's deteriorating posture. Worse, bvFTD stole the joy from one of our longtime favorite rituals: eating dinner together. Thanks to Barbara's love of cooking and her culinary skills, dinner had always been the highlight of our day. When she stopped cooking nearly two years before, I took up the mantle she had carried with such panache, trying to deliver a similarly positive experience for us every day.

This particular evening, I made a chicken, broccoli, and rice dish Barbara loved, hoping as I did each night for an enjoyable meal together. I brought our plates into the dining room, dropped Barbara's off in front of her, then headed to my chair across from her. When I looked up from placing my napkin in my lap, all my hope and joy vanished. In less than a minute, Barbara's mouth had become so full of food, her cheeks looked like chipmunks devouring their last meal before hibernation. My cheeks flushed brightly while my stomach churned. The frequency of Barbara's near-choking episodes had been increasing; I feared any meal could be her last. Before I could respond, Barbara stuffed another forkful in her mouth, the new rice kernels instantly falling out of her mouth and back onto her plate. *I can't take this anymore.*

"Goddamn it, Barbara! We've talked about this!"

I jumped up, grabbed her plate away, wrenched the fork out of her hand, and stomped into the kitchen, slamming her plate down on the counter. Walking back into the dining room, trying to control my anger, I found Barbara standing up and reaching across the table trying to grab my plate. My mother's catchphrase, "Where there's a will, there's a way" popped into my mind, but I wasn't amused. I picked up my plate and walked into the kitchen without a word, determined to eat standing at the counter so I didn't have to look at Barbara anymore. I couldn't stomach this new facet of FTD Barbara.

As I admitted this to myself, I recalled a similar incident with Barbara's parents. Seven months after her mother's dementia diagnosis, the four of us were eating dinner at their house in Pennsylvania during a weekend trip. Barbara's father had made dinner, a first in Barbara's life. As soon as he set the plate down in front of his petite, slender wife, she started cramming food into her mouth like she'd been starved for weeks. Seeing this, Barbara's father jerked the plate away from her.

"Peggy!" he hollered. "You're being a glutton again! I told you I wasn't going to feed you if you kept eating like that!"

I stayed silent, not moving a muscle. Having been called a glutton as a teenager when my thin frame increased by fifteen pounds, I knew the humiliation such words could cause. Barbara immediately jumped in to protect her mother.

"Dad, stop! That was completely uncalled for! You should apologize! Mom can't help it!" she had argued.

Barbara grabbed the plate back from him, pulled up a chair beside her mother, and began offering her small, reasonable bites to chew and swallow. I could still see them smiling at each other throughout the remainder of that meal. But I wasn't Barbara. I didn't have her inner calm and grace. Fear of Barbara choking to death and me not being able to save her had overtaken me. And fear was hard for me to release. Calling from the dining room, Barbara's voice broke through my ruminations.

"Give me my food!" she insisted.

I walked back into the dining room with only my plate in hand. I didn't want to upset her by abandoning her at the table, but I also couldn't give her plate back to her. The risk was too high.

"Where's *my* food?"

"I can't have you feed yourself anymore. So, you have to wait until I finish eating, and then I'll feed you."

As I chewed my food with her staring at me, I couldn't believe what I was doing.

Am I intentionally punishing her?

"I'm afraid you'll choke," I explained further, addressing my growing shame rather than Barbara's question.

But this weak retort didn't quiet my inner voice. I had to admit the truth to myself. I did want to punish FTD Barbara—for scaring me, for changing so dramatically right before my eyes, for reaching a stage of decline I never wanted to see.

My meal suddenly tasted like dust instead of the deliciously spiced dish I'd wanted us to enjoy together. I picked up my full plate and walked into the kitchen. I returned with Barbara's plate and fork, pulled up a chair next to her, and scooped a small bite of food onto her fork. I tried to smile as I approached her mouth, but the smile never reached my face.

Barbara's face, by contrast, was alight with a full-blown grin. She opened her jaws to take in the reasonably-sized bite. She chewed with her eyes still smiling. She was My Barbara again, not the ravenous FTD monster I didn't like.

I'm such a jerk. She doesn't deserve punishment!

I hung my head as I used Barbara's knife to push another mouthful onto her fork.

"Where's your dinner?" she asked, concern filling her voice.

"I'm not hungry," I said, still not looking her in the eye.

"But I want you to eat with me, like always," she replied.

"I can't feed us both at the same time," I stated in a flat voice, a mixture of exhaustion, defeat, and deep sadness.

"Yes, you can. One and one. First me, then you."

It sounded so simple and clear when she said it like that. I just stared at her, fork hanging in midair. I was incredulous at the wisdom she still had. *Why didn't I think of that?*

I instantly knew why. I'd been so determined to give Barbara independence and choice over her life, as I'd promised her I'd do, that I'd unwittingly been fighting against myself on every daily task—feeding, toileting, all of it.

I've been blinded by my singular focus of caring for Barbara "correctly." Correctly, to me, had meant putting as much control over daily life tasks in Barbara's hands as possible. Even as her ability to manage her own care declined, I'd persisted in maintaining her sense that she was the one in charge of her life circumstances, regardless of the cost to me. I'd continued giving her the fork to manage her own eating even as her near-choking episodes increased and caused me high stress. I desperately did not want to take away this fundamental act of her feeding herself. "Not able to feed myself" had become a haunting declaration from Barbara's advance directives. Yet, my good intentions had resulted in me disliking Barbara and then myself, creating an unpleasant experience for far too many nights.

Barbara's practical suggestion provided a way out of my self-imposed hell. It wasn't that Barbara couldn't physically feed herself anymore; her impulsivity just made it dangerous for her to do so. Those were not the same thing. I had conflated them out of fear that I would be triggering her advance directives if I took over her feeding. I leaned over and kissed Barbara on the cheek as this insight caused my jaw to slacken and finally relax into a smile.

"Okay, honey, I'll go get my plate and we'll eat together."

One and one.

||||||||||||||||||||||||

We traveled to UPenn in late June for Barbara's one-year checkup. As usual, the MRI, EKG, lumbar puncture, and vitals went without a hitch. When Dr. Irwin conducted a thorough assessment of her muscle and motor functions, I became increasingly alarmed by what he documented: no reflexes anywhere, difficulty standing fully upright, and increased hand tremors. For the cognitive function tests, she redrew the abstract figure Dr. Irwin had shown her seven minutes prior almost exactly. Barbara also had given her amazing English-major style answers for "words that begin with *f*," spouting off *fortitude, ferocious, feral,* and *fantasy* rather than *food, friends,* and *family.* Even Barbara's ability to follow the instructions to alternate between a letter and a number had shown improvement. Her cognitive capabilities were no longer in decline, and some had even improved.

Thrilled with her cognitive functioning, my focus drifted back to the physical changes Barbara exhibited. Her left foot no longer aligned directly in front of her body. The intermittent tremor in her left hand persisted for longer stretches. Her standing torso bent forward almost forty degrees. *What has happened to her?*

"Okay, Susan, you wanted to talk. Let's go next door while the coordinators finish up with Barbara," Dr. Irwin's soft voice interrupted my musings.

Barbara was so absorbed in her tasks she didn't even notice us leaving.

"I don't understand the physical changes I've seen in Barbara since we were here in April," I jumped right in when we got into the adjacent exam room.

I described the day she couldn't lift her foot. I identified her shuffling walk, drooping head, stiff neck muscles, difficulty swallowing pills, and her spontaneous coughing that turned into near-choking episodes whenever she drank or ate. I emphasized my shock and dismay over her posture.

"What's going on with her?" I asked with desperation.

I wanted an honest answer but hoped I'd be told I needn't be concerned. Dr. Irwin held my eyes.

"We've observed these changes too," he said.

I crumpled into my chair as my last shred of hope vanished.

"Sometimes with FTD, though not usually with the *GRN* variant, we see extrapyramidal (EP) dysfunction," he continued.

I had no idea what that meant, but I knew it was bad. My confusion must have shown on my face. Dr. Irwin simplified his language.

"Barbara has developed a parallel movement disorder, separate from her bvFTD. It originates in the basal ganglia, causing resting tremors, constant muscle restlessness, loss of facial expressions, and trouble with tongue control, including swallowing and word formation problems. While it co-presents in less than one-quarter of bvFTD patients, Barbara definitely has this secondary disorder."

My cheeks reddened as I recalled my tirade the night Barbara relentlessly thrashed her legs in bed. But I couldn't indulge my self-berating; I had to focus. There was more.

"This EP disorder also causes locomotion difficulties and decreased posture control," he concluded.

"Is that why Barbara can't stand fully upright anymore, and also has constant swallowing issues?" I asked.

"Yes."

My vision blurred and my mind blanked. For once my medical curiosity was quelled. Both my mind and body had retreated into numbness.

"Barbara's motor function losses will only continue to get worse," Dr. Irwin added.

Although I welcomed his honesty, I couldn't fully process this frank statement. We sat in silence for a minute with my head hanging low and my energy depleted. I almost missed Dr. Irwin telling me occupational and speech therapy could keep Barbara functional for longer. My attention snapped back with his last statement.

"Unfortunately, there is no curative treatment."

He had a look of profound sadness on his face that nearly broke me. I didn't want to hear any more. This was already too much for me to process. *How am I going to tell Barbara this news? Her strong, graceful body is failing her, just like her brain did.*

"I know this is a lot to take in. If we can help you in any way, please let us know," Dr. Irwin continued with compassion.

I couldn't respond to his kindness. For once in my life, no words formed in my brain. I nodded affirmatively and finally eked out a weak "thank you." I wanted to run out of the building and scream at the top of my lungs, but I couldn't. I had to stay strong for Barbara.

I returned to the cubicle where she was still completing her tests. As I came into her view, Barbara broke into the warm, love-filled smile she gave me every time I reentered her sightline. My heart simultaneously soared and faltered.

On the way back to the hotel, I silently rehearsed ways to deliver the disastrous news Dr. Irwin had just given me. "Honey, you've developed a movement disorder" would be such a harsh message to deliver to someone whose brain already failed them. I struggled to find a kind way to convey what fundamentally would be so unkind, so heart-wrenching. Barbara had been heroic in her efforts to function as normally as possible despite her FTD diagnosis. She cried several times over her back pain but never once had broken down from the weight of living with FTD.

While it helped that people with bvFTD typically didn't recognize their own behavior changes, Barbara had never received negative responses from the people around her. This was probably because she hadn't manifested the significant socially destructive behaviors this brain disease typically caused. However, I feared the added diagnosis of motor dysfunction would prove too much for Barbara to bear.

When we got back to our hotel room, I decided to let her rest before delivering the news. I settled her on the couch and turned on the HGTV channel.

"I'm going to go out and pick up lunch for us. You just relax; maybe take a nap," I said.

She nodded, acknowledging I had spoken, but was already absorbed in the dynamics of the *Good Bones* crew working to fix yet another run-down house. I reached over to stroke Barbara's hair but had to quickly leave the room before I broke down. At least I didn't have to worry about her wandering anymore, a cruel result of Barbara's escalating movement difficulties.

I walked the four blocks to Rittenhouse Square, dazed, tears streaming down my face, oblivious to everyone I passed. As soon as I reached a bench, I dropped down and doubled over in a wail. An older woman walking her Cavalier King Charles spaniel stopped in front of me.

"Are you okay?" she asked.

I looked up with my reddened eyes and gave her a weak smile.

"Yes, thanks. I just need to cry right now. Don't worry."

She patted my arm.

"You'll be okay. Crying out your sorrows helps to keep you going. Trust me, I know," she continued with a smile full of light. "Remember what really matters—love and kindness—and your life will be rich."

As I watched her small, white-haired frame walk away, my tears dried. The vibrant flowers around me came into focus, and the joyful laughter of nearby children hit my ears. The universe lifted me up, and my spirit began shifting to a new state of calm. With the help of a stranger, acceptance and peacefulness slowly permeated my being. I had the strength I needed to talk to Barbara.

When I returned to the hotel with lunch, I found Barbara still engrossed in her TV show. She had improved concentration since her gene therapy. Unwrapping the Greek salad, I used our new strategy to feed us both at the same time. Barbara finally had accepted my slower pace of feeding her, so our meals had a significantly more relaxed tenor than before.

When we finished eating, I turned off the TV and told Barbara we needed to talk. I pulled up a chair in front of her, so we were eye to eye, and reached for her hands. She worked to entwine her fingers in mine, a move that used to be so natural but now required a focused effort. When she had our hands the way she wanted them, she looked up at me with her curious, trusting eyes. I reported the news with the honesty her trust required.

"Dr. Irwin told me today that the movement problems you've been having—your left foot, your changing posture, your swallowing challenges, and those coughing, choking fits are because you have a motor disorder as part of your FTD. They all originate from a network of brain structures primarily involving the basal ganglia and their connection to the cerebral cortex and thalamus. It's happening in parallel with the loss of brain cells in your frontal lobe."

I hesitated.

"Because of this condition, your physical problems will keep getting worse," I made myself finish.

Barbara's eyes stayed locked on me the whole time I spoke, but her lids began fluttering when she heard me say "keep getting worse." She looked down at our hands before speaking in a quiet voice.

"I know I have trouble walking and my posture's not great

anymore. I see my hand tremors sometimes. But what about the new gene in my brain? Won't that new gene fix this?" she asked.

All the effort she had put into the clinical trial flashed before my eyes like a time lapse, each frame threatening to break me apart.

"I'm afraid not. The study drug has boosted your healthy gene. That's what it was designed to do. But the physical problems you're having suggest motor parts of your brain in the brainstem and spinal regions are having difficulty, and your new gene wasn't designed to fix those problems," I responded, struggling to steady my voice.

Barbara broke eye contact and nodded, indicating she understood. I continued explaining the science of this diagnosis to keep from dissembling in front of her.

"The doctors don't know why this happens in about 20 percent of bvFTD patients, but the why doesn't really matter. It's happening to you."

Barbara looked up at me. The deep sadness in her eyes was so hard to bear.

"Is this what caused my mother's body to end up in a fetal position?"

The changes in Peggy's body, and especially the way she physically curled into herself in the last eighteen months of her life, had haunted Barbara for decades. Her mother had been a vibrant athlete and a semipro tennis player, yet she ended up a small ball of bones, tissue, and skin with no physical capacity, kept alive by a feeding tube. This horror was still seared into both our brains.

"Yes, I think so. Some aspects of FTD are still unpredictable and mysterious. This is one of them," I said.

"Can they give me anything for it?"

The pleading expression on Barbara's face broke me, yet I couldn't fall apart. I had to hold strong for her.

"No, my love. There are no curative treatments."

What a cruel reality to convey to someone who already had endured so much with a smile. I never felt so dispirited in my life. Squeezing our hands even tighter together, Barbara bowed her head, her difficulty holding it upright now apparent to both of us. We sat for a while in silence, trying to absorb this horrific new world we had entered. Finally, Barbara looked up at me with steely determination in her eyes and spoke clearly.

"This changes everything."

ACT FOUR

FACING REALITY

Early July 2022
–
Early January 2023

Love wins every single time.
Love wins by lasting through death.
Love wins by loving more,
loving again, loving without fear.

—Kate O'Neill

CHAPTER THIRTEEN

DETERMINATION AND DIAPERS

When Barbara hit the one-year mark following her original therapy dosing in July 2021, we were released from trips to Philly for six months. We planned to spend that time in San Miguel de Allende, but first we made a weeklong stop at our condo in New Orleans to regroup—any longer in the sultry summer days of swamp country would be miserable. Plus, we both yearned for our new home in Mexico.

One morning on our stopover, I left Barbara in the capable hands of her home care aide and embraced some cherished walk time in the French Quarter. The intense humidity pressed against my skin in the same way Barbara's ominous words in our Philadelphia hotel room had gripped my heart. I knew exactly what her words meant.

As a product of several generations of highly determined and intentional women, I knew what could happen when a determined woman received fatal health news. My beloved grandmother died of a massive heart attack in the exam room while the doctor stepped out of the room to tell my aunt her mother's heart would soon fail. My own mother, upon learning that lung cancer infested her body and couldn't be removed, died in the hospital two days later. I didn't expect Barbara's end to be as quick as those, but I understood the immense combined power of intentionality and willfulness. I had long known of Barbara's fierce determination not to linger in illness for years as her family members had. Like me, Barbara believed there were fates worse than death. My mind whirled as I walked.

I have to get prepared. But how?

Dig deep. You have to find the strength.

I kept repeating the last dictum to myself, my heels hitting hard on the pavement to drive home the point and its urgency. My intuition told me Barbara only had a short time remaining. As I walked, I questioned the extent of my own strength. *Do I have the fortitude to support Barbara on her next journey, to give her permission to leave me?*

||||||||||||||||||||||

As our taxi entered San Miguel on a mid-July afternoon, we were greeted by bright pink bougainvillea, the ochre shades of the

Colonial palette, and the ringing of a triangle heralding the coming garbage truck. Despite living here only a few months at a time over the past two years, Barbara and I felt the joy of coming home.

We had agreed San Miguel was where we wanted to be for the remainder of our lives together, however long that would be. Any health care Barbara needed would be provided here with competence and heart, and the colorful surroundings in this *pueblo mágico* would bring her continuous joy. I looked over and saw Barbara smiling as we passed people descending the steep hills of Colonia Ojo de Agua at a pace almost as fast as our shuttle. The driver braked frequently to minimize the jostling created by the round cobblestone streets of this old section of town.

"Are you happy to be back in San Miguel?" I asked.

I needed affirmation of what I was observing. Barbara turned to me and her smile deepened.

"Yes. Thank you for bringing me home."

I winked at her. Her clarity filled my heart with serenity.

"I'm excited to see the renovations done on our house this winter. What about you?"

"Mostly I can't wait to see the hummingbirds in our courtyard."

This exchange highlighted our differences. I needed my indoor living spaces to reflect my aesthetics, while Barbara focused on creating beauty outside. Our house in Mexico already had beautiful outdoor spaces and gorgeous foliage when we bought it, so all she had to do was enjoy them, and she yearned to do so. When the shuttle pulled up to our house, the melodious church bells in nearby Colonia San Antonio welcomed us with a saintly tune.

"*Buenas tardes*. It's good to have you home!" one of our neighbors shouted and waved as she walked past us with her dog.

I returned the greeting and helped Barbara out of the van. My spirits deflated as I watched her struggle to move her once-limber, agile body. When I finally had her standing and steady on her feet, I enveloped her in a hug to give us both strength and comfort. We walked through our entry courtyard arm in arm. As we opened the door, we exclaimed with delight at the sight of our new porcelain floors, which were so much lighter and brighter than the previous dark red tiles.

Barbara walked into the living room while I supervised the luggage delivery and paid the driver. When I came into the house, I found Barbara in our new kitchen, stroking the new mesquite wood cabinets.

"Wow! These new counters and cabinets are beautiful," she said. "We picked out this countertop together, didn't we?"

The ironic juxtaposition of Barbara's renewed cognitive abilities and her dissembling body never failed to jolt me, but I refused to be derailed from the joy of our return. I wrapped my arm around Barbara's shoulders and pulled her close.

"Yes, my darling. We did it together six months ago!"

I took in our new mesquite cabinets and black-patterned countertops, then slowly spun Barbara around so she could see the decorative red knobs on the handcrafted china cabinet behind her.

"Look at these knobs you picked out. They're perfect!" I exclaimed.

Barbara walked closer to the cabinet and took one of the knobs in her left hand. She nodded and looked up at me.

"I have good taste, don't I!"

Ignoring how she repeatedly opened and closed the glass-front cabinet door, I simply matched her grinning face with my own.

The next morning the buzzer at the front gate sounded promptly at 9:15 a.m., signaling that Barbara's new caregiver had arrived. I came down the stairs as our housekeeper, Maria, answered the door.

"*Hola! Buenos días! Cómo estás?*" greeted Maria.

"*Muy bien,*" replied Elena, Barbara's new helper.

"*Hola, Elena. Cómo estás?*" I fell in step with the traditional greeting.

I shook hands with the smiling, petite, salt-and-pepper-haired woman in blue scrubs. She had been recommended by our doctor here, and I immediately took a liking to her. Her eyes exuded both confidence and kindness, exactly the combination I wanted for Barbara.

"I'm doing well. It's wonderful to meet you," Elena replied in faintly accented English.

We spent some time going over the details of Barbara's diagnoses, her health history, her current state of behavioral and physical challenges, and her specific care needs. Then, we went upstairs to wake Barbara and begin what I hoped would be a long and mutually caring relationship. When I opened the door to our bedroom, Barbara popped her head out from under the covers. I had briefed her the previous night about Elena coming today, and she remembered.

"Hi! Is Elena here?"

I moved aside so Barbara could see the small woman following right behind me. When I finished introducing them to each other, Barbara grinned at Elena.

"Your hair is beautiful! You're beautiful!"

Elena's eyes twinkled and she reached for Barbara's hand.

"And you . . . your eyes . . . and smile are so beautiful," Elena replied.

They exchanged a warm, caring silence.

"Okay, let's get you up and get your day started!" Elena prompted.

This exchange melted away the tension in my neck, shoulders, and back. I looked up at the ceiling and offered my silent appreciation to everyone and no one in particular.

A week later, at the request of Barbara's two best friends from high school, I set up a video call for the late afternoon when we would be alone in the house so Barbara wasn't distracted. These days I couldn't be sure how online interactions or phone calls would go, as Barbara didn't initiate much in either format. But Barbara's friends wanted to see her, and for once she wanted to be part of it on her own.

I sat Barbara down in the dining room chair in front of my computer. I'd already connected to the link they sent me, but they hadn't started the session yet. There were no familiar faces looking back at Barbara, just the message: Waiting for host to start the session.

"Why am I here?" Barbara asked in an irritated voice. "There's no one on the other end."

Wow, our roles have reversed completely. For forty years, Barbara had been the patient one and I'd been the one irritated by the slightest inconvenience. Now irritation was a regular response from her, so I didn't bother to address it.

"They'll be on soon," I assured her as I sat holding her hands, trying to keep her calm and present.

Her friends' faces finally popped up on the screen and the conversation began.

"Barb, you look so snazzy with your blonde highlights," one mentioned.

A few days in the bright Mexican sun had heightened the honey blonde streaks Barbara's hairdresser had added to her dark auburn hair at her most recent appointment.

"Yeah, don't you know blondes have more fun?" Barbara quipped.

The three of them devolved into comfortable laughter. I left the room as both of her friends started talking simultaneously and Barbara fell into her typical role of listener in the presence of these extroverts. Not having heard Barbara's voice for a while, I came back into the dining room about fifteen minutes later. I wanted to be sure the online link was still working.

"Here's Susan now," Barbara said. "She'll explain it to you."

I came closer with a quizzical look on my face. Barbara turned to me.

"They want to know what the doctor told us at UPenn last month. I told them it wasn't good news, but I couldn't explain it."

I pulled up a chair next to her, wrapped my arm around her shoulder, and kissed her on the cheek before turning to the screen.

I slowly inhaled and exhaled, relying on my scientific mind to speak our still-raw reality.

"Barbara had a movement disorder added to her diagnosis, and it's causing an accelerating decline in her physical functions," I explained, giving them a few more neurological details as I hugged Barbara closer to me. She started to wiggle away from me, and I realized I'd been squeezing her too tightly, as though holding her in place next to me would protect her (and me) from what lay ahead. I released my grip and reached for her hand.

"Barbie, I'm so sorry," one friend said.

Barbara looked up at me as though seeking guidance on how to respond, but I didn't want to make assumptions about her feelings, so I stayed silent. She turned back to the screen.

"Don't worry. Susan's taking good care of me. And so is Elena, my nurse, and Maria, our housekeeper. I'm fine," she said.

My eyes widened as I stared at this brave, resolute woman before me. *She's at peace with this. I've got to catch up with her, but can I?*

A few weeks later, I found myself confronting the difficulties of being Barbara's primary caregiver again. My challenges seemed to come in waves, and Barbara's increasing bowel incontinence made this wave feel like a tsunami. I never questioned my commitment to care for her. I still loved Barbara with all my heart, but loving and caretaking differed greatly for me. Being affectionate and tender with Barbara came as naturally as breathing; daily management of her bodily functions did not. *Do I need to expand the home care service hours?*

Before Barbara's physical caretaking became so challenging, I hadn't considered having a caretaker in our home all day, much less into the evenings. A paid person in our midst made it hard for me to be as physically connected to Barbara as I wanted to be. I could still sit with her and hold her hand, but it made me self-conscious and didn't feel as intimate.

I had to think this through, as the trade-offs were significant. On one hand, I would have to do basic toileting tasks for Barbara in the afternoons and evenings to have more personal time and togetherness with her. On the other hand, I could hire a trained caretaker until the end of the day or even into the evening hours, freeing me of those physical care tasks, but impacting our "us" time.

When I juxtaposed my choices like this, the decision became clear. I wanted as much intimate time with Barbara as I could get for as long as I could manage without someone else always around us. However, I recognized this needed to be Barbara's decision, not mine. I had to provide the best care for her, and she had the right and ability to tell me what would be best. When Elena left that afternoon, I shared my struggles with Barbara. I felt she already knew them, so I spoke my truth directly.

"I'm struggling with your lack of bowel control. Even though you're wearing diapers now, you still have accidents and I'm not managing them well," I told her.

"What do you mean? You clean me up right away," she said.

"Yeah, but sometimes I can't hide how hard this task is for me. I can't stop my gag reflex, and I don't like you having to experience my reaction. I don't want to make you feel bad about something you can't control."

"I know," she said, reaching for my hand.

"I probably should hire someone to care for you in the after-noons and evenings too. You'd get better care and wouldn't have to deal with my challenges," I offered.

"No," Barbara stated quickly and emphatically, looking me in the eye. "After everyone leaves, I like being together. I like you holding my hand while we stream a show. I like you putting me to bed at night."

Tears sprang to my eyes. It wasn't what I did or how I did it that mattered to Barbara. She simply wanted me to be connected to her, present and caring. And if Barbara could stay connected to me despite bvFTD trying to destroy her caring capabilities, I cer-tainly could and would do the same, upholding my part of our long mutual relationship.

"Okay, my love. We'll leave things as they are."

One early August night we proceeded through our regular bedtime routine without a hitch. Barbara took her shoes and socks off by herself. I helped her remove her clothes, put on a sleep shirt, change into a nighttime diaper, and brush her teeth. The last step of our nightly ritual involved Barbara swallowing her sleep medicine. Tonight, she took the small 50 mg trazadone pill from my palm, placed it in her mouth, and took a big gulp of water. I watched carefully, as always, but this time I didn't see any sign of her throat muscles moving. Barbara turned her head from looking at herself in the mirror to looking at me, her pupils enlarged.

She's in distress. She's not swallowing!

"Swallow, my love," I said quietly, masking the terror rising in my body. "You have to swallow the water and pill in your mouth."

Nothing. No muscle actions. Barbara's pupils grew even bigger as she stared at me. I struggled not to meet her moment of panic with my own terror. I continued coaxing her to swallow while massaging her throat in downward strokes. I hoped I could manually trigger her swallowing reflexes. I didn't know what else to do. When my stroking didn't work, I pushed Barbara's chin up, hoping the elongation of her throat muscles or gravity would enable her to swallow. Nothing.

I fought to stay steady.

"Just relax, honey, and let the water slide down the back of your throat."

Finally, Barbara's throat moved.

"I swallowed," she said, reaching for her glass of water.

I suspected the pill had somewhat dissolved before she swallowed it, leaving a bitter taste in her mouth. As she took in another gulp of water, I held my breath. This time her swallowing happened automatically and she smiled at me. The edges of my mouth upturned slightly, but inside my heart raced and my head throbbed.

If she can't swallow, she can't eat. If she can't swallow, I have to deal with her end-of-life wishes! I wrapped Barbara in a close hug, and she hugged me back hard. When I felt our shared fear dissipate through our bodies, I let go. Clasping hands, we walked into the bedroom. I helped her get into bed, swinging her legs up as I now did every night, all the while debating with myself.

Should I check in with her about this swallowing challenge?

Remind her of her advance directives?

Is she still capable of having a discussion like this?

Is this the right time?

As Barbara's head hit the pillow, she gave me her usual heart-melting smile. It took all my willpower not to break down at the cruel situation I was facing. This loving, precious woman still gave her heart and soul to me while degenerating day by day, robbed of one involuntary movement function after another. I kissed her on her forehead and lips, tucked her in, and sat down beside her. The words *integrity*, *forthrightness*, and *mutual respect* scrolled across my mind. I reached for her hand.

"Do you remember when we updated your advance directives right after your FTD diagnosis?"

Barbara quickly nodded up and down. She used words more sparingly now because she sometimes slurred them. I could tell she understood, so I continued.

"It's not unusual for people to change their thinking as they get closer to their death. We've talked about this before, like the time Kevin wanted extensive treatment for his esophageal cancer after telling us multiple times he would never do chemotherapy."

She nodded again.

"People change."

A simple, yet profound truth we both knew.

"Yes. So, I need to know how you're feeling now. You said in your advance directives you didn't want to continue living if you couldn't swallow. Witnessing the problem you just had with your pill, I need to know if you still feel the same way."

"Yes," she answered immediately, faster than I thought possible given the complex, hypothetical nature of the question I just asked.

I kept my face as blank as possible and my voice light, not wanting to signal any of my own feelings.

"Why, hon? Why do you feel this way?"

"Because . . . then I'd have peace."

My heart swelled and dipped as a roller coaster of emotions raced through my body. Gratified she still knew and could articulate her deep wants, I felt punctured to the core by the meaning of those words.

She's ready to go.

I squeezed her hands, unsure what would happen if I tried to speak. I believed unequivocally, on both an intellectual and spiritual level, in everyone's right to a dignified end of life. Yet, how could I willingly let go of my beloved? Barbara's eyes stayed locked on mine, no evidence of fear or anxiety on her face. I briefly wondered whether she'd lost the ability to worry, but she interrupted my musing.

"Will you help me?" she asked, keeping her gaze steady.

My heart instantly answered, *Yes, always, whatever you need,* but no words came out of my mouth.

"Will you be able to let me go?" Barbara pressed.

My diaphragm contracted. I heard no sounds and had no sense of time or place. The two of us existed alone at this moment.

Barbara's searching eyes were all I saw. Deep love requires immense courage. I released my breath.

"It won't be easy, but I'll be ready when you're ready."

This was the only lie I ever told Barbara.

CHAPTER FOURTEEN

COCKTAILS AND CATHEDRALS

We hadn't had friends or family stay with us since the previous December, and now it was mid-August. I didn't know how it would be to have friends stay in our home, but I was eagerly looking forward to our visit with New Orleans pals the following week. Always so kind and caring, I knew Gary and Izzy could handle most things. Truth be told, Barbara had become a wild card.

I didn't leave for my walks anymore until our housekeeper Maria arrived. My walking time had to change after I returned from an early-morning trek the week before and found Barbara stranded on the toilet. She'd awakened unusually early that morning and managed to get out of bed herself, which had become more difficult for her. Unfortunately, she couldn't get up from the toilet by herself. Her brain no longer communicated with her leg muscles. By the time I found her, Barbara's face had become distorted with panic and her feet were numb. I had to half carry her to the bench in our bedroom and rock her until she calmed down. This experience devastated me. I chastised myself for days after.

Now, returning from my vigorous uphill walk in the cool mountain air, our housekeeper Maria greeted me with her arm outstretched and her index finger pointing to the TV room at the back of the house.

"*Señora* Barbara," she said.

I walked toward the TV room with trepidation. Anything could be awaiting me, including another bowel incontinence episode. I grappled constantly with the cruelty of Barbara's physical losses contrasted with her restored cognitive awareness. I thought it must be torture for her to consciously experience her own physical demise, especially for a person like Barbara, who had always been so connected to her body.

Entering the room, I saw Barbara standing at the French doors, seemingly engrossed by the abundance of flowers in the courtyard outside. The sun streamed in, contrasting Barbara's blonde highlights with her natural auburn hair. She was wearing her favorite sleeping shirt with "The most important things in life are not things" on the front. What must have disturbed Maria was the pink nighttime diaper peeking out from under Barbara's robin's-egg blue nightshirt. It most likely was full since she didn't get on the toilet by herself anymore since the stranding episode. She turned as she heard me enter.

"Where have you been? I've been waiting for you!" she admonished.

"You're up early," I said nonchalantly as my thumping heart slowed.

Barbara responded with a wide grin. Whatever emotion she'd been having disappeared now that I was with her. I didn't want to chastise Barbara for getting out of bed on her own, but walking around the house in her diaper wasn't ideal, especially with company coming. The melodious cooing of doves that floated in from the outside patio calmed me. I reached for Barbara's hand and gently squeezed it before speaking.

"It's not a good idea to come downstairs in just a diaper, my love. I think you embarrassed Maria."

"Oh," she replied with a quizzical look.

This had never occurred to her.

"And remember, Gary and Izzy are coming today," I continued. "If they had been here, they'd be embarrassed too."

Her smile returned.

"No, they wouldn't. They'd just laugh!"

I looked into her twinkling eyes and started to chuckle.

"You're right," I conceded.

Maria and I had been shocked and embarrassed by Barbara's unconventional behavior. Yet, it wasn't embarrassing to her and it wasn't hurting anyone. We needed to let her be. I didn't want to spend our remaining time together controlling Barbara's behavior or disciplining her like a child. Once again, Barbara taught me what really mattered, and it wasn't *What will people think?* like

I'd learned as a young child. My mother had been obsessed with being judged—maybe because she had a tendency to judge others. Concerns about other people's assessments of mine or Barbara's behavior had never dominated our thinking, but others' opinions now ceased to hold any import whatsoever. End of life had a way of clarifying what really matters.

A week later, we took our friends to the Luna Rooftop Bar at the top of the Rosewood Hotel for an evening of drinks and tapas. We did this with everyone who visited because it was sentimental for us. Barbara and I had stayed at this hotel during our first trip to San Miguel, spending many nights on this rooftop absorbing the stunning views of La Parroquia, the parish church and signature icon of San Miguel de Allende.

"Wow, what a view," Gary gushed. "You get a full three-sixty from up here!"

The low sunlight reflected from the western mountains and illuminated the unique pink cathedral, spires rising toward the heavens. The sky was darkening from a pending storm, so the pink spires of the sunlit church sparkled especially bright. This was the best sunset view in town.

I couldn't take my eyes off the scene before me, and I didn't want to. "Heavenly" is not a word I use often, but it fit this scene. *I'm so glad we moved here. Such beauty!* Finally, I turned back to our guests.

"Amazing, isn't it?"

"Quite!" they replied in unison.

Another minute of silent appreciation passed before we turned our attention to the cocktail menu. We ordered drinks and tapas, plus a spicy mocktail for Barbara. When the waiter left, I encouraged Gary and Izzy to walk around for the full sunset view of the town from every vantage point. While they were gone, I checked in with Barbara to be sure she had everything she needed. We hadn't been out of the house in the evening for the six weeks we'd been back in Mexico because I couldn't manage Barbara by myself in a public space. I hated having to think in terms like this, but this was life at the moment.

"Thanks for bringing me here," she said, a faint smile on her face. "I forgot how beautiful this town and the church could be. It's probably the last time I'll see the church like this."

I stared at her with my mouth half open, not knowing what to say. It hadn't occurred to me Barbara might be processing her "lasts," even though she'd told me a few weeks ago I needed to let her go. I'd treated her statement as a moment in time—a discussion I'd initiated that wouldn't continue in Barbara's thoughts. And since she no longer shared her inner thoughts with me unprompted, I'd operated under the false impression that Barbara didn't have many inner musings anymore. Clearly I was wrong.

Just then, the waiter walked up with our drinks and our friends returned. I fought back tears as I drank my Mexican mule. *I might need lots more of these tonight!*

I wanted oblivion to numb my aching heart. I smiled at appropriate times in the ensuing conversation, but my mind remained stuck on Barbara's words. "The last time." It played like a vinyl record hitting a scratch; the needle skipping over and over at the same spot. We ordered a second round of drinks, including another jalapeño-hibiscus mocktail for Barbara. I half listened until one of our friends' stories made Barbara let loose her deep belly laugh. I hadn't heard this precious sound in so long. It instantly brought me back. *Forget the future. I've got to make sure I don't miss out on the joy of the present!*

As if to celebrate my gratitude for this moment, a huge gust of wind sent everyone's paper napkins flying in the air like confetti.

"Wow, look behind y'all!" Izzy exclaimed.

We turned to face the blackest cloud I'd ever seen.

"We're about to have a major thunderstorm!" I proclaimed unnecessarily as the sky let loose a torrent of rain followed by a simultaneous crack of lightning and thunder.

Everyone on the rooftop raced to the elevator except us. Three of us were survivors of years of hurricanes and wild thunderstorms in New Orleans, and Barbara always loved a good storm. There was no need to run; we had the protection of a covered roof. Soon, as the wind strengthened and the rain began blowing sideways, our cover felt more meager. We scrambled, drinks and all, to the elevated tables protected by plexiglass on three sides. Five minutes later, the level where we'd been sitting was flooded.

"Are you okay?" I yelled into Barbara's ear over the roaring storm.

"I'm good," Barbara responded with a sweeping grin on her face, fully wrapped in her serape. "It's a big storm like we used to have at our lake!"

I laughed and pulled her close, delighted she still had access to those precious memories. All thoughts of Barbara's "last" pronouncement vanished as the four of us huddled together against the rising wind and dropping temperature. We grinned like fools as we enjoyed the pounding torrents of Mother Nature.

The sky changed colors as the storm moved over us and the final thunder cloud scurried toward the horizon. The rays of the setting sun flashed through the sky one last time, leaving behind brilliant reddish-orange clouds just for a moment. As we lingered, relishing the rare opportunity to occupy the rooftop by ourselves, we enjoyed the midnight blue of early nightfall softened by the gleaming lights of La Parroquia. Sitting in mutual silence, we felt privileged to be taking all this in, content to be witnesses to nature's light show.

Two weeks later, memories of our friends' visit fading, Barbara and I returned to our daily routine of sitting together on the couch after dinner watching TV and holding hands. My shoulders and back stiffened reflexively when a new ad for hospice services came on the TV screen. *When did they start advertising hospice on TV?*

Sweat broke out on my neck and palms. I looked up at the revolving fan blades above me, afraid to look at Barbara. A beat later, I slowly turned my head in Barbara's direction as I inhaled deeply through my nose. Her eyes were glued to the screen. When the ad finished, she turned to me.

"I like hospice," she stated with no emotion in her voice.

I'd known Barbara's positive views of hospice for decades from her mother's declining years. Yet, I didn't know how to interpret her statement at this moment in our lives. I needed clarity.

"Do you want hospice?" I probed. "For you?"

"I already told you. I'm ready to die."

My mouth dropped open and I forced a gulp down my throat. We'd been distracted by our visit with Gary and Izzy, so we hadn't discussed this topic recently. I hadn't been able to wrap my brain around the enormity of Barbara's intention, much less act on it. But she hadn't lost focus on her end of life. She insisted on telling me exactly what she wanted.

"Why?" I choked out.

When she didn't respond, I asked again.

"Why do you want this?"

"Because I'll be at peace," she replied, consistent and determined. *She knows what she wants.*

I licked my lips as I collected my thoughts. I tried to speak, but my mouth felt like sandpaper. I cupped Barbara's right hand in between my own as I struggled to express myself. Finally, I turned to face her.

"I . . . I want you . . . to have ownership . . . command . . . of your life . . . and your death. And I want to . . . honor your wishes. It's just—" I attempted.

She interrupted me, impatient to be heard.

"Tell them I'm ready. Don't let them deny me just because of my diagnosis. I know what I want."

Before I could respond, Barbara continued.

"And don't make me wait too long."

I didn't know if she could tell me what "too long" was, but I didn't ask. I wasn't ready to know. All I could do was nod as I looked at our hands.

"Okay. I hear your resolve," I finally said. After a pause, I added, "And I accept it."

She squeezed my hands in unspoken appreciation.

The next morning, I took the first steps in orchestrating Barbara's endgame. I researched hospice services in San Miguel. While I discovered there was a fledgling movement of death doulas, as well as at-home hospice services in our town, I learned these services weren't typical in Mexico. I didn't believe we needed hospice yet. Well, honestly, *I* wasn't ready to invoke this service. Still, it comforted me to know it would be available to us when the time came, whenever the dreaded day would be.

I placed a call to the executive director of the 24 Hour Association in San Miguel. Barbara and I had read about this organization when we were deciding whether to buy our house. This membership group handled expat deaths in San Miguel, including working with a local funeral home responsible for removing the body from the home and processing it according to the individual's wishes. This group also explained how to notify the American or Canadian consulate responsible for issuing death certificates for their citizens when they died abroad. Knowing this organization existed had been one of the deciding factors in our move to San Miguel. I recognized we needed a firm plan in place for whenever we died. Joining this organization was a key action I needed to take now.

The director informed me we could have our ashes interred in a niche in the expat section of the local cemetery. This sounded like the right solution for us, and I wanted to run it by Barbara before

I took the next step. The following day after Elena left, I took Barbara into the living room. Once we were comfortable on our couch, I broached the subject of our ashes. As always, I was direct.

"I've learned we can have our ashes interred in a niche in the old cemetery here in San Miguel, after we die. Would you like your ashes to be here, surrounded every year by all the love and music and good energy of Día de Los Muertos?"

Barbara looked at me quizzically, like she didn't understand. Then I saw the recognition come to her face.

"You mean all those skeleton puppets dancing?"

Now it was my turn to be quizzical. I cocked my head as I pondered her question, then a memory popped up. Last fall, the holiday parade had a whole troop of larger-than-life skeleton puppets, and Barbara remembered them.

"Yes, exactly!" I exclaimed, always thrilled when she could access positive memories.

"Then, yes," she said with a smile. "It's the next best thing to a New Orleans jazz funeral."

I agreed. I'd always thought having a jazz funeral would make dying worth it, especially the second-line parade where even strangers off the street joined in and danced along with the funeral band and loved ones on the way to their postburial reception. The idea of being surrounded by the energy of Día de Los Muertos comforted me just the same.

"Okay, let's do it," I concurred, my eyes twinkling in response to Barbara's grin. "Our ashes will be buried together here in San Miguel."

To my surprise, I didn't break down in tears with the finality of this decision. Instead, my muscles relaxed as a sense of lightness permeated my body. Barbara leaned toward me, and I embraced her fully. Our last end-of-life planning step completed, we held each other with gentle urgency.

CHAPTER FIFTEEN

ACCEPTANCE AND ANGELS

By mid-September, I couldn't keep Barbara's intentions to myself any longer. I had to tell our close family and friends Barbara was ready to die. I didn't relish making those phone calls, but it would be selfish not to give her closest family and friends a chance to say goodbye.

What do I tell them? There is no good way.

Before I called anyone, I considered how to give key friends and family the opportunity to see Barbara one last time without creating pressure. Barbara's sister-in-law had quashed her brother's wish to travel to San Miguel, citing his FTD diagnosis as the reason. His decline was not happening as rapidly as Barbara's even though he had not elected to join the gene replacement trial. His diagnosis had occurred earlier in the degeneration process than hers, so his decline was delayed by several years. Still, I knew how difficult it could be to travel with someone who has FTD, so I understood this decision.

I also knew disease, death, and grief could be powerful distancers. People often shied away. I learned this lesson multiple times in my life. Some people just didn't have what was required to be so close to death. I hold no judgment about this; it's merely an observation. I didn't want anyone to feel obligated to visit us if it proved too hard for them for any reason. Fortunately, I knew the three Maine couples we were closest to didn't have these issues, so I started with them.

"Karen, I'm sorry to have to make this call to you, but Barbara told me she's ready to go. She's at peace with dying," I ventured.

"Oh, my God, no! Has she really declined so fast?"

I almost lost my composure, her despair threatening to crack mine wide open.

"She's not in a steep decline yet. But I believe when people are truly ready, deep in their soul, death will come sooner than we expect. I don't know when, but I would guess she'll be gone by early next year."

"She doesn't want to have a long decline like her other family members did. She's made that clear many times," Karen answered in a quiet voice.

My voice was equally subdued.

"Yeah, and she's made me promise I wouldn't let her linger."

"Of course she did. She chose you a long time ago because you're able to love her in this way. Remember, she chose you. She knew you could and would do what she needed when her time came," Karen comforted.

I broke into the sobs I'd been holding back for a month. Karen listened in silence while I poured out the most current wave of my grief. When my tears slowed, she continued.

"I know you'll do what you need to do to honor Barbara's wishes. And please don't think you're alone. We'll make time to come see you guys before the year ends."

I knew this visit would probably be a burden for her and Carol because the fourth quarter brought increased work-driven stress into their lives.

"We could always arrange an online call if it's easier," I offered.

"No. Not if it's the last time. I have to see Barb and hug her . . . lots. We'll make it work. I'll let you know when."

After we signed off, I breathed more easily. True friends had long been a blessing in our lives but never more than now. The second call came a little easier.

"Norine, I'm calling with some difficult news."

I explained Barbara's state of mind and gave Norine all the options of where we would be over the next three months—back to our New Orleans condo in November to enjoy the jazz and food scene together one more time; Philadelphia in early December for Barbara's six-month safety check; then back to San Miguel in mid-December. Before she could state a preference, I asked for what I really wanted.

"I don't know if it's too much to ask, too selfish, but I'd love for y'all to come to Mexico for your birthday."

She and I both understood this meant for Christmas, a holiday that already held an emotional charge for me. In 2006, I lost my mother the day after Christmas. Ever since, I'd scheduled a new adventure during this holiday to mask my dread of the day she died. This year we couldn't go anywhere, so I needed the adventure to come to us. I didn't share these thoughts with Norine, but my voice must have conveyed the urgency of my ask.

"Great idea! I'll talk to Cheryl and get back to you. Please hold it for us," Norine responded before I could take back my request.

I glowed with gratitude for the friends we had.

Just one more Maine couple to contact. They had retired recently, and I caught them at home together. I directed the planning more now, telling these friends the best time to see Barbara would be in Philadelphia after her December checkup. They immediately agreed to be there, as I had expected they would.

"We don't want this to be true, Susan, but we're grateful you are giving us the chance to say goodbye to our darling friend," they said.

Of course I had reached out to the people closest to Barbara, providing them with an opportunity for a face-to-face farewell. Barbara had not just been my spouse and soulmate. She was a sister, aunt, cousin, and loving friend. Everyone who knew her would grieve her loss deeply. I braced myself for the hardest calls of all to our nephews and nieces.

They're going to be heartbroken.

I had the most concerns about their availability. They were millennials, deep into their early careers and young families with little free time. Barbara's remaining time had become limited, so I formulated a plan in my head. Instead of arranging three separate visits, I decided on a joint gathering. Being together as a family would help us support each other at this most difficult time.

I emailed them an invitation to a group weekend in Philadelphia in early December, preceding our checkup at UPenn. Philly provided the perfect midway point between their homes in Washington, DC, New York, and New Jersey. Explaining Barbara's decline in general terms, I had no doubt they would make arrangements. I didn't tell them the whole story, as I had to tell them about Barbara's end-of-life readiness in person.

||||||||||||||||||||||||

By the end of December, exhaustion from all our travels and the difficult goodbyes with friends and family held me in its grip. I'd tried to imagine my future without Barbara everywhere we'd gone in the past three months, from New Orleans, to Philadelphia, and back to San Miguel de Allende. It proved impossible and deeply enervating. We'd been committed to each other since I was twenty-nine, and in just under three months I would be seventy-one years old. We'd had a lifetime together. I didn't remember me without her.

Barbara's wise counsel had accompanied me through life's twists and turns. Her adventurous spirit had joined mine in all manner of escapades. Barbara's infectious laugh and joy for life brought out my bright, mischievous side, saving me from perpetual seriousness. Would I be a dull, sad lump without her? Would I even want to go on after she died?

When we were at UPenn earlier in the month, Barbara told her clinical coordinator she wanted to go to sleep and not wake up. Dahlia whipped around to me, a startled look on her face. I met her look with a weak smile and a calm voice.

"She knows she's declining. She's accepted it. She's ready to go," I managed.

I struggled to get there. I couldn't imagine waking up and not seeing Barbara's smile. Going through a single day without getting hugs from her, much less no hugs for the rest of my life, proved unimaginable. I'd told Barbara over and over I would be ready when she was ready, but my declaration felt like a lie every time.

I supported Barbara's desire to depart her physical form. She had long felt angered by the loss of dignity her family members suffered during their long years of decline. Now she was experiencing the same indignities with her physical decline, and those indignities plagued her more and more. She had difficulty swallowing her food and her medicine, causing both of us to panic. She even choked when simply drinking water now. Most days, she didn't have enough stamina or coordination to walk around our cul-de-sac or to the nearby park she loved without resting. Every day had become predictably simple and boring: wake up, shower, read, watch TV, go to sleep. This limited daily routine was insufficient for a creative, active, and curious spirit like Barbara.

The heaviness of our current lives weighed on me even more than usual on this New Year's Day. For the past thirty years, I'd started this auspicious day in a spiritual practice using *Sacred Path Cards* written by Jamie Sams. These cards had been my tool for self-discovery. I used them to understand the personal and societal issues I might encounter in the year ahead and chart a course for success. When I pulled out the *Sacred Path* deck in my usual fashion to start this year, I couldn't open it. I no longer had a reason to look ahead.

My empathic antennae had reached high alert the previous week. Holding Barbara's hand while we watched TV together, I realized she wasn't clasping my hand tightly like she'd always done. I had enough experience with death to know what this meant. Aching inside, I recognized Barbara had begun disengaging, preparing to leave me. Her time drew near.

I walked into the courtyard and turned on our fountain. The sound of soft gurgling water soothed me. Sitting in my favorite chair, I looked around in gratitude at the beauty around me—wispy palms, red bougainvillea, green poinsettias, and orange chandelier plants all helping to calm my knife's-edge nerves. Barbara's intentionality and courage had given me this beautiful home. I owed her so much.

Please let me find the grace I need for our next dance together.

As I watched Barbara sleeping soundly on the morning of January 3, I recognized how much I needed to have a joyful time with her. But what to do? Everything had become a challenge. We needed to go to a garden. She'd always loved the park near our house, but walking there had become impossible for her and we didn't have a car.

After Maria and Elena left for the day, I called a taxi to take us the two blocks to Parque Guadiana, our neighborhood park in San Miguel de Allende. Although it was winter, flowers thrived in the perpetual spring weather of the *alto plano*, the high plain of the Colonial Highlands. Bright pink bougainvillea were the first to catch Barbara's eye as we left the taxi and entered the park.

"Look, Susan, the flowers are the color of my scarf!" she exclaimed, holding her Barbie-pink scarf up against the closest blossom.

She was right; they matched perfectly. A warm calm shot through my body, and I hugged her close. *This is what we both needed.* We walked the few steps to a bench situated near the first water fountain in the park and sat, holding hands. To our left stood a large statue of Our Lady of Guadalupe, perpetually adorned with vases of flowers at her feet.

"Those are gerbera daisies," Barbara stated, her knowledge of plants still intact.

Our eyes brightened as we connected with each other in silence, cherishing the love flowing between us while the bubbling sounds from the fountain enveloped us. We didn't need to talk. We sat content in the comfort of a lifetime of commitment and caring.

"Let's go to the other fountain," Barbara declared after a few minutes.

Her restlessness couldn't be contained even though her spirit was content and walking was challenging for her body.

"Are you okay walking to the other end?" I asked.

"I am if I hold on to your arm. And if we need to stop, there's more benches on the way."

Barbara's practicality and determination shone through all her travails.

"You can always hold on to me," I assured her.

I pulled Barbara up to a standing position using my left arm. My right shoulder had become even more compromised due to a fall I'd taken three weeks prior.

"Okay, let's go. Bench to bench," she said. "We have all the time in the world."

Except we don't. I sucked in a quick hit of oxygen to counter my sudden lightheadedness. Determined not to fall apart, I dismissed the truth piercing my heart, joining in Barbara's fantasy instead. We made our way past lines of plants and trees, including six-foot columns of fencepost cacti lining the steps and a jacaranda tree. Barbara suddenly stopped.

"Look at those tiny red flowers!" she exclaimed.

I looked around but didn't see what she saw. This fact came as no surprise to either of us; Barbara always had been more attentive to details than me.

"Where do you see them?" I asked, never doubting they were real.

"On the ground. Look, they're part of the groundcover," she said pointing straight down. "So tiny and so bright."

She leaned over to pick a flower, something I knew we weren't supposed to do. I didn't intend to police her. Not now. I just held on to her waist to make sure she didn't fall. We walked on and came to a bench near the larger fountain. The water was louder here and didn't provide as melodious a background as the smaller one. It still comforted me somehow. As we sat in silence again, holding hands, several groups came and went. A mother and her young son carrying a large backpack. A white-haired woman walking her small dog. A teenage couple holding hands and seeking a secluded spot for kissing. Suddenly, the normalcy around me became too much.

My life will never be normal again! My heart started racing in response to this unwelcome thought. I jumped up, surprising myself and Barbara.

"I have an idea!" I exclaimed to hide my agitation.

"Every time you've ever said those words, it's turned out wonderfully for us. What's your idea?" Barbara said, letting out a little chuckle.

I kissed her on the forehead, appreciating how she had always trusted my ideas and spontaneity.

"This isn't a big idea, but it's a tasty one. I'm going to get us some mango *paletas*—those blended frozen fruit pops on a stick."

Barbara nodded in agreement, a broad smile emerging.

"You stay here," I said, even though I knew Barbara couldn't get off the bench by herself. "I'll be right back."

The *paletas* shop was only half a block away from the park so I returned quickly. Barbara hadn't seen me approaching. She had been intently watching two little girls dipping sticks in the water, twirling, and flicking the water all around them. Her interest immediately relaxed me. She wasn't agitated by my absence.

"Hey, I'm back."

Barbara's head whipped around, and her eyes locked on the yellow-orange frozen delights I held in each hand.

"Give it to me!" she demanded, her compulsivity taking over her normally polite demeanor.

I quickly unwrapped the colorful and delicious *paletas*, handing one to her with a napkin wrapped around the stick. Biting down voraciously, Barbara devoured a third of the icy treat at once while I'd only managed to take a few licks. I didn't care. Not even her compulsive eating could change the positive mood this park had brought me.

"Oh! Oh!" she exclaimed with her frozen treat suspended mid-air, eyebrows raised and pupils enlarged.

I let out a quick chuckle.

"Did you give yourself a brain freeze, honey?"

Recognizing her mistake, Barbara let out her wholesome deep belly laugh.

"Yeah, I guess I did."

Barbara's laugh had always been contagious to me, so I followed suit, unable to stop once I started. Sticky liquid rolled down my palm and across my wrist. I barely noticed; our enjoyment was too precious to squander.

Later in the evening we sat on the bench at the end of our bed as we had done so many nights before. I removed Barbara's sneakers and socks for her; she could no longer do it herself. As I finished the task, Barbara placed her hand on my arm, and I turned to look at her. Her electric smile never ceased to warm my whole body.

"I had fun today," she said.

I wrapped Barbara in a big hug, and we held each other until I could find my voice again.

"Me too. I'm glad we went to the park. It's so beautiful there."

I started to rise and position myself to help her stand up when Barbara grabbed my hand and squeezed hard. I sat back on the bench with a quizzical look on my face. I noticed tears in the corners of her eyes, something I hadn't seen since we talked about her movement disorder six months before.

"What's up, my love?"

Barbara grabbed my other hand, enfolding both of my hands in hers without speaking. She looked down at our entwined fingers and stroked my hand over and over, her brow furrowed. I gave her all the time she needed to say whatever churned in her mind. Finally, she looked up at me and spoke quietly.

"I don't know if I can let *you* go."

My throat closed. My breathing stopped. I didn't know what to say. I couldn't speak anyway. Tears slowly dripped down my cheeks. Barbara looked directly at me, seeking guidance like we'd always given each other in difficult situations. *Can I do this? Am I strong enough to help her right now?* I wanted to pull Barbara back from death and never let her go, but my deep love wouldn't let me pursue this selfish desire. Instead, I looked Barbara in the eye, tears still falling, and squeezed her hand until the right words came to me.

I knew what I had to say.

"I don't ever want you to let go of me either. But there are other ways of being with me besides sitting right next to me."

Barbara's eyebrows arched. I took a deep breath and continued.

"You can let go of your body and be my angel instead."

Barbara's face lit up. She believed in angels, as did I.

"Yes! Yes! I'll be your angel!"

EMBRACING SPIRIT

January 2023
—
September 2023

Goodbyes are only possible for those
who love with their eyes.
For those who love with heart and soul,
there is no such thing as separation.

—Rumi

CHAPTER SIXTEEN

REASONS AND REFLECTIONS

awakened on January 6, 2023, to dawn light streaming through a crack in the curtains. It was the morning after Barbara's death. My eyes instantly spotted the metal heart from our wedding cake adorning the top of the fireplace in our bedroom. I reached my arm out toward Barbara as I'd done every morning before this one, momentarily forgetting she wasn't there anymore. Suddenly, the absence of any other living energy in our bedroom rocked my senses, overwhelming me. A spasm gripped my chest, and I turned away from her side of the bed. The ache grew, reverberating throughout my whole body.

Deeply alone for the first time in forty-two years, with no partner and no purpose, I didn't know what to do next. *Who am I without Barbara?* I felt as though I had awakened without my legs.

How can I possibly move forward in my life? How can I navigate even one day?

Lying there, curled into a fetal position, I couldn't stop my brain from replaying her death. I had bolted upright in the predawn hours the day before, awakened by sounds of Barbara choking. I jumped up and raced to her side of our bed as the sound changed into a loud gurgle. I stopped short when she came into my view. Her face had been transformed—eyes shut, color drained away, and the dreaded downturned mouth locked in place. Barbara had lapsed into a coma; her death was underway.

Part of me wanted to leap into action, do CPR, anything to keep Barbara here with me. Yet, I took no action. I had promised Barbara the right to choose her end time. I also wanted to celebrate her in this moment of my worst fears. I admired Barbara's determination to die on her own terms and not to endure a slow, tragic death like her family members. I had agreed to support and witness her bravery, so I sat down on the bed beside Barbara and gently held her hand. Her periodic breathing struggles were difficult to hear, yet I persevered. I wasn't going to leave her side.

I had feelings to share with Barbara while she could still hear my voice. I told her how grateful I always would be for our ability to navigate the challenging times of her illness as a couple, to stay connected even though her disease wanted to separate us. *We* won, not FTD. We had lived our love and triumphed, remaining connected and committed to the end. I told Barbara she had lived intentionally, as she wanted, touching so many so deeply. Now she could rest. She could release herself from the body and brain no longer serving her. She could go with her work here completed. Then I spoke my final promises to Barbara, letting her know I would survive her death.

I promise you I'll live as fully as possible, even in my grief.

I'll continue to enjoy what we loved to share together.

I'll do this because it would be disrespectful to you if I did otherwise, squandering the time in front of me your genes denied you.

Your indomitable spirit will be my constant companion always.

When I finished speaking, I played Peder Helland's gentle piano music. Barbara sang in a Threshold Choir for years, her resonant voice accompanying many people on their journey from this physical world. I wanted the music she loved to escort her in death. Barbara's breathing relaxed as we absorbed the music into our souls, quiet together for the last time.

The faintest dawn light seeped into the room as I completed my pledge to Barbara. I mustered the courage I needed to call our San Miguel doctor, which would trigger a subsequent call to the hospice doctor as Barbara and I had agreed months prior. We knew, from our experience of Peggy's death, the dying process could be weeks long. Barbara didn't want to undergo that torture or to put me through such needless pain. She wanted the hospice doctor to come to the house and hasten her dying, giving her a dignified death by releasing her from her body as peacefully as possible. It was the hardest phone call of my lifetime, yet I made it.

Over the course of Barbara's illness, my days had revolved around her. Without her, what shape would my day take? I had never been a routine person, but my creative, explorative nature had taken a back seat to Barbara's daily needs. And what about the years ahead of me? I'd promised Barbara I would continue to live fully after she died, but would it really be possible? I'd been sharing my dreams and frustrations with Barbara since I was twenty-nine-years-old, a novice in the world. We'd happily navigated life together. I felt safe and confident with her by my side. *Now what? How can I manage alone?*

I had the physical ability to get up, shower, and dress; I just wasn't sure *why* I would want to do any of those things anymore. What was my reason for living? My life would never again be as rich as it had been, so why go on? This wasn't a melodramatic, poor me question. It was the existential question that had been present with me since I watched the undertakers carry Barbara's body away.

The physical void Barbara's death created and the aloneness I felt overwhelmed me. Even as a strong introvert, the thought of so much silence in my life terrified me. I had many dear friends and family members who wanted me to survive this loss. I just didn't know if their desires for me to live would be reason enough. Without Barbara's beaming face to light my days, I wasn't sure what would motivate me to keep on living, enjoying life. Had I lied to Barbara for a second time?

I understood death and grief well enough to know the answers to my questions would not come quickly or easily. I would wear my grief—grief that made every breath a herculean accomplishment—for a long time, probably for the remainder of my days. *Can I find a way forward through this immense pain?* Lying in bed that morning, I understood why many spouses died soon after their partner departed.

To stop grief from debilitating me, I practiced yoga breaths. My body relaxed slowly. I uncurled my legs, extending them downward under the covers. I turned over to face the sliding doors, and a hint of the fuchsia-colored bougainvillea blossoms on the outside balcony came into sharp focus through the crack in the curtains. Those flowers called up memories of Barbara's joy in planting and nurturing gardens. I remembered the calm energy I felt around Barbara as she died. *She's at peace now. She's where she wanted to be.*

I reflected on Barbara's excitement at the idea of being my angel. *Your bond with her is permanent. Remember that.* I recalled a Rumi quote I often repeated to Barbara from my hotel room when I traveled for work, "Your body is away from me, but there is a window open from my heart to yours." In my soul, I believed Barbara and I had shared lifetimes together, and we would again. With Barbara's body gone now, I needed to use all my senses and spiritual energy to establish and sustain a new type of connection with her.

To stay sane, I also had to move my body. On this first morning and for months after her death, I walked with no specific destination or purpose. I walked wanting the feeling of my feet meeting the hard stone of the San Miguel sidewalks to pound some energy back into my dulled body and brain. Some days I intentionally sought out the steepest hills in town and scaled them with the hope my physical pain would override my psychic pain.

Each walk I took eventually led me to Parque Guadiana, the last place I had been with Barbara outside our home. I sat on the same benches we did with the nearby fountain gurgling in rhythm with my flowing tears. I conjured Barbara's physical presence, desperately wanting her back on the bench with me, her hands in mine. My wanting was so fierce I thought it would burst through my body, creating a physical hole the world could see. Grief had become my essence. How could I possibly hide it?

Within three weeks of Barbara's death, shame and its accompanying sidekick blame overtook me. Repeatedly, I berated myself with these words: *Barbara deserved the best possible caretaking and you couldn't deliver.* My deep shame followed me twenty-four hours a day. I tossed and turned each night reliving every miniscule failure over the years. The scene of me pounding my fist into Barbara's thigh in the middle of the night and of me withholding her food replayed in an endless loop as though these were the majority of our interactions, not the single events they were.

I became sleep-deprived and lost all perspective on the consistent, heartfelt care I'd given Barbara. I felt only my deficiencies. No matter what friends and family said to me about my loving care of Barbara, I countered with evidence of my failures. I spiraled out of control, self-hate intertwining with deep grief. I needed help traversing through the shame entrapping my mind and body.

I sought help from my primary doctor, who connected me with

a psychologist who practiced cognitive behavioral therapy. This pragmatic, short-term therapy can be a powerful tool for addressing acute emotional situations, especially ones that trap people in negative thought cycles. I immediately made an appointment. The first moment I sat down with Michael, I felt safe. He had a calming energy and a caring smile.

"Tell me about Barbara," he invited, his eyes sparkling with interest.

Leaning in, I began to explain her brain disorder. He interrupted.

"No, tell me about Barbara as a person, not a disease."

I leaned back and stared at Michael as he held my gaze, his face open to learning about the woman I grieved. This would be the first time since Barbara had died, since FTD had started taking her from me, that someone had given me a platform to conjure up her whole being, her predisorder personality. I felt my shoulders drop as I allowed positive memories to flood my mind.

"She had confidence in herself even as a young woman. The most curious, open-hearted person I've ever known, Barbara wanted to know everyone she met. Yet, she didn't suffer fools. She laughed heartily with her whole body. She didn't talk much in group settings, but she always had a pithy quip to summarize any topic or situation being discussed. Barbara was widely loved."

"She sounds incredible. Tell me more."

I shared with Michael all of Barbara's qualities, including the ones I admired and the ones that frustrated me, explicating her fierce independence as well as her difficulty sitting through extended after-dinner conversations. I told him about Barbara's many talents and her love for learning new skills. When I finished my long recitation, I felt a warmth permeate my body. I had transformed Barbara from a disease-bound person into the full-color, spirited woman I'd known and loved for so long. I had gotten My Barbara back.

Face flushed and feeling newly content, I expressed my appreciation to Michael.

"Thank you for helping me reconnect to all of Barbara. I didn't realize I'd lost so much of her over these FTD years."

Our next two sessions focused on the nature of my forty-two-year partnership with Barbara, highs and lows included. I realized I had been aggrandizing Barbara since she died, making her into a veritable saint and overlooking the difficult challenges her FTD behavior had created. By contrast, I could only see myself as wholly deficient in my caregiver role, even though I had provided Barbara with years of loving care. The truth of her FTD years required a more balanced view on both sides. Each of us had our challenges and triumphs. Explaining them to Michael as honestly and openly as I could brought me slowly back to center. My self-berating began to subside.

At the start of the fourth session, Michael asked me to describe what I did best as Barbara's caregiver. Pausing, I scanned my memories.

"I loved her unconditionally, even as she changed in sometimes embarrassing and difficult ways. I stayed committed and connected to her."

Michael leaned forward.

"And what were the three most egregious things you did during the three years you chose to be Barbara's caregiver?"

I paused as my clasped palms began to sweat. I had come here to release my shame, yet the thought of exposing my worst behavior caused my throat to constrict. I swallowed hard, then launched into my answer, recalling my three most shameful moments: slamming my fist into Barbara's thigh, eating in front of Barbara after removing her plate, and continuously gagging as I cleaned her up after bowel incontinence episodes. I told him every sordid detail of my failures to keep Barbara's needs front and center. Michael listened intently, nodding but never interrupting. When I finished talking, he held the silence for several beats before speaking.

"So, in other words, you're telling me you're human."

I don't know what I had expected Michael to say when I finished my recitation of failures, but those words had never crossed my mind. Repeating in silence, *You're human*, I felt a wave of energy emerge from my core and travel through my body, cracking open the shell of shame I had built around me.

"Did Barbara ever complain about how you treated her?" Michael asked with his eyebrows lifted.

I scanned my memories.

"Well, no. We always talked about the times I let her down . . . when I didn't do my best. I wanted to change those situations every time. She never did," I responded slowly.

A weak smile crept onto my face as I remembered one key episode.

"Except, Barbara did insist I give her plate back the time I took her food away."

Michael chuckled.

"From everything you've told me about her, don't you think she would have spoken her mind if she needed you to treat her differently?"

Pondering his question, my whole body began gently rocking back and forth. A full-blown smile emerged as I thought of Barbara's straightforward nature.

"Yeah, she would have."

"Then, in Barbara's absence, I'm here to say you need to let go of the shame you're carrying. It's not warranted. Of course you weren't perfect in your caregiving; no one is. What's most important, though, is Barbara didn't expect you to be. She just needed your love, and you gave her that every day," he said.

As he spoke, the dark shadow of self-blaming and shaming lifted from my body and swirled away, flying through the open windows of his office. In their place, a flood of gratitude surged through me—gratitude for the privilege of caring for my beloved through the end.

CHAPTER SEVENTEEN

TRIBUTES AND TRAVELS

In May 2023, I held a Gathering of Remembrance for Barbara in Portland, Maine. Planning this sacred event had sustained me throughout the winter I spent in San Miguel grieving Barbara's physical absence. To best reflect Barbara, I designed a stylish, well-orchestrated, and emotionally meaningful celebration devoid of sappiness. Hundreds of people attended in person or via Zoom to honor Barbara, as I had expected they would. Along with myself, four of Barbara's closest friends spoke about her five most essential qualities—intentionality, authenticity, friendship, courage, and joie de vivre.

Most memorable to me are the words spoken by her childhood friend Lisa, who reflected on Barbara's multiple forms of courage.

"Barb was always present in the moment, ever willing to step up to the plate, and fully prepared to tolerate uncertainty," she said. "As anyone who shopped with her knows, she loved coaching friends out of their comfort zones, encouraging each of us to be a bit more daring in how we perceived and presented ourselves. But hers was not the kind of bravery that needed to be in the foreground. Her courage was a quiet emanation from within, which informed everything she thought and every action she took. Barbara has always been a still pond, reflecting back something deeper than appeared on the surface."

The highlight of Barbara's gathering was the music. Sixteen accomplished singers came to Barbara's remembrance celebration from Maine, Washington, DC, and as far away as California, Minnesota, and North Carolina to sing a cappella in honor of Barbara's lifelong accomplishments as a singer. Barbara had studied and performed with these singers across a twenty-year period. They sang nine of the songs she most loved, including "True Colors," "Lean on Me," Sweet Honey in the Rock's "Breaths," and Cris Williamson's "Song of the Soul." The outpouring of love and support from these accomplished singers delivered an incredible testament to Barbara and the way she built lifelong relationships.

On the day of Barbara's gathering, the singers' magical voices penetrated my grief and filled my heart with joy for the first time in months. I wished Barbara could have been there in person to share the experience with me, like we had shared so much music in the past. Instead, I was comforted by the presence of her spirit. When the first chords of the final song, "The Water Is Wide," reached my ears, I could hear Barbara's resonant tenor voice filling the room as it had done so many times when she performed lead on this song. On her remembrance day, and many days before and since, a cappella music connected me to Barbara's essence.

The reception following the program afforded me the opportunity to receive much-needed hugs from friends and family. I was especially grateful for the presence of my young cousins who traveled from Colorado and Idaho. They stayed by my side even as I received love from both longtime friends and more recent ones, like the UPenn clinical coordinators. While many tears were exchanged, they were primarily of joy. Barbara, of blessed memory, was a source of love in life and in death.

IIIIIIIIIIIIIIIIIIIIIII

Muscles taut, I gazed out the window as my plane descended into De Gaulle Airport outside Paris in early June. I still carried the pain and joy of Barbara's Gathering of Remembrance with me. I hadn't intended to travel so soon after, but I'd been invited to a writing retreat at a countryside château in the southwest of France and couldn't say no. I intuitively felt drawn to this adventure focused on my first passion of writing. Besides, only one person in the group knew me, so I could share as much or as little of myself as I wanted. Still in a state of grief, my natural introversion had been guiding my choices and actions more and more since Barbara's death.

As the wheels hit the runway, tears rolled down my cheeks unbidden while questions exploded in my mind. *What are you doing? Why did you decide to visit Paris?* Paris had always been *her* city. I could find Barbara everywhere in the city of love. *Is this what I need? To feel her all around me?*

I don't remember what convinced me to add Paris to my itinerary. At some point, I'd reasoned walks along the Seine and time spent with some of my favorite art would soothe me. I figured if I could travel alone to Paris, I could travel alone to anyplace on the planet. Now I questioned my decision. *Is this self-torture or a brave act of respect?* It felt like a little of both.

After settling into my hotel room on the Right Bank, I raced out of the building into the sunshine, striding the few short blocks to the banks of the Seine. Grief pulsed strongly through my head and heart. I needed to calm myself, and water usually helped. Seeing the river swirling before me, I focused on its flow. My breathing began to slow. I closed my eyes and inhaled deeply. *I'm okay.* Releasing my breath, I assured myself with a new belief. *Barbara will protect you.* I didn't know where this idea came from, but it gave me what I most needed in the moment: comfort. I stretched my arms up to the sky and leaned my head back slightly, feeling my back relax as I brought my arms down slowly to my sides.

I began to stroll along the riverbank, opening my senses to my surroundings. Suddenly the numerous houseboats moored just below me came into focus. I imagined what it would be like to live on one of them. As my vision sharpened even more, I admired the distinct decor of each boat. I challenged myself to pick out the boat best reflecting my taste and the one most representative of Barbara's. My style was more Victorian townhouse, while hers could be called Bohemian atelier. I only found one boat I loved but many she would have claimed.

Thinking of us in this way gave me a spark of joy. We had always laughed at how different we were. Those differences could have made our lives difficult, but they didn't. They caused us to listen to each other more, seek more understanding of our differences and their origins, and to find and hold on to the essence of our connection. Appreciating our differences once again, my whole body calmed, and I smiled my first real smile in five months. I stared at the Seine and thanked the Celtic water goddess, Danu, for her wisdom and her help in finding my balance.

The next day I walked across the pedestrian bridge from the Right Bank to the Left Bank, on my way to the Musée d'Orsay. My appreciation of art began with my relationship with Barbara, and I intended to honor her tutelage. I had a mission to visit my favorite impressionist paintings at the d'Orsay and once again stand in the grandeur of this converted train station. Maneuvering through the crowd to find the handrail for the stairs down to the main floor, I recoiled from the bodies jostling me. I felt light-headed and folded inward. *Too many people here. I don't remember it being like this.*

I calmed myself by looking out over the grand design of the building. I found it as awe-inspiring as the first time Barbara brought me here, though the vibe felt totally different. The energy of the crowd felt frenetic, which was not as I remembered it. So, instead of descending to the main floor, I headed to the upper floors and my imagined safety from the crowd around me.

When the elevator doors opened, my hopes shattered. Multiple languages emanating from this packed room hit my ears at once. I exited the elevator anyway, determined to see my favorite paintings. Jockeying for position in front of Monet's *Regattas at Argenteuil*, I realized the peace I'd hoped to find in this museum could not be. My throat constricted. My arms and hands tingled. Sweat formed on my lip. I had to get out of there.

Exiting the museum, I zigzagged through the narrow streets of the Left Bank in the general direction of the Luxembourg Garden. Not sure exactly where I needed to go, I kept up a rapid walking pace to release the panic dogging me. Before long, I recognized my surroundings and stopped walking. I focused my eyes and saw, across the street, the entrance to the Hôtel des Marronniers, where Barbara and I stayed during our first trip to Paris. *How did I end up at this place I most wanted to avoid?*

Surprisingly, being here didn't upset me. I felt Barbara had brought me to this place to let me know I didn't have to avoid my memories. I stared at the entrance as calm returned to my mind and body. I didn't need to go inside. I still remembered every inch of the tiny room we had, the sweet courtyard where we rested in the afternoons, reading and sipping cappuccinos. I crossed the street and leaned against the building. The warmth of the sun-kissed stone penetrated my back as I closed my eyes and breathed in the memories we had made there. I thanked the spirits around me for the reminder not to stay stuck in recollections of the previous year and all the difficult aspects of Barbara's secondary movement disorder. Instead, I needed to focus on our longer life and travels together, those places and times where the beauty of our relationship resided.

I crossed back over to the corner brasserie for lunch, ordering *poulet frites*, roast chicken with shoestring fries, and a side salad. Savoring the classic French vinaigrette on my salad, a familiar taste Barbara had served me often, I replayed multiple food adventures I had with her. My first street crepe on Rue Saint Jacques near the Sorbonne. Breakfast on the balcony of our hotel in Venice as we watched the Vogalonga regatta parade down the Cannaregio Canal. The flash-fried seafood and vegetables we consumed over a long lunch in Barcelona. The fresh Greek salad, taramasalata, and grilled lamb chops we enjoyed on Santorini. I didn't hurry this Paris meal as I had all the others I'd eaten alone since Barbara died. And I didn't cry either. As the saltiness of the fries and delicate sweetness of the chicken hit my tongue, I revisited my memories with quiet joy.

My last stop for the day was the Luxembourg Garden. The beauty and intentionality of formal gardens always moved me. As I crossed Rue Bonaparte, my eyes focused on a banner announcing the art collection of Leon Monet, Claude Monet's brother, at the Musée de Luxembourg. My curiosity piqued, I bought a ticket and had one of my best museum experiences ever. The collection included pre-Impressionist landscapes, early cartoon-style drawings, and brightly colored Asian-style paintings done by Claude Monet, works I had never seen and didn't even know he had done.

Sitting in the gardens afterward by the Statue de la Liberté I realized my life presented a clear choice to me. I could wither in my pain, or I could use my bounteous memories with Barbara to propel me into new experiences. Either way, my loss would always be with me. Continuing to travel, even if alone, offered new adventures to layer onto the richness of my life with Barbara. And truth be told, even in my grief, I was still the venturesome soul I'd always been. I wanted to honor myself and Barbara by living as my true self. I hoped I could.

CHAPTER EIGHTEEN

DREAMS AND DANCES

Light bounced on Great Pond one early September morning, diamond-like in its sparkly shimmer. I rocked on the porch of my new lake cottage in central Maine, sipping my morning tea. An osprey cry caught my attention. I watched as it floated on the gentle wind before pulling in its wings and diving head-first into the water, its prey caught in a flash of speed and fishing prowess. The breeze kicked up into a short gust of wind, rustling the pines and maples at the water's edge. I gave myself a mental pat on the back for how right my decision to buy this lake cottage had been for my healing. Just like I had shifted my heart closer to Barbara when the neurologist confirmed her bvFTD diagnosis, I recognized my need to physically shift back to Maine for part of the year—to the place where our history resided—so I could stay close to Barbara's energy.

My return to Maine had been serendipitous; it was a dream I didn't even know I had. The dream manifested in mid-June after a Celebration of Life ceremony in Belgrade Lakes Village for the husband of a longtime friend of mine. He was a man I turned to often for advice, both business and family. The shock of his sudden, unexpected death still gripped me three months later. *Why did this have to happen?* There could be no real answer to such a question. Death comes when it comes, especially after we and our loved ones hit seventy years of age. We're not privy to the whys and wherefores. We're just left to deal with the aftermath. For reasons I can't explain, I'd come into this life with the strength and intention to face whatever came my way and to emerge whole.

The afternoon following Cary's Celebration of Life, as I waited to visit with my dear friend, I stopped for a coffee at a nearby café and began to search real estate listings, as friends of mine had their lake cottage on the market and wanted my opinion of their listing. After reviewing theirs, I turned to the competition. The listing for the cottage I now own hooked me with the view of Great Pond from the porch. More perusing revealed this property had all five features Barbara said a lake cottage needed for a whole summer's stay:

1. An easy stroll from the cottage to the water (no steep steps)

2. A view of the lake from the primary bedroom

3. Guest bedrooms on the main floor (no lofts with ladders to climb)

4. A long view of acres of water from the dock

5. No neighbors in sight from the porch

I called the realtor immediately, not realizing it was Sunday. As my good real estate karma would have it, the buyer's broker was in the office that day, trying to catch up on her paperwork. She arranged a showing for the same afternoon, and my heart made a decision to buy this property as soon as I walked through the front door. The golden tongue-in-groove pine walls instantly reminded me of the cottage Barbara and I had had on this same lake for twenty-five years. Joyful memories flooded over me. I knew I wanted to spend the rest of my summers in this spot. I put in an offer, furniture and all.

I didn't think I'd ever have a place in Maine again once Barbara and I had decided to make San Miguel our home. I've learned, though, life never unfolds as planned. San Miguel will remain my primary home so I can be close to Barbara's remains and absorb the beauty and graciousness of our Mexican town and its people. Eventually, I will join Barbara, our ashes together in one niche in the expat section of Nuestra Señora de Guadalupe cemetery. There, we can revel for eternity in Día de Los Muertos celebrations. Yet, Great Pond in central Maine also holds Barbara's spirit. She drew me back. So, once again, I shuffled my living plans, selling my New Orleans condo and closing on a seasonal cottage.

Having been in my lake cottage for a month, I was enjoying the familiar, relaxing rhythm of the waves lapping the stones on my shoreline. I spent hours on my new dock, replaying the many times Barbara and I kayaked around the islands I could see from this vantage point. I laughed out loud when I remembered the time we kayaked up the shore from our cottage and a sudden squall darkened the sky, the cloudburst drenching us to the bone. We laughed like little children, absorbing the pouring rain with delight.

I couldn't remember how long it had been since I'd been able to laugh like we had that day. Even as I closed on this cottage, I was afraid the void of Barbara's physical body with me in this sacred place would wrench me apart. The opposite happened. This special place and the joyful memories we made here gave me a way back to my deep connection with Barbara.

I wanted more memories, less pain, even though I knew the deep ache of Barbara's physical absence would never leave me. Truth be told, I didn't want this ache to disappear. It felt like a badge I had earned by loving Barbara so fully.

One morning, I awakened to an unexpected surprise—a great blue heron standing at the water's edge in front of my cottage. This majestic bird had delighted Barbara and me for years when it glided past our old cottage at dusk every day, returning to roost in trees above a shallow, secluded cove at the end of our road. Its flight stunned us every time. The wingspan and grace of the great blue was awe-inspiring. But those flights provided only momentary delight. The heron's wings propelled it over long distances in a flash of elegance, taking it out of our view as abruptly as it had arrived.

I'd never had the opportunity to view this prehistoric treasure for a long duration. Now, she stood right in front of me without a concern in the world. I didn't know if this bird could see me through the window where I lay in bed, but I didn't want to find out. Great blue herons are incredibly solitary, skittish birds, so I feared I would lose her if I moved at all. I communed in silence, content to send her telepathic messages of appreciation for her beauty, her grace, and her majestic stillness.

Sitting on the dock reading the next day, I flinched when the same heron flew by me on the way to a stream to my west. She appeared abruptly, the whooshing sound of her enormous wings so close to me I instinctively ducked as she passed. I thought she gave me a tip of her wings, as if to say, *I see you. I'll be back.* The heron's brief flight of grace reminded me of a day at the lake decades before when Barbara agreed to show me the underwater ballet routines she did as a teenager. She'd been a competitive swimmer as well as a competitive underwater ballerina, representing two sides of her I loved—her strength and her elegance. I grinned at the joyful memory and went back inside the cottage to find the meaning of great blue herons among spirit totems. While not one to appropriate other people's culture, I had had such a meaningful encounter with a red fox on my fortieth birthday that I claimed them as my totem. Barbara had never been able to settle on hers, but with the exchanges of the last two days, I had started to think the great blue might be Barbara's spirit totem.

As I read my book on spirit totems, I vigorously nodded up and down. The great blue heron represented to Indigenous peoples the traits of grace, beauty, and patience, all traits Barbara had had in spades. Reading further, my mouth gaped open.

> *Those who have the blue heron as their spirit totem need to follow their own unique wisdom and path of self-determination. These individuals know what is best for themselves and need to follow their hearts rather than the promptings of others.*[*]

These words described Barbara exactly, both the way she lived and the way she died. A warm energy began vibrating in my heart and spreading throughout my body, causing my ears to tingle. I felt a vibrational shift.

A few days later, I walked into the living room from the kitchen and came to a sudden stop as my eyes gazed out toward the lake. The great blue heron had returned. This time, she stood in the middle of my yard at the edge of my deck, closer than I'd ever seen this skittish bird get to a human habitat. At this close distance, the heron stood so large I became mesmerized. I stared, mouth open in shock.

---

[*] These words are my paraphrase of what Ted Andrews says in his book *Animal Speak: The Spiritual and Magical Powers of Creatures Great and Small* (Llewellyn, 2002), 157.

As I continued watching from the living room, this majestic creature began to lope around the yard with slow-motion steps and a plunging neck. I moved a few steps with her, positioning myself to take a photo through the glass. I knew no one would believe what I was experiencing without evidence. I couldn't be sure I believed it myself. Great blues just didn't intentionally get so close to humans. Suddenly, the truth permeated my thoughts.

Barbara is communicating with me through this bird!

Tears welled in my eyes. Just before I snapped the picture, the heron turned and looked directly at me. Afterward, I lowered my arm and met her gaze. We held eye contact for what felt like an hour but could not have been more than a few moments.

In no hurry to leave, the great blue treated me to more strutting motions. My eyes followed her every action. I began to move my body along with the heron, making slow sweeping motions with my arms and loping with my legs. I did a slow twirl around the room, keeping one eye on the heron. I hadn't startled her. Instead, the great blue stayed in parallel motion with me for several turns.

We danced . . . together . . . just as Barbara and I had done through the ups and downs, the joys and the sorrows we shared for so long.

RESOURCES FOR PERSONS WITH FTD AND THEIR FAMILIES

I've been fascinated by the human brain, its capability and its quirks, for as long as I can remember. The challenging times I experienced with Barbara's genetic brain disorder haven't diminished my fascination; they have enhanced it. The human brain houses our essential self, our personality, and the cells governing our attitude and our behavior. Yet, despite the fact this organ ensures our very survival, most humans don't understand or even think much about their brain. Fortunately, there are neuroscientists, neuropsychologists, and a myriad of other complementary scientists focused on exploring and uncovering the secrets of the human brain.

I am indebted to many of them for Barbara's gene replacement therapy, which gave me extra time with Barbara. If a secondary movement disorder hadn't taken away her critical functions, including swallowing, walking, and bowel control, we would have lived many more years and possibly decades together after she received the new gene in her brain. For this reason, I want to provide others impacted by familial or nonfamilial FTD with some insights about FTD research, clinical trials, and services for patients and their families.

It is my hope everyone who needs assistance will seek out scientific breakthroughs and/or crucial support services to make their journey with FTD even more successful than Barbara's and mine. I am not an expert, but I can connect you and your loved ones with caring, competent professionals who are. I recommend you start by exploring three key areas of need: the FTD diagnosis; genetic counseling and testing; and engagement in FTD research and advocacy.

THE DIAGNOSIS

Frontotemporal degeneration (FTD) is a debilitating neurodegenerative disorder or dementia often misdiagnosed, as well as underdiagnosed. An important reason for this diagnosis problem is FTD can cause multiple changes in a person, including changes in behavior, personality, and/or language, which most people don't associate with a diagnosis of dementia. Additionally, the symptoms of FTD can overlap with symptoms of other illnesses, such as Parkinson's, bipolar disorder, and depression. Another key reason is that too many medical doctors as well as psychologists are not yet sufficiently knowledgeable about this rarer form of dementia. Due to these factors, it takes an average of 3.6 years for an FTD patient to receive an accurate diagnosis. The consequences of such underdiagnosis or misdiagnosis are unnecessary agony and the loss of valuable time in limbo for both the person with FTD and their families.

Changing the current state of FTD diagnosis requires more people to become alert to the facts about FTD. For one, FTD manifests at a younger age than other dementias, most often between the ages of forty and sixty-five. And it can cause one or more of the following categories of symptoms:

- Impaired cognition, especially executive functions like judgment, planning, and decision-making

- Apathy, emotional blunting, and lack of motivation

- Impulsive and repetitive behaviors

- Changes in eating habits, including overeating and preference for sweets

- Uncharacteristic actions, language, or moods caused by changes in personality

- Social disinhibition and loss of empathy

- Language difficulties, including both expression and comprehension of words

- Movement problems, including muscle weakness, rigidity, and poor coordination

If you or a loved one exhibits any of these symptoms, even if no one else in your family has done so before, make an appointment with a neurologist and ask this doctor if they are knowledgeable about the brain disorder known as FTD or frontotemporal degeneration. If you want a second opinion in the diagnosis process, there are some specialty clinics around the world you can contact. Within the United States, the three most prominent ones are:

1. University of Pennsylvania (UPenn) FTD Center
   215-662-3606 [New Patients]
   https://www.pennftdcenter.org/contact

2. University of California San Francisco (UCSF) Memory and Aging Center
   415-353-2057
   https://www.ucsfhealth.org/conditions/frontotemporal-dementia

3. Mayo Clinic
   https://www.mayoclinic.org/diseases-conditions/frontotemporal-dementia/care-at-mayo-clinic/mac-20354745

In addition to these prominent centers of FTD research and medical practice, patients and their families can find more diagnostic resources on The Association for Frontotemporal Degeneration (AFTD) website at this URL: https://www.theaftd.org/what-is-ftd/research-and-medical-centers/.

GENETIC COUNSELING AND TESTING

Approximately 15 to 40 percent of all FTD cases have a genetic cause due to a single gene variant. The majority of genetic FTD cases are due to an illness-causing mutation in one of three genes: *GRN, C9orF72,* or *MAPT.* These genetic mutations can be hereditary or environmental. Determining whether you or your loved one has a genetic form of FTD requires specialty testing.

Before undergoing such genetic testing, genetic counseling is highly recommended. A genetic counselor who specializes in neurodegenerative diseases like FTD can assist you in understanding and adapting to the medical, psychological, and familial implications of having a brain disorder caused by a gene mutation. Genetic counselors can be found at the three FTD centers listed in the preceding Diagnosis section and through the AFTD website explained in more detail in the following section.

FTD RESEARCH AND ADVOCACY

Advancing scientific and care knowledge for people with FTD and their families, including the availability of FTD therapies and treatments, requires more research and advocacy for this little known and poorly understood neurodegenerative disease. The organization doing the most across the world to advance both FTD research and advocacy is The Association for Frontotemporal Degeneration or AFTD.

Online at theaftd.org, this organization is the largest national nonprofit devoted to providing resources to help families affected by FTD today, and to advancing research to foster accurate diagnosis, treatments, and cures. AFTD is driven by a devoted staff along with thousands of volunteers and donors who reflect a community's profound determination to #endFTD. With the FTD Disorders Registry, AFTD is proud to partner with families, researchers, biopharma companies, state and federal policymakers, and health professionals across the country to improve care for people and families facing FTD—efforts that could ultimately be important to all persons facing dementia or other types of neurodegenerative disease.

AFTD RESOURCES

- AFTD website: www.theaftd.org
- AFTD HelpLine (translation services available): 866.507.7222 / info@theaftd.org
- Diagnostic checklists for those concerned that they or someone they love has FTD: https://www.theaftd.org/what-is-ftd/ftd-diagnostic-checklist/
- Nationwide support groups led by AFTD-affiliated volunteers: https://www.theaftd.org/living-with-ftd/aftd-support-groups/

The QR code to the right will take people to the AFTD home page without having to type in the URL.

ACKNOWLEDGMENTS

First and foremost, I want to honor my beloved life partner and spouse, Barbara B., who asked me to write this memoir so more individuals diagnosed or undiagnosed with *GRN*-FTD, as well as their families, could benefit from our experience and be treated with improved medical care and eventually a cure.

I also want to thank our dearest friends and family, only some of whom are named in this book, for all the love and support they gave us throughout our forty-two years together, and especially during the most difficult times of Barbara's declining years. In addition, I want to voice my heartfelt appreciation to the friends who got me through my deepest phases of grief, especially Lynne J., Cheryl and Norine, Karen and Carol, Gary and Izzy, and Griselda and Cacho.

I want to express my sincerest appreciation for my friend Susan Page, owner of the La Calavera Catrina art piece featured on the cover of my book, who gave me permission to use this image to express a beautiful view of death befitting to Barbara. Susan has many wonderful pieces of folk art at her Galeria Atotonilco located outside of San Miguel de Allende, Mexico.

Importantly, I never could have undertaken or completed this memoir without the skilled assistance of my initial writing teacher, Laura Davis; my two developmental editors, Katie Bannon and Nadine Kenney Johnstone; numerous workshop leaders at the San Miguel Writers Conference and Literary Festival, including Danielle Trussoni and all of the women (you know who you are) in my three writing feedback groups. I also want to give my wholehearted appreciation to April Eberhardt, an agent extraordinaire, who guided me often and who opened up the opportunity for me to attend a writing retreat in France when I most needed a new perspective and a change of scenery. And Lessie Schrider, I couldn't have had a better final book editor than you!

Another person I could not have gotten to this point without is Dr. Tayler Friar, an art historian and communications genius. She revamped my LinkedIn profile, taught me how to get the algorithm to pay attention to my posts, and also created my author's website. She has become a cherished friend who brings sparkle and joy to my life.

Last, but definitely not least, I want to thank all the members of my publishing team at Greenleaf Book Group/River Grove Books who believed in this book and guided me so graciously and skillfully through the editing, design, branding, and marketing process needed to bring it to readers' attention. You all helped my dream—and Barbara's—come true.

AUTHOR Q&A

Q: **What did your writing process look like for *Dancing in the Face of Death*?**

A: When I go through difficult times in my life, I always use journaling to help me sort out my feelings and find the clarity I need to guide me forward. From the moment I recognized changes in Barbara's behavior and attitude, I made journal entries almost every day, writing only when she was sleeping. Then, one morning after Barbara's diagnosis of behavioral variant FTD (bvFTD), I was writing in my journal when she walked into the living room. "Are you writing about me?" she asked. "Well, about both of us," I replied. Then she said these prescient words, "You should write a book about us, about this disease, about our path through it." I looked at her in astonishment, and at the same time, I knew I would do as she instructed because I trusted her wisdom. So, if you felt the tension and the pain and the joy of this time in our lives as you were reading, it's because none of these emotions were filtered by time. I wrote every part of this book as it was happening—except for Act 5. It took me almost nine months after Barbara's death to know what kind of life I would have without her, and whether there would be anything significant for me to convey to readers.

Q: Where did the title come from, and what significance does it hold for you? What role did dancing play in your relationship with Barbara, and how does it relate to the way you both navigated this time in your lives?

A: After a year of friendship, Barbara and I fell in love dancing together. From that first time, we sought out every opportunity to dance, including dancing around our house or in clubs or at weddings or anywhere else music moved us. And our dancing didn't stop when Barbara started declining. In fact, I made it a point to dance with her several days a week, even when all she could do was sway with me as she began losing the capacity to move her legs. Barbara's sense of rhythm was second to none, even at the end.

Q: What was your favorite memory to revisit when writing this book? What was more difficult to return to and put down on the page?

A: I love every memory I have with Barbara, so it's difficult to pick a favorite, especially between our travels together and our time on

Great Pond in central Maine. If I have to pick one, though, the memory of us paddling alongside each other as we swam across the cove in our early forties is a special one for me. That day, we were both healthy and alive with the possibilities of life individually and as partners. And our encouragement of each other as we each swam the distance of the cove and back reflects the way we championed each other in every endeavor we undertook.

As to the difficult memories, there unfortunately were so many that I can't pick just one. The first one that stands out for me was the afternoon where Barbara kept picking a scab on her arm until it bled, and she ended up begging me to tie her hands. Reliving the pain I felt when she acknowledged her inability to control her destructive behavior was especially difficult for me, as I also had to relive how helpless I felt to stop her in any humane way.

The second difficult memory was the night I resorted to hitting Barbara's continuously moving leg with my fist out of frustration. This episode was hard for me to admit to myself, much less to readers, even though I know intellectually that frustration and anger cannot be avoided in difficult caregiving situations. For me, the integrity of my entire story rested on my willingness to share the most personally embarrassing moments of our journey through the challenges of dementia.

Q: **Many memoir writers believe they need to portray themselves in only positive ways. Yet your memoir is honest in areas where you found yourself coming up short—whether it was worrying about being a caregiver, having moments of**

weakness when faced with the changes you saw in Barbara, or struggling with anxiety when thinking about life without her. Why did you feel it was important to include those parts of the story alongside the beautiful moments?

A: From the beginning, I decided this memoir would only be worth writing if I was willing to do it with full integrity. I knew it wouldn't be easy for me, as I have long wrestled with the pretense of perfection, even while knowing I could never achieve it. But living with and caring for a person with bvFTD strips everything down to its rawest form. I eventually understood there was no way to be a perfect caregiver for a person with FTD. Everything becomes so unpredictable, so heart-wrenching. So, I had to learn to care less about how perfectly I was providing for Barbara and instead focus on how lovingly I connected with her, even in the most trying of circumstances. I didn't always succeed in my efforts, but I wanted to draw attention to this shift in my focus in hopes it would help other caregivers and family members of persons with FTD, especially those with the behavioral variant. I want other caregivers to give themselves grace when they encounter the challenges this disease inevitably presents.

Q: What is the most important thing you learned about yourself through this journey? How did you grow as a person, both throughout Barbara's diagnosis and after she died?

A: I learned so many things about myself during the three-and-a-half years between my recognition of Barbara's FTD and her death, and so much more in the three years since her death. The most important lesson I learned during her years of decline was that love lives deeply within me, as it did within her. No disease was capable of snatching love away from us, even as that cruel disease took so much of Barbara's brain and related behaviors and functions. It wasn't easy, and sometimes I was too tired to even try, but staying connected with the essence of the Barbara I knew so well—My Barbara as I came to call her—enabled me to traverse all of the challenges we encountered.

In many ways, the harder road for me came after she died. We had been together for so long, I didn't know who I was without her. I didn't know if I could—or even if I wanted to—go on without her. Yet, when I turned seventy-one only ten weeks after she died, I realized that I had more living to do and she would want me to continue living fully. And through my grief, I have slowly reconnected with myself as a whole human being, with life as a gift not to be squandered, and with love itself.

Q: Throughout the book, you beautifully describe the various pieces of art, culture, and music that played a role in your and Barbara's life together. What was your favorite activity to do together? Why was it important to you—and Barbara—to continue integrating these elements into your lives even as her condition advanced?

A: Barbara and I flourished when we were sharing artistic activities of any kind, whether visiting museums and galleries, enjoying concerts and live music together, reading and discussing all types of books, or going to plays and movies. We both valued human creativity deeply and wanted to experience and celebrate it as often as possible. We also learned about life, ourselves, and each other by exploring the arts and culture in all forms and across as many parts of the world as we could visit. Staying focused on sharing those fulfilling experiences added to the normalcy of our lives together up to the end.

Q: Can you speak more about the meaning of La Calavera Catrina and your San Miguel home in your and Barbara's life?

A: La Calavera Catrina, the symbol of Mexico's Day of the Dead since the 1910s, was first presented as an etching by lithographer José Guadalupe Posada and published in a broadside by the Vanegas Arroyo family. For us, it captured the mix of joy, beauty, choice, and grief, which death contains if you don't fear it.

As to San Miguel de Allende, Barbara selected this *pueblo mágico* as our home because of its visual beauty and her affinity for colorful flowers, people, language, and culture. Ironically, I began to love this place more after Barbara died because on my walks around town, I so frequently encountered the beautiful spirit of this place and its people, native Mexicans and gringos alike. In many ways, this town and its residents brought me back to enjoying life again.

Q: As you mention in the book, you've experienced several losses throughout your life. How did those experiences shape how you approached Barbara's care and your own emotional management?

A: My first experiences with serious disease and death came when I was eight and nine years old, and they involved my forty-one-year-old father and my eight-year-old cousin, respectively. Our extended family sought every possible medical solution to cure each of them—my young cousin from childhood leukemia and my father from a rare autoimmune blood disease. My father was successful in receiving experimental solutions, although never a cure, that kept him alive for the next thirty-four years. My young cousin lost her battle with a disease that now has a cure in most cases.

While it may sound odd, I have always been grateful that I experienced both chronic illness and death at a young age because those experiences taught me several important lessons. First, to always fight for a medical cure, no matter how remote the chances. Second, that life and death are inseparable, so there inevitably will come a time to let go and allow your loved ones to be released into the death that they choose.

The third lesson is this: If you live an engaged life, you will feel deeply for others and one of those deep feelings will be grief. Grief, after all, is the price you pay for allowing love into your life. And for me, grief is a price well worth paying for love, no matter how uncomfortable grief can be.

Q: In chapter 4, you describe the excitement you experienced when first learning about the clinical trial for the behavioral variant of FTD. How did you balance both the hopefulness and fear you felt when doing this initial research?

A: Because of the experiences with my family, and also with Barbara's brother who died of melanoma, I had had several opportunities to learn about and advocate for participation in clinical trials for rare and/or incurable diseases and health conditions. And because I also value medical science and what it has done, for the most part, in advancing the quality and longevity of human life, I never felt fear when I was researching clinical trials for Barbara. Even when I found an option for her and understood that she was entering a phase 1 trial where her safety was not guaranteed, my strong intuition was that she would not be harmed and that doing nothing was a more fear-based approach than her participation in the clinical trial. I experienced the whole process as hopeful and hope-driven, the preferred way we both led our lives.

Q: How did you manage your own sadness and anxieties around Barbara's changing behavior?

A: Throughout Barbara's decline, I let myself feel the sadness and anxiety as much as possible without burdening her with it. I would release my emotions on walks or in times I spent with friends while Barbara was receiving home care. As my friends can attest, I sometimes broke down completely when I was with them. Their love and support helped put me back together to face another day or week of the ongoing grief I lived with for all those years. I could not have survived with any form of love or grace to give to Barbara if it had not been for my closest friends. They remain my rocks, and I try to be the same for them.

Q: You and Barbara maintained such courage, strength, and love for each other throughout this difficult time. How did you face these challenges with such grace and steady determination?

A: Both Barbara and I are direct and intentional in our relationships with other people, and we developed a foundational trust between us in the earliest months and years of our relationship that served us well through all sorts of difficult times, including her years with FTD. Across four decades, we never once ended a day together with any difficulty left unspoken or without the commitment to work together to resolve it. I believe this core connection we built and intentionally reinforced across the years was what enabled us to stay aligned and determined to meet the challenges of FTD together.

Q: Throughout several moments in the book, you describe how intentional you and Barbara were when discussing her end-of-life wishes and other aspects of care. How did you approach these conversations, and what advice can you offer to readers who are similarly navigating difficult conversations about health and life?

A: Neither Barbara nor I lived a fear-based life. Both of us were committed to having a connection based on integrity, intentionality, and the courage to love fully. From the time her mother's early onset dementia was first diagnosed, Barbara and I shared the pain of multiple FTD disease and death scenarios in her family and talked about our thoughts and feelings throughout those multiyear experiences. By the time her FTD symptoms surfaced, we had established a decades-long pattern of open communication and straight-forward discussions about every aspect of life and death. While I'm not in the advice business, I would encourage everyone to do the hard work of establishing honest, trusting relationships with the people who are most likely to be your care partners later in life. Understanding each other's mindsets when you're younger, before you need to have the difficult conversations about end-of-life wishes, makes those discussions easier.

Q: In chapter 16, you briefly discuss your experience in therapy after Barbara died. How did this help you work through your grief and to remember Barbara as a whole person—not just defined by her diagnosis?

A: The short-term therapy I did after Barbara's death using cognitive behavioral therapy (CBT) techniques was essential to my mental health at the time as well as my general well-being today. Without doing that work right away, shame, guilt, anger, and other negative emotions could have overtaken my psyche and caused me to spiral into an emotional abyss for years. And this struggle didn't occur because I was a poor caregiver to Barbara—in fact, I was a loving, capable caregiver throughout her declining years. The source of my shame was an unrealistic drive for perfectionism I had carried throughout my life. The CBT technique of reclaiming Barbara as a whole person with whom I had had decades of a healthy, loving relationship was also essential to me reclaiming myself as the whole, capable person I am without the need to be perfect. This therapeutic technique gave me back a grounded reality so I could grieve Barbara's death in a healthy way and not from unwarranted shame or guilt.

Q: You describe a beautiful moment with a great blue heron in chapter 18, when you felt that Barbara was communicating with you through the bird. In what ways do you continue to feel Barbara in the world around you now?

A: I am strongly intuitive and I feel Barbara's calm, loving energy around me often, whether it's when I'm enjoying a walk in the woods or a park, when I hear certain music, or when I'm feeling stressed and remember to relax and breathe. There is no doubt in my mind that she is an angel guide for me as I navigate my new life.

Q: As you explain in the resources section at the end of the memoir, FTD is a little-known and poorly understood neurodegenerative disease. How do you hope that your and Barbara's story adds to the research and advocacy around FTD?

A: We both wanted our story to be compelling enough to bring attention to this "cruelest disease you've never heard of" so other people who struggle for years to get an accurate diagnosis can find assistance sooner and with greater accuracy. In addition, all of the proceeds from the sale of this memoir are going to the UPenn FTD Center to support further research for cures of all forms of FTD but especially the behavioral variant that has plagued Barbara's family.

Q: What resources did you find most helpful when learning about FTD and stepping into a caregiver role? Do you have additional recommendations for readers?

A: The Association for Frontotemporal Degeneration (AFTD) and the UPenn FTD Center were bedrocks of support for me throughout Barbara's FTD journey, and they continue to be so. I especially urge all FTD caregivers to participate in the AFTD Annual Education Conference each spring and in UPenn's Annual Caregiver's Conference, which is often accessible online.

Q: What piece of advice would you offer someone who finds themselves in a similar situation as you—caring for a loved one facing a life-changing diagnosis?

A: Two points come to mind: Be gracious with yourself as you navigate the challenges you will encounter, and make sure you have sustained personal support. Your role and the tasks it requires are difficult, especially on a long-term basis.

Q: What do you hope readers take away from your and Barbara's story?

A: The most fundamental takeaway for me is that the effort required to build an intentional, honest, and committed relationship with another human being is worth it, even if you have to experience deep grief when that person dies, because the love you receive along the way is irreplaceable.

Q: Is there anything you didn't get to say in _Dancing in the Face of Death_ that you would like readers to know?

A: I have continued to gain insights about love, grief, courage, relationships, and caregiving in the years since my memoir ended. You can access my thoughts on these and other topics via the blog I post on my website at www.susankoen.com.

ABOUT THE AUTHOR

 SUSAN L. KOEN, PhD, was born and raised in the southern United States, especially her adopted home of New Orleans, but as an adult chose to make New England her home for forty-four years. She especially loves Maine, where she still has a summer cottage. In 2020, she became a permanent resident of Mexico and now resides most of the year in the *pueblo mágico* of San Miguel de Allende in the Central Highlands north of Mexico City.

Dr. Koen is an organizational psychologist, entrepreneur, and author/creator of both leadership and workforce training programs that utilize applied neuroscience. For decades she was an internationally known expert in optimizing worker health and safety and preventing human errors in twenty-four-hour and 24/7 workplaces, including manufacturing, mining, energy, and utilities operations.

Since retiring, Susan has focused her time on writing creative nonfiction, including her memoir as well as essays published in *The Sun Magazine* and other journals. You can also find her thoughtful writings in the blog section of her website at https://www.susankoen.com and in her LinkedIn posts at https://www.linkedin.com/in/susan-koen/.

Dr. Koen is available as a podcast guest on topics of healthy love/healthy grief, caregiving for a spouse with dementia, behavioral variant FTD, death with dignity, long-term lesbian relationships, and personal courage.